NETWORKING WITH THE AFFLUENT AND THEIR ADVISORS

NETWORKING WITH THE AFFLUENT AND THEIR ADVISORS

Thomas J. Stanley, Ph.D.

McGraw-Hill

New York San Francisco Washington, D.C. Auckland Bogotá
Caracas Lisbon London Madrid Mexico City Milan
Montreal New Delhi San Juan Singapore
Sydney Tokyo Toronto

McGraw-Hill

A Division of The **McGraw·Hill** Companies

This publication is designed to provide accurate and
authoritative information in regard to the subject matter
covered. It is sold with the understanding that neither the
author nor the publisher is engaged in rendering legal, accounting,
or other professional service. If legal advice or other expert
assistance is required, the services of a competent
professional person should be sought.

*From a Declaration of Principles jointly adopted by a Committee
of the American Bar Association and a Committee of Publishers.*

Library of Congress Cataloging-in-Publication Data

Stanley, Thomas J.
   Networking with the affluent and their advisors / Thomas J.
Stanley.
     p. cm.
  Includes index.
  ISBN 0-07-061048-7
   1. Rich as consumers—United States.   2. Social networks.
3. Financial planners.   4. Investment advisors.   I. Title.
HC110.C6S69   1993
658.8'348—dc20   92–44105

Printed in the United States of America
   0   FGR/FGR   0 9 8 7 6

This book is printed on recycled, acid-free paper containing a minimum of 50%
recycled, de-inked fiber.

For Janet, Sarah, Brad, and Molly

PREFACE

Why write a book about networking with the affluent and their advisors? The top 1 percent of the households in America account for nearly 40 percent of the wealth. Traditional methods of marketing, selling as well as advertising, are often ineffective determinants of the patronage behavior of the affluent. The affluent respondents whom I have interviewed report that interpersonal endorsements (also known as "word-of-mouth endorsements") were most influential in their decisions to patronize a variety of product and service providers.

Interestingly, some people, including many affluent individuals, serve as patronage opinion leaders. They exert considerable influence in this context. Why? Because they are viewed as having high credibility and intellect in judging the quality and character of those who intend to supply the affluent. Cultivating the endorsements of these opinion leaders is a very productive way to address the affluent market.

Why do opinion leaders go out of their way to endorse one offering but not another? Readers, you may be thinking that you deserve all the endorsements. Why? You feel that you are number one! You contend that your brand of product and service is the very best. After all, you graduated near the top of your university class. However, such attributes as good intellect and high-quality products and services are basic requirements. Most of the people who target the affluent must have these attributes. But these are core features, and it takes additional features to succeed in this market. The possession of these additional features often explains why some of your competitors enjoy higher sales volume than you. Those who have no Phi Beta Kappa pins may have two or three times the number of customers or clients than you have because, unlike you, they have the endorsements of the key patronage opinion leaders who influence the affluent.

More often than not, people endorse those who do more for them than provide conventional or core products or services. There are several methods of encouraging patronage opinion leaders to endorse one's offerings. These methods all come under the heading of networking. There are eight dimensions or faces of networking with the affluent and their advisors.

The most powerful way to network is to enhance the revenue of opinion leaders. Realize that before receiving business-related endorsements, you must first "send business." Revenue enhancers are more likely to gain important referrals than are those who merely tell people about their product and even about their Phi Beta Kappa pin. In fact, not one of the extraordinary networkers profiled in this book graduated at the top of his or her college class!

If you are the best or nearly the best in your field, you must take the initiative of telling key opinion leaders. You must cultivate their endorsements. But if your business revenue is not at the top for those in your field, don't despair. There is always hope. Encourage the market and its influencers to respond to your offering in a positive way. Network. By doing so, you can become a success in a small fraction of the time that is often required otherwise.

Without important endorsements, it is difficult to succeed in targeting the affluent and their advisors. Perhaps an analogy from our nation's military history can illuminate this point. Many historians feel that John Paul Jones was the finest officer who ever captained a U.S. naval ship. His extraordinary talents were well documented even prior to the Revolutionary War. On the day that the Continental Navy was formed, political opinion leaders (members of the Continental Congress) ranked each captain in our small navy. The rankings were supposed to be based on the so-called objective qualities of naval officers. Where did Captain Jones, the father of our navy, rank among the 24 captains?

In reality, the rankings were not based on objective criteria. They were based on the principle called "localitis." The 17 captains ranked ahead of John Paul Jones were all first endorsed by their respective "hometown political opinion leaders." The members of the Continental Congress received no such endorsements on behalf of Jones. According to his biographer, Samuel E. Morison, Jones "was the maverick of the navy," with no influence network, no support, no endorsements from shipbuilders, family, or community upon which to lean. Of course, Jones never spent much time or energy in attempts to influence the influential. He assumed, incorrectly, that those with the best core qualities would always be ranked at the top of their respective cohorts. Therefore, despite his talent, he was assigned to captain a small sloop, regarded as the "18th-best ship" in the U.S. Navy. All of those who were ranked above him were assigned larger/better vessels.

Readers, where do you and your offerings rank in the eyes of important patronage opinion leaders? Encourage these leaders to rank you high. Cultivate their endorsements. Become a vital part of their influence networks. Without their support, you may be assigned a small piece of the affluent market.

ACKNOWLEDGMENTS

The information contained in this book was gathered from conversations, interviews, and the case studies of hundreds of marketing, sales, and new business development professionals who network with the affluent and their advisors. Most successful networkers are very unselfish people. They are determined to do more for clients, prospective clients, and patronage opinion leaders than merely provide a core offering. Their willingness to share is greatly appreciated.

I am indebted to my wife, Janet, for her honest evaluations of case studies and for her patient guidance and assistance in the development of the manuscript.

Special thanks are accorded to Ruth Tiller for her extraordinary help in editing and word processing.

Finally, I wish to acknowledge the contribution of Sarah and Brad Stanley, who always gave "their candid insights about the true value of countless networking concepts and case scenarios."

Thomas J. Stanley

CONTENTS

CHAPTER 1

INTRODUCTION

"You must give before you receive."

WHAT IS NETWORKING?

Networking is the essence of high-performance marketing. It is the highest form of professional selling. Networking is influencing the people who influence the patronage behavior of dozens, hundreds, even thousands of affluent prospects.

Ordinary sales professionals target ordinary prospects. In sharp contrast, extraordinary networkers target prospects who are opinion leaders of affluent affinity groups. Imagine the impact on the revenue of an ordinary sales professional if he is endorsed by the president of a trade association whose members include hundreds of millionaires. In fact, such an endorsement was recently given at a trade conference.

How does an endorsement of this kind come about? The transformation of an ordinary sales professional into an extraordinary networker begins with targeting. The very best networkers identify and then prospect the advisors and role models of the affluent.

Numerous surveys of the affluent reveal a strong positive relationship between the level of an affluent person's wealth and that person's use of opinion leaders in selecting financial consultants, financial planners, bankers, insurance providers, attorneys, accountants, health care professionals, architects, home builders, artisans, and automobile dealers. In addition, opinion leaders have a significant influence on the choice of suppliers by affluent business owners and self-employed professionals. Supplier selection is typically associated with moderate to high risk. Hence, many members of the affluent population attempt to reduce the risk of hiring an incompetent supplier by choosing suppliers that opinion leaders endorse.

Eight years ago, frustrated by his low productivity, a young life insurance agent considered changing his occupation. But, luckily for his company, he never stopped making sales calls. And today he is at the very top of the productivity scale. How did he achieve this radical changeover? He will tell you that the most important call he ever made was to the president of a trade association with several thousand wealthy members. The agent gained the president's endorsement, and today his clients include more than 150 members of the trade association. How did he gain the president's endorsement? Not by immediately attempting to sell the president life insurance. The agent's initial proposal was to help the president meet his obligations to the membership of the trade association.

There are many ways to influence the opinion leaders of the affluent. This book discusses eight roles that networkers can play in influencing the influential. During their entire careers, most networkers play only one or two of these roles. However, a truly gifted networker described in this book plays all eight roles.

Some Basic Premises
Several basic premises should be comprehended before one attempts to network with the affluent:

1. Most affluent people are members of one or more affinity groups. These groups include trade associations, professional societies, retiree/senior citizen/mature citizen organizations, ecologically defined associations, political groups, and alumni associations.

2. Information about the quality and integrity of suppliers, including referrals and endorsements, diffuses much more rapidly within a group than between groups. In other words, the speed of intragroup word-of-mouth recommendations is many times faster than the speed of intergroup communication. The best networkers cultivate intragroup referrals and endorsements. Consider how long it would take the average sales professional to meet with 300 affluent prospects. The most optimistic observers would say months; others would say a year or more. But a sales professional was recently introduced to 320 affluent business owners in 2½ days. The president of a trade association made these introductions.

3. The affluent market segment is growing seven times as fast as the household population in this country. Dollar for dollar, the most productive way to penetrate the affluent market is to network with its members, their advisors, and key members of their important affinity groups. In spite of these facts, more than 90 percent of the sales and marketing professionals who target the affluent do not network. Why? Most of these people do not know how to network. Others are too impatient to network.

4. High-performance networkers gain endorsements for reasons that go beyond the basic product or service they offer. They do extraordinary things. For example, many enhance the revenues of prospects. In other words, they sell the prospects' products. They give this help before asking prospects to become clients. The affluent will go out of their way to endorse you if you do extraordinary things for them. Eight categories of these extraordinary things are described in this book.

5. High-caliber networkers focus their efforts. They first target those who will give the greatest return. Directly analogous to this networking approach is a military example. Sergeant Carlos Hathcock (USMC) was our nation's top marksman in Vietnam. Early one morning on patrol, he discovered 150 NVAs marching in an open valley. Who was the target of his first shot? The leader of the group. His elimination had an immediate and profound psychological effect on the other NVAs. During the three-day battle, Sergeant Hathcock and his companion, Corporal John Burke, were then able to eliminate most of the members of this affinity group. (See Charles Henderson, *Marine Sniper* [New York: Berkley Books, 1988].)

THE EIGHT FACES OF NETWORKING

Networkers can influence the influential in eight ways. This book discusses these eight faces or dimensions underlying influence networks. The following chapters contain case studies of some of America's top-rated networkers. Most of these networkers employ more than one of the eight dimensions. However, each is classified according to the major dimension of influence that he or she utilizes. The extraordinary networker described in Chapter 8 actually employs all eight dimensions. However, his major dimension of influence is that of someone who saves considerable money for clients and prospective clients. He does so by negotiating the purchase of expensive automobiles and homes for them.

Face One: The Talent Scout

Most affluent individuals are either successful self-employed business owners or self-employed professionals. They are in constant search of quality suppliers. Now consider for a moment the number of quality suppliers that sales and marketing professionals prospect. Productive networkers come into contact with hundreds, even thousands, of suppliers each year.

Why not act as a Talent Scout for clients and prospects? They will appreciate the efforts of networkers who play this role. However, truly enlightened networkers focus their energies when playing this role. They provide Talent Scout services to people who influence large numbers of affluent prospects. By targeting in this way, a young sales professional recently gained the endorsement of a millionaire who headed an important trade association.

This sales professional, a financial consultant, successfully targeted important opinion leaders who represented the most affluent industries within his trade area. How was this accomplished? He established an "Industry Advisory Council" that provided top-notch speakers to these affluent affinity groups free of charge. The "Council" also made available the names of top-ranked suppliers/ industry experts to members of the trade association. The experts he provided included leaders in such fields as advertising, estate planning, commercial real estate, marketing, public relations, production management, and materials procurement.

How was this sales professional rewarded for referring these top suppliers to industry leaders and other prospects and clients? His revenue was enhanced, the main topic of Chapter 3. The suppliers felt indebted to him, and many of them became his clients. Within 14 months, he was no longer a six-hour-per-day, cold-calling, low-level producer. He is now viewed as a Talent Scout and investment expert by members of one of the most affluent affinity groups in America. Most recently, he was asked to manage the investments of a trade association that represents thousands of affluent members.

Chapter 2 contains several important concepts regarding the

way in which a high-grade networker generated significant sales volume via the Talent Scout strategy. In addition, a portion of Chapter 8 details the Talent Scout activities of the Ace of Aces of Networking. His list of talent suppliers has 80 categories!

Face Two: The Revenue Enhancer

What is the most powerful method of influencing those who influence many other affluent prospects? As a general rule, it is the dimension of networking called "revenue enhancement." Ask most successful business owners, professionals, and other self-employed prospects this simple question: "What is your number one need?" Most will answer, "Revenue enhancement." Given a choice, would these prospects prefer to patronize a supplier who provides only a core product or service—that is, the basic or conventional offering—or one who provides more than the core?

Dull, normal truck dealers offer only trucks; unenlightened accountants offer only accounting services; run-of-the-mill attorneys offer only legal advice; and so on. Truly gifted suppliers, however, offer more than the core. For instance, consider the truck dealer who goes out of his way to find business and customers for his clients. Also note the business generated by Father Fred, a construction equipment dealer who lives by the networker's creed: "You can't sell construction equipment to contractors who have no contracts."

Father Fred is a master of networking via the revenue enhancement mode. This strategy accounts for a major portion of his own revenue. Prospects have sought him out. Influential clients have gone out of their way to refer business to him. Why? Because he enhanced their revenue. He is in constant contact with major contractors who employ his customers. Most of Father Fred's customers are subcontractors. On their behalf, he debriefs contractors about their needs for subcontractors. Thus, Father Fred creates his own demand. He enhances the demand for his clients' offerings. In turn, the enhanced demand for those offerings enhances the demand for Father Fred's construction equipment.

There are thousands of equipment dealers in America. But there are only a few Father Freds. If you needed equipment, what type of dealer would you seek?

Revenue enhancement is not limited to the construction industry. Look at the case of a truly enlightened auto dealer in Texas. To target top sales professionals from the investment industry, he networked with a regional sales manager from a brokerage firm. The sales manager referred his top producers to the auto dealer. Why? Because the auto dealer enhanced the sales manager's revenue.

The auto dealer not only referred his top suppliers to the sales manager. He also sent the sales manager the names of people who had recently been awarded major construction contracts in Texas. Almost all of these winners had bids in the over $1 million category.

How did the auto dealer obtain this information? He once asked a euphoric customer why the customer had purchased a top-of-the-line model. The answer was quite simple: "I just won a major construction contract!" He then asked the customer another question.

AUTO DEALER:

Sir, is there any publication that lists all of the people in your business who won construction contracts?

CUSTOMER:

Why, yes. Read "The Big One" section in the weekly publication called the *Texas Contractor*. It lists a dozen or more big winners each week!

Not far from the city where this took place, another revenue-enhancing networker, a young financial consultant, recently landed a $15 million account. His client was the owner of a successful welding company. When this financial consultant first visited the owner, what did he say?

Two of my most important clients own hundreds of oil-drilling platforms. They are looking for a welding company to service their platforms. I would like to put you in touch with them.

Both owners of oil-drilling platforms did, in fact, hire the welding company. And in turn, via the revenue enhancement strategy, the owner of the welding company opened a major account with the financial consultant.

In another case of revenue enhancement, a young sales professional enhanced the business of major suppliers to the food industry. These suppliers included leading industry experts on such matters as advertising, public relations, marketing, business valuation, estate planning, production planning, and commercial real estate.

How did the sales professional identify these experts? They all published articles in the top food industry trade journals.

When the sales professional in this case first prospected owners of food companies, they often said, "At the moment I don't need what you're selling." His response was quite simple: "What are your most pressing needs?" If the prospect stated that he needed an advertising agent, the sales professional made a referral to the advertising agent who was published in the trade journal. The advertising agent reciprocated by opening an investment account with the sales professional and by referring his food industry clients to the sales professional.

The top networker who employs revenue-enhancing strategies once stated:

> The most important thing you can do to convert a prospect into a client is to say: "Give me a stack of your business cards. I have many clients who are likely to buy from you."

Revenue-enhancing methods are simple, logical, and highly productive. Why, then do sales professionals use them so infrequently? Because these professionals lack empathy for the real needs of prospects. Fortunately, that empathy can be acquired. Revenue enhancement is the central topic of Chapter 3.

Face Three: The Advocate

The affluent in America typically agree with the following statement: "Although thousands of well-qualified accountants, attorneys, architects, financial consultants, bankers, and other types of professionals can provide basic services, few of those professionals have demonstrated any interest in supporting the causes that are really important to me."

The two service professionals described in this section are skilled in their respective disciplines. However, their success in generating endorsements from key patronage opinion leaders is explained not only by their core skills but also by their advocacy of the needs and rights of their targeted audiences.

Mr. Alan is a successful financial consultant. He helps clients and prospective clients by providing them with quality financial advice and investment management services. But he also plays the role of Advocate. Take a recent situation as an example.

One of Mr. Alan's best clients is a timber grower. This client owns thousands of acres of high-grade forest and periodically harvests timber from various tracts. But the client's livelihood is being threatened. Mr. Alan discovered this because he is a strategic reader of the editorial sections of both local and national newspapers.

Recently, he read a letter to the editor of his metropolitan newspaper that proposed banning the harvesting of timber in the state. This completely one-sided letter was written by an advocate of woodpeckers' rights. The letter stated that keeping woodpeckers in the forests was of more importance than the needs of landowners. In a letter to the editor of the same newspaper, Mr. Alan advocated a more balanced approach to the issue. He pointed out that earning a living was a basic democratic right and that "not even timber people are exempt from having to feed and clothe their children."

Mr. Alan mailed copies of his letter to all the timber growers and trade association officers listed in *Who's Who in Timber* and to selected lawmakers and clients. He attached this note to each copy that he mailed to members of the timber industry:

> I trust the enclosed letter will help your cause. If I can be of any
> further assistance to you and your colleagues, please let me know. I'm
> a strong supporter of the rights of business owners. Any comments or
> suggestions will be appreciated. Please call or write me.

Several timber growers called Mr. Alan to thank him for his kind support. All of the others took his telephone call immediately or returned the call within a day or two. Several eventually became his clients. A steady stream of prospective clients has been referred to him by the timber growers listed in *Who's Who in Timber*. How many other professionals who service the members of *Who's Who in Timber* played the role of Advocate? According to Mr. Alan, the answer is zero! And only Mr. Alan reaped the benefits that advocates receive. He has been endorsed as an outstanding financial advisor and asset manager by an increasing number of industry opinion leaders.

Mr. John is a landscaper whose case history is similar to Mr. Alan's. Although only in his mid-20s, Mr. John is already an accomplished networker and marketer of his services. As an example of his high level of networking, consider his recent role as an advocate of the rights and freedoms of senior citizens.

During a recent visit to his grandfather, Mr. John learned that his grandfather was quite upset by an article that had appeared in the local newspaper. The article argued that seniors were unable to operate motor vehicles safely and suggested that they be required to take a driver's test every year. Yet the author of the article provided no hard statistical evidence to support his contentions.

On behalf of his grandfather and all the other seniors who operated motor vehicles in the community, Mr. John wrote a letter to the editor of the newspaper. The letter advocated the right of seniors to retain their driving privileges and provided statistical evidence documenting the ability of seniors to drive in a safe and prudent manner. That evidence was gathered and disseminated to seniors by the state's Mature Citizens Association.

Mr. John sent copies of his letter to all of the senior citizens among his clients. Enclosed with the letter was this note:

> Most of my clients are seniors. I really appreciate your business and hope that the enclosed letter will help your cause.

A copy of Mr. John's letter was placed in his firm's "New Business Development Dossier," also known as a "promotional packet." The letter was also published in three area-based newsletters to which seniors subscribed. Mr. John's trade area is in the center of affluent retirement communities, and when Mr. John's firm submits a written proposal to the managers of these communities, it encloses something that none of his competitors can match—Mr. John's letter to the editor, which documents his role as an Advocate of the causes of senior citizens.

Mr. John also provides free landscaping services to two rest homes for underprivileged senior citizens. This contribution is noted in his dossier. Mr. John is quite frank about his view of landscapers. He will tell you that scores of qualified landscapers within his trade area are skilled in the development and decorative planting of gardens and grounds. Beyond this core service, however, only Mr. John distinguishes himself as an Advocate of his target market.

Chapter 4 details several examples of the advocacy role played by innovative networkers.

Face Four: The Mentor

Many top-grade networkers play the role of Mentor for clients. But only a much smaller number have been clever enough to play that role for the entire membership of an affluent affinity group. Bart Carr is one of them. He is the Mentor to the members of several dental societies.

Mr. Carr is not just a financial planner. He is also a skilled business consultant. His consulting specialty is enhancing the productivity of professional practices.

How did Bart establish himself as a Mentor to dentists? He asked the various officers of the endodontist society and other key informants this all-important question:

What do endodontists really need?

Interestingly, Mr. Carr's survey of key members proved that financial planning and insurance issues were not at the top of his target audience's list of needs. What issues were at the top of the list? Two of the most important were:

1. How to make the dental practice more productive.
2. How to value/sell the dental practice.

Mr. Carr proposed to the leaders of the endodontist profession that he and another expert conduct seminars on these issues. He persuaded the nation's leading expert on valuing/selling dental practices to conduct seminars with him, not by offering to sell him life or disability insurance, but by offering exactly what the expert needed—an opportunity to address thousands of prospective clients.

To date, thousands of endodontists have heard their message, a message from mentors. This is why so many endodontists have sought Mr. Carr's advice concerning financial and insurance matters. Would this have happened if he did not first position himself as a Mentor to the leaders, the society, and the rank and file of the endodontist profession? No is the answer he gave to this question.

But Mr. Carr is not the only networker who has served as a Mentor before receiving the benefits gained by mentors. A young top-producing financial consultant recently asked me to send an autographed copy of my book to the owner-manager of a luxury automobile dealership. I asked him why he was being so kind. He told me that he had developed an interesting method of generating new business. He conducts "Selling to the Affluent" seminars for selected automobile dealers and their sales professionals. In essence, his task as a Mentor is to teach clients and prospects how to fish.

At the end of each of these seminars, this financial consultant is given time to lecture on investment-related topics. Each time he converts a dealership owner into a client, he asks, "Do you know any other dealers who might benefit from my services?"

A financial planner is even more resourceful. He had the courage, intellect, and audacity to network with the regional sales manager for a manufacturer of luxury automobiles. What was the theme of his letter?

> According to a recent newspaper report, the public views most automobile salesmen as being unprofessional (copy of trade article enclosed). People in my industry have long faced the same problem. Along these lines, I conduct seminars on "How to Put Professionalism Back into Selling." I'm sure your dealers could benefit from my message. I have been a mentor to many people who today are truly sales professionals.
>
> Hopefully, we will be able to discuss these and related issues in person. I will call your office next week.

The regional sales manager did not wait until "next week." He took the initiative of contacting the Mentor in this case. Why? Because the Mentor offered to help solve a major problem facing him and his industry.

Yes. It is often productive for sales and marketing professionals to become mentors to influential people. Most networkers are, by definition, influential. So consider the value of becoming a Mentor to networkers. This is truly a worthwhile vocation.

The Dean of Networking, the Networker of Networkers, is Ms.

Genie Johnson of Dallas, Texas. A recent news release featured her contribution to this growing field.

> Genie Johnson may not have invented networking, but she perfected it.
>
> In February of 1988, Genie left her own investment advisory firm and concentrated on networking full time. She started a company called CEO Network. CEO Network's mission was to enhance the professionalism of networking as a potentially unlimited means of generating business. With the capitalization provided by member dues, many new and exciting networking concepts were initiated. In just three years, over $24 million in new sales were generated among the members of CEO Network!
>
> Networking works! A network group is a marvelous asset for each member. The group commits to helping members generate clients; members actually become a prospecting force for each other.

Why does the Johnson system of networking produce good results for its members? Because Ms. Johnson actually custom-designs each network group. For instance, take a moment and place yourself inside the shoes of a CPA who wishes to target surgeons. Ms. Johnson will recruit members who can help in this regard. She will find noncompeting professionals and other types of suppliers for a network group. But not just any noncompeting professionals and suppliers. The members she recruits will already have many clients/customers who are surgeons! And ideally the CPA will already have a client/contact base that he will share with the other members of his network.

It is Ms. Johnson's hands-on approach that makes her networking system so productive. Her proactive role as a Mentor to affluent networkers also bears fruit for the Johnson system. As a direct result of her personal efforts, many influential people go out of their way to refer business to her.

As an example of high-caliber mentoring, consider the following case study of how a Johnson network operates:

> The Plastic Surgeon in the network gave a lead regarding a vineyard owner to the network's Commercial Real Estate Agent. The Real Estate Agent helped the vineyard owner select a site for a wine shop with a tasting room in Dallas. After choosing the wine shop location, the Real Estate Agent passed the lead to the network's Advertising Agent, who, in turn, recommended its Printer and its Property and

Casualty Insurance Agent. Each network member landed the vineyard owner's business. The vineyard owner was happy dealing with vendors who knew one another and cared about his success. The members of the network felt that it had put forth a collective effort from which all of them benefited.

All the members of this network are taught by their Mentor to give first rather than to receive first. Most people fail in their attempts to network because they violate this procedure. Chapter 5 details the strategies of several mentors.

Face Five: The Publicist

Generating publicity and related endorsements for others is often more important than promoting oneself. This view is part of John Gorsline's philosophy of doing business. It is one of the major reasons that Mr. Gorsline is regarded by many as the premier supplier of life and disability insurance to world-class race car drivers.

The concept of insuring high-risk athletes is a very interesting one. It is especially interesting to the reporters who cover auto racing. Many of them have written feature articles about Mr. Gorsline's commitment to insuring race car drivers. Such articles have appeared in *Auto Week, On Track, USA Today,* the *Detroit News,* the *Montreal Gazette,* and *The New York Times.* In the 17 paragraphs that the *New York Times* devoted to telling the Gorsline story, the reporter posed an interesting question:

> Who in his right mind would sell a policy to someone who makes his living weaving through traffic at speeds that often exceed 200 miles per hour?
>
> John Gorsline is one who does. In fact, the Rochester-based insurance broker specializes in life and disability coverage for racing drivers.
>
> The key to Gorsline's success is the individual approach he takes to assessing risk. Insurance companies customarily evaluate and rate the riskiness of whole categories of people, but Gorsline has persuaded several underwriters to insure his clients on a person-by-person basis.

New York Times, July 26, 1987.

But person-by-person evaluation is not the only reason for Mr. Gorsline's success. Many world-class race car drivers refer their peers, other colleagues, and up-and-coming drivers to Mr. Gorsline. Why? When these world-class drivers were novices, he helped them with more than their insurance needs. He went out of his way to endorse them. He made important referrals on their behalf to writers, reporters, sponsors, team owners, and race car owners. In fact, several of the top race car drivers in this country will tell you that Mr. Gorsline helped them obtain their so-called rookie test. Passing this test is required to obtain a race car driver's license.

Mr. Gorsline has very close ties within the car racing community. He serves on several important boards that represent the car racing industry. But perhaps most important in terms of networking, he is a key source for the car racing media. He goes out of his way to supply ideas, wisdom, and case studies to various reporters. In essence, many members of the press rely on him for provocative case studies and new ideas for their articles.

Many members of the car racing media are in Mr. Gorsline's debt. He always makes himself available to the press for interviews and debriefing sessions. In regard to the car racing circuit, he is a cosmopolitan man. Last year he logged over 300,000 miles flying to car races all over the world. He also spends considerable time debriefing other key informants about "current events" in car racing.

Mr. Gorsline is an information and influence conduit within the car racing industry. So when he endorses a novice driver to the car racing press, sponsors, and other important players in the industry, that driver is likely to be recognized as a future superstar.

Interestingly, Mr. Gorsline does not limit his endorsements to his clients. In fact, he endorses any driver who he feels has exceptional talent. His integrity in this regard is one of the most important reasons for his success in networking.

It took Mr. Gorsline many years of hard work and dedication to become a distinguished member of the car racing community. Do all sales and marketing professionals have to wait for years before they can benefit from networking via the Publicist role? No. Several of the successful publicists mentioned in Chapter 6 are relative newcomers to networking.

Face Six: The Family Advisor

Most accountants, bank credit officers, financial planners, financial consultants, and life insurance agents can estimate the costs that clients are likely to incur in providing their children with a college education. But funding may not be the major issue in this matter. Some children of the affluent do not generate good high school grades. Thus they may be unable to gain admittance to the college of their choice.

Developing an investment plan for funding Johnny's college education makes little sense if Johnny cannot get into college. Several innovative networkers therefore play the role of Family Advisor to affluent families by helping them to get him into college. Chapter 7 addresses this and other problems that the affluent family may face. The problems include:

- The wish of children to move back home after completing their undergraduate or graduate programs.
- The drug or alcohol dependency of children or other family members.
- The wish of grandparents to move into the home of a son or daughter.
- The inability of adult children to provide for the education of their offspring.
- The conflict of children or grandchildren over the allocation of the proceeds from the liquidation of the family business.

At the very least, networkers can help families solve these problems by referring them to skilled specialists, thus playing a role akin to that of the Talent Scout. Influential clients will go out of their way to endorse the networkers who helped Johnny get into college.

The role of Family Advisor is also discussed in a section of Chapter 8.

Face Seven: The Purchasing Agent

Even extraordinary sales, marketing, and new business development professionals never fully utilize their skills and inherent talent. This statement holds especially true for the dimension of networking that relates to acting as a Purchasing Agent for clients.

Do you want to attract and retain an increasing number of important clients? Do you want to influence opinion leaders of the affluent? Do you want these opinion leaders to go out of their way to refer affluent prospective clients to you? If your answer to all of these questions is yes, then consider playing the role of Purchasing Agent.

If you're even moderately successful in selling, you are by definition an accomplished negotiator. Selling is, in essence, negotiating. Each year you negotiate the sale of your offering with hundreds, perhaps thousands, of clients. Are you tired of always playing the role of seller? Why not reverse that role from time to time? Act as a buyer, working on behalf of clients, prospective clients, and other influential people.

What is the most distinctive role played by the marketing professional whom I designated as the Ace of Aces of Networking? He often acts as an informal Purchasing Agent for clients (see Chapter 8). Follow his lead.

How can you acquire the knowledge you need to become an astute buyer? You already have it. List the tactics that your toughest clients and prospective clients employed when you negotiated with them as a seller. Use these tactics when you make purchases for clients who are not skilled buyers.

Compare your skills and experiences with those of your clients. Most of them lack your skills in relating to people. And many of them don't have the time, interest, or courage needed to ask sellers for a so-called better deal.

Most of your clients are not seasoned buying professionals, yet these clients often make both personal and business purchases. Many of them lose thousands of dollars each year by "cutting bad deals." Describing his own experiences with such clients, the Ace of Aces of Networking notes that

> many of my clients find it demeaning to ask the seller for a discount. This applies to the purchases of everything from expensive homes, luxury automobiles, commercial real estate, even businesses. That's where I come in. I offer my skills free of charge as an informal purchasing agent. It's a lot easier to negotiate on behalf of a client than to negotiate even for yourself. I have saved my clients thousands and thousands of dollars. It is just part of my commitment to clients.

There is another benefit of being a Purchasing Agent for clients. How difficult is it for a client to ask you to reduce your fees? It may be very difficult if you recently saved that client $70,000 by negotiating the purchase price of a home offered at $1.1 million. Not long ago, the Ace of Aces of Networking cut this deal for an influential client. No, the client never asked him for a discount on his fee. But he did refer several important prospects to him. Whom would you like to represent you? A professional who provides only the very basic service or one who will negotiate aggressively and wisely on your behalf?

Chapter 8 provides a profile of the best networker in the context of a summary of the eight faces of networking. While this networker often acts as a Purchasing Agent for clients, he also plays the seven other roles.

Face Eight: The Loan Broker

Mr. W. Robert Williams is no ordinary attorney. He is a senior partner of a highly successful law firm. Mr. Williams will tell you that he owes his success to providing clients with more than mere legal advice. Take, for example, some of his recent exploits in the role of Loan Broker. Keep in mind that credit is one of the most important needs of affluent business owners and professionals.

Recently, Mr. Williams contacted the publisher/editor/owner of a fledgling trade journal directed to owners of family businesses to propose that the journal publish his article on estate planning. However, before discussing his own objective, he debriefed the publisher and discovered that the trade journal was suffering from growing pains. Although the journal clearly had significant potential for making considerable profits, it was in dire need of a short-term credit infusion. Two local banks had turned down the publisher's loan applications; another financial institution had agreed to lend him money, but he felt that the loan rate and the origination fees were far too high.

Mr. Williams, a highly skilled negotiator and networker, offered the publisher his assistance in obtaining a loan at a competitive rate. He said:

> I often help my clients obtain competitively priced loans. . . . I do it all the time. I work with over a dozen enlightened bank officers. . . . I

send them a lot of business. They owe me a lot of favors. So they
rarely turn down an application that has my endorsement. . . . If
they turn down someone I recommend, I never send them any more
business. And they know I'm a man of my word.

As a result of Mr. Williams' loan-brokering activities, the publisher obtained a short-term loan four days after applying for it. (In
fact, several financial institutions competed against one another in
attempting to obtain the publisher as a client.)

Mr. Williams also benefited from this arrangement. The publisher had Mr. Williams' firm develop an estate plan for him. Eventually, the publisher also endorsed Mr. Williams and the firm to all of
his major suppliers—printers, office equipment dealers, media sales
representatives, graphic designers, and so on. And perhaps most
important, the publisher proposed that Mr. Williams write a series
of short articles about the estate planning needs of owners of family
businesses and a column responding to readers' questions about
such topics as minimizing estate tax, transferring the family business to the next generation, and dealing with insurance and estate
tax liabilities. The publisher also invited Mr. Williams to share his
booth at his industry's national trade association meeting. At that
meeting, Mr. Williams' theme, once again, was "Ask the Expert
about Your Estate Planning Needs." How should Mr. Williams
have responded to the publisher's proposals? How would you have
responded if you had been in his position?

Today more than 10,000 owners of family businesses subscribe
to the once struggling trade journal. Several thousand people attend
the industry's national trade association meeting. As a regular con-
tributor to both the journal and the trade association meeting, Mr.
Williams can invite other noncompeting, networking professionals
to access members of his targeted affinity group. In this way, he can
give visibility to top-notch accountants, public relations experts,
marketing consultants, and so on.

Mr. Williams' networking efforts are not limited to "for profit"
organizations. When he moved into a new home several years ago,
Mr. Williams also changed churches. He contributed his talent and
skills to his new church. The minister asked him to serve on its
executive committee. The executive committee consists of more

than 150 church members, most of whom are successful self-employed business owners and professionals.

The church's credit problems were discussed during the first executive committee meeting that Mr. Williams attended. The church had an outstanding million-dollar note. This loan was used to complete the church's Youth Center. The interest rate on the note was well above the current norm. However, the minister informed the executive committee that the lending institution holding the note "absolutely refused to lower the interest rate."

After the executive committee meeting, Mr. Williams obtained the minister's agreement to arrange another meeting with the officers of the lending institution. He accompanied the minister to this meeting. Within 10 minutes, the church was no longer burdened with an unconscionable interest rate on the note.

Why did the lending institution lower its interest rate? Mr. Williams explained to its officers that he had contacted several other lenders and that two of them were already committed to lending the church money at "one over prime." One of these lenders happened to be the major competitor of the lending institution. Thus Mr. Williams' network of sensitive lenders "contributed to a higher cause."

Mr. Williams was ultimately rewarded for his efforts. To date, more than two dozen members of his church have become clients of his firm. Positive word-of-mouth endorsements spread very rapidly through tightly knit affluent affinity groups. But what was the cornerstone of the rapid diffusion of positive information about Mr. Williams? Remember that people will go out of their way to endorse you if you do things that go beyond the core offering.

During a recent executive committee meeting, the minister told the members:

> I have some important news. . . . We have recently been informed that the interest rate on our note has been substantially lowered.

He then went on to acknowledge Mr. Williams' efforts. He introduced Mr. Williams as

> an estate attorney who obtains credit for noble causes and even clients. It's all part of his service commitment to our church and community.

Mr. Williams' estate planning business is a very successful one. But his estate planning skills do not fully explain his success. Much of his business is generated by his efforts to cultivate strong relationships with what he calls "enlightened credit sources."

Chapter 9 details the Loan Broker concept.

CHAPTER 2

THE TALENT SCOUT

"He developed a list of the top suppliers to the industry that he targets. Now an increasing number of the industry's members are seeking him out. They ask for and are given access to this information. They often reciprocate by purchasing his core offerings and referring their colleagues to him."

NELSON PARAMUS IS A SUPPLIER OF TALENT

When I first came into contact with Nelson Paramus, he had been in the investment business for about six years. I found his marketing methods to be extremely primitive.

Nelson was working long and hard but never generating a very large income. In his best year, he made about 40 percent of $155,000 in gross brokerage commissions, or only about $62,000. Why? Because he was not focused. Nelson prospected "all forms of human life." In other words, he categorized anyone who was breathing as a prospect. Thus most of his prospects and clients were far from affluent.

Moreover, Nelson's clients had nothing in common with one another. He had several hundred clients, but they were from several hundred occupational/industry categories. Also, only a small minority of his clients invested more than a few thousand dollars with him.

For these reasons, Nelson decided to change his marketing and selling strategy. He decided to target the affluent investor and promised himself that he would begin to focus on high concentrations of affluent prospects via networking. Within one year, his commitment to this marketing strategy began to bear fruit.

It is interesting and enlightening to reflect on Nelson's transformation from a "smiling/dialing cold-calling solicitor" into a sophisticated networker. Remember, Nelson, like many other extraordinary sales professionals, began his transformation from very near "ground zero." None of his friends, associates, or relatives were wealthy. And when his transformation began, he had few affluent clients.

How did Nelson become a friend, a service provider, an apostle to the members of an affinity group that contains a very high concentration of millionaires? He did so by positioning himself as a Talent Scout for his target market. His case study should be required reading for all professionals who wish to enhance their production. His system is applicable to a wide variety of professional services, including accounting, investment services, legal services, architecture, real estate sales, management consulting, banking, insurance, and public relations. Professionals who have suffered from low sales production in spite of hard work will derive the most benefit from Nelson's techniques. But even professionals who are just beginning their careers will benefit from the Talent Scout concept.

THE ANATOMY OF WEALTH

A key issue in targeting the affluent population is understanding the anatomy of the wealth contained in one's trade area. Most of the wealthy people in America are self-employed business owners and professionals. Thus, before you develop an affluent market strategy, you need to address this question: What types of industries within your trade area contain the highest concentrations of millionaires? A crude but effective way to obtain the answer is to contact your local Chamber of Commerce or the Industry and Trade Bureau in your state. Those groups should be able to tell you your trade area's top 10 or 20 industries in terms of sales revenue. Their ranking is not always a precise match of the actual ranking of the industries that have produced millionaires in a specific area. But, it is a reasonably good match in most instances. Many of the suppliers to the top 10 or 20 industries are also affluent.

So where should professionals like Nelson Paramus begin? How should they develop a marketing strategy? First, "Know thy trade area and thy client base.'' Trade and professional associations represent the top industries within one's trade area, yet few professionals ask their current clients whether they are members/officers of such affluent affinity groups. Moreover, few professionals capitalize on the affinity that their current clients have with these groups. Many times, a professional's current clients are members of these groups and can assist him or her in gaining access to other members. So first look at your trade area's anatomy of wealth and at the industries with which your current clients are affiliated.

Nelson followed this suggestion. I told him that the processed food and food distribution/service industry was an important affluent segment of his trade area. Yet it appeared that no other financial consultants were specifically targeting this affluent affinity group. Although my assessment was based on observation and not on a survey, it proved to be correct.

On three occasions within a 12-month period, I had been present at hotels in northern New Jersey when they hosted conferences of food industry trade associations. Thousands of affluent owners of food industry businesses had attended these conferences. During these three conferences, how many marketers of investment products were present? How many marketers of any professional service were present? How many marketers who believed they targeted the affluent took advantage of these opportunities to mingle with one of the highest concentrations of affluent prospects in America? Zero.

When I shared these observations with Nelson, his eyes lit up. Then I asked him whether any of his current clients were in the food processing/distribution/service business. He said that he had only one client of this kind—the owner of a small food distribution company. Today he has many more.

SYNERGY WITHIN THE CLIENT BASE

Once Nelson realized the enormous potential of the food industry, he began to construct his influence network system. Nelson interviewed the previously mentioned client to obtain his insights about the industry. During the course of the interview, Nelson learned several important facts about the food industry. One of these facts concerned readership habits. What did Nelson's client read? *Food Distribution Magazine!* The client gave Nelson a copy of this periodical, and he closely examined its contents. As he expected, there were no articles about investments, money, pension plans, and so forth. But this omission was about to be rectified. Nelson became the first professional in the investment field to publish an article in *Food Distribution Magazine.*

> I called the editor up. I said, "Ms. Editor, I have some articles to contribute to *Food Distribution Magazine.* Would you accept them?" She said, "No problem!" I faxed over a couple, and she published my first article two months later.

Nelson's first article in *Food Distribution Magazine* was entitled "Simplified Employee Pension–Individual Retirement Accounts Offer Small Business Owners Convenience and Flexibility." This simple, straightforward, one-page article described the benefits of various types of pension plans available to business owners. The article was a foundation stone of the network system that Nelson constructed. It enhanced his credibility with a very affluent segment. It established him as a person interested in and concerned about the investment needs of the business owners in a specific affluent affinity group.

NELSON'S NETWORK

Shortly after Nelson's first article in *Food Distribution Magazine* was published, he capitalized on it. He sent reprints of the article to the presidents of 25 local/regional food industry trade associations. Accompanying each of these reprints was a letter announcing the establishment of the Food Industry Advisory Council, also known as "Nelson's network."

How did Nelson locate the heads of these trade associations? For $100, he purchased a directory entitled *Who's Who in the Food Industry.*

> I did all the legwork. . . . I bought the book. [It listed] every single [executive,] company, association, media [trade journal], distribution, ice-cream maker that existed in the region. . . . I'm now a member.

Armed with the names and addresses of these affluent opinion leaders, Nelson decided to approach them with the Talent Scout theme. Most sales professionals focus solely on their own needs. But not the new Nelson.

> I said . . . I'm not going to go back to the same routine and cold-call these people. . . . I wrote them [the heads of local/regional trade associations] a little letter that . . . announced the formation of the Food Industry Advisory Council.

PRO FORMA LETTER ANNOUNCING NELSON'S NETWORK

Dear Mr. Smith:

I am writing to you to announce the availability of the Advisory Council for the food industry.

For some time I have been providing investment advice to many people within the food industry. I have also been writing articles that have appeared in *Food Distribution Magazine.* Because of my interest in the food services industry, I have had individuals come to me seeking speakers for association functions. In response to this evident need, we have developed the Food Industry Advisory Council.

Current members of the Food Industry Advisory Council include CPAs who will speak on the subject of business valuation and personnel tax management; insurance executives who are authorities on the subjects of buy/sell agreements, estate protection, etc.; professional money managers who are familiar with the needs of individuals in this industry; financial planning specialists who can provide help with retirement plans, 401K plans, and executive investment counseling; and others.

It is our intent to offer the services of the Advisory Council to food industry associations such as yours. You may wish to consider using one or more of these speakers for your future meetings. We can provide résumés and biographies detailing the expertise of these individuals. I hope that you will contact me in the near future if you wish to take advantage of this service.

My association with the food industry is a pleasure. Hopefully, this Advisory Council will make a positive contribution to the industry. Let me know if we can help.

Very truly yours,

Nelson Paramus
Financial Advisor

Nelson initially sent out this letter to the heads of 25 food industry trade associations. Within one week, the head of one of the most important food industry trade associations wrote to Nelson.

Dear Nelson,

We need a speaker to address the attendees at our [trade] show on Wednesday, August 21, at the civic center.

The subject is "The Impact of the Financial Market and Wall Street on the Food Industry."

Can you help?

Thanks.

Sincerely,

Marv
Executive Director

Working from ground zero a week before sending the letter, Nelson was now on a first-name basis with Marv. Would this have been the case if Nelson had contacted him via the traditional smiling and dialing assault method? I doubt it.

Upon receiving Marv's letter, Nelson offered Marv the services of a top food industry investment analyst as a featured speaker. He met with Marv several times to make sure that Marv's need for a speaker would be satisfied.

Marv informed Nelson that the members of the food industry

association were the owners and senior executives of food wholesaling companies, distribution companies, processing companies, and retail stores. The association's membership list reads like a who's who of the food industry! In fact, the association is one of the most affluent affinity groups in America.

How was Nelson rewarded for playing the role of Talent Scout? Marv endorsed Nelson to many of his associates in the food industry. In fact, thanks to Marv's kind endorsement, Nelson left his first food industry trade association meeting with 320 business cards from the affluent business owners who attended the meeting. Nelson was introduced as the "Talent Scout" who went out of his way to find a speaker.

The speaker whom Nelson had enlisted to address the meeting did an excellent job. Many members of the trade association felt indebted to Nelson for this quality program. After all, without Nelson's help the trade association might have had to pay thousands of dollars for a speaker of similar caliber.

Marv was so impressed with Nelson's credentials and with his contribution to the food industry that he opened an account with him. Consider the benefits of having a client who is an industry executive and an opinion leader. This client not only is a multimillionaire but also a living endorsement for Nelson. He is a part of Nelson's network. And he has introduced Nelson as his financial advisor to many of the affluent attendees at meetings of the trade association. Most important, Nelson's calls are now welcomed by hundreds of members of this affluent affinity network. The results of Nelson's first efforts within the network testified to his rising reputation. Of the first 50 prospects from the attendee list that he contacted, 10 opened accounts with him.

ENDORSED BY A LEADER

Why did Marv, a multimillionaire and a recognized industry leader, respond so positively to Nelson's offerings? Why did so many other financial consultants fail to capture Marv's business? Marv, like most affluent business owners, respects those who respect him. He responds favorably to those who empathize with his needs. So what does Marv need? Surely not one more cold call with the me-me-me message. He finds this approach offensive. Cold callers have little credibility with him because they usually have nothing in common with him.

Marv will typically turn down cold callers because they rarely mention the four needs of affluent/successful business owners. Few cold callers have ever said to a prospect:

> I'm a devoted supplier of your trade association. I also want to be a Talent Scout to you and your membership. I have an affinity for your organization. You're the head of one of the most important trade associations in your industry. I'm sure that your members expect great things from your administration. I imagine it's lonely at the top sometimes. I would like to help you meet the needs of your membership. I can supply you with a highly qualified speaker. He can address the future of "our" industry. He is a top analyst. There will be no charge for this service.

Marv wanted Nelson to help manage his investments because Nelson addressed Marv's needs as the head of a trade association before mentioning his own service offering.

Nelson does not actually manage his clients' investments. He often represents more than 100 of this country's premier independent investment managers, and he helps match them with his clients. In essence, these investment managers are also part of his influence network. And so are various other qualified professionals who have earned his endorsement. Among the high-grade professionals that Nelson has scouted are accountants, attorneys, insurance underwriters, commercial real estate specialists, loan officers, estate planners, and a variety of food industry specific experts. These professionals, in turn, have often referred/endorsed Nelson to their affluent clients.

THE NEED OF THE AFFLUENT

Once an individual like Marv has accumulated considerable wealth and perhaps distinguished himself as the founder and head of a highly successful enterprise, what does he still want to accomplish? Like many other successful people, he still wants to help others, to self-actualize. This desire explains why so many successful people become heads of trade and professional organizations. They want to help their industry or profession and its members. This desire transcends money and business success. For the Marvs of the world have already met their money and business goals.

Yes, recognition of success and revenue enhancement are important issues in the context of an effective sales message. But even more important for the Marv type are the issues that surround self-actualization. Marv had a problem. He wanted to do all he could for his trade association and its members. Nelson provided a solution to that problem. He helped Marv find an outstanding food industry expert who brought important insights to the association's members. And what does Nelson see in his future concerning trade associations?

> I'm not going to be their broker! I'm going to be their consultant. I'm the person [the consultant/apostle] who solves problems. You've got a mortgage problem, a plant relocation problem, call Nelson for this, call Nelson for that. I take lots of nonbusiness calls. But there are going to be some business calls too. We provide speakers, suppliers, consultants, help, recommendations, and advice. . . . No charge for any questions. Call our Food Industry Advisory Council. No charge.

THE QUESTION OF WHEN

Are you thinking about starting your own influence network? Nelson will tell you not to wait too long. It often takes several months, even a year, before you start to enjoy revenue enhancement via the influence network. Once your network has been established, however, you will probably have clear access to high concentrations of wealthy prospects. To establish the network, you must be prepared to work hard, focus on the real needs of your market target, and be patient.

RECRUITING INFLUENTIAL WRITERS

What has Nelson done since he published his first series of articles?

MR. PARAMUS:

> I also scouted other contributing writers, the other experts who wanted to participate in this industry. I called them and said, "We're trying to do the same thing. Let's get together. You give me clients, and I give you clients." One of them, Mr. H. H., happens to be one

of the premier consultants within the food industry. So I was calling the other day on a prospect in the food industry who was looking for a food consultant. And I said, "Well, call up Mr. H. H. He's the best in 'our' industry." They got together. They are now working together.

DR. STANLEY:

Nelson, in other words, were you just talking to a prospect who said he needed a food consultant and not an investment advisor?

MR. PARAMUS:

Yes. And I was able to put him in touch with a top food consultant. I focused on the needs of the prospect and brought Mr. H. H. and him together. Mr. H. H. was very appreciative. In his words, he said, "Nelson, keep them coming."

And he also said, "I want to offer discounts to your association." So I arranged for Mr. H. H. and Marv to meet. Now . . . they're putting a marketing package together to give [members] discounts on travel, discounts for this, food coupons, and bartering deals with members. Guess who's going to be the financial consultant for this group? Nelson, Nelson. First I'm a financial consultant for Marv, now for Mr. H. H. and many more to come!

DR. STANLEY:

What are you doing for them?

MR. PARAMUS:

Just traditional investing. I buy big market bonds for them, manage money, IRAs. Suggest some other things as well.

DR. STANLEY:

Whatever happened to the fellow from the food industry who called you and said, "Nelson, I want to move my plant to New Jersey"?

MR. PARAMUS:

I called the top commercial realtor in our area and put them together. They are both affluent. And they will both be clients someday.

THE NELSON PARAMUS PRO FORMA DIALOGUE

What does Nelson say to prospects when he first contacts them? Remember that prospects and clients are not the only people who are important in terms of his campaign. He must focus on their needs, he must often focus first on the needs of the secretaries/ interceptors of prospects, of the suppliers to prospects and clients, and of the members and potential members of the Paramus influence network. When he initially telephones a prospect in the food distribution/food processing industry, 9 times out of 10 the call will be taken by the prospect's secretary. Only one time out of ten will the call be taken directly by the prospect. A pro forma dialogue follows.

MRS. GRAHAM:

Good morning. Mr. Acme's office. Mrs. Graham speaking. How can I help you?

MR. PARAMUS:

Good morning, Mrs. Graham. This is Nelson Paramus. I would like to speak to Mr. Acme. Is he available?

MRS. GRAHAM:

Will Mr. Acme know what this is about? May I ask about the purpose of your call?

MR. PARAMUS:

Mrs. Graham, I met Mr. Acme last month at the Food Industry Association's national conference. I hope he remembers me. I'm the financial writer. You may have seen some of the articles that I have written in *Food Distribution Magazine*. I help business owners who are part of our Food Industry Advisory Council with pension planning and consulting.

MRS. GRAHAM:

Mr. Paramus, if you will hold for a moment, I will see if Mr. Acme is available.

MR. ACME:

This is Roger Acme.

MR. PARAMUS:

Mr. Acme, good morning. This is Nelson Paramus. I met you last month at the national conference.

MR. ACME:

Ah . . . I'm sorry. I met so many people at the conference.

MR. PARAMUS:

You may recall that Marv, the president, introduced us. I'm the fellow who supplied the speaker from Wall Street. I write the financial column in *Food Distribution Magazine*. I hope you have not forgotten me already.

MR. ACME:

Of course, of course. I remember you. Marv thinks a lot of your work. I have not read them yet, but didn't you just send me some reprints of your articles?

MR. PARAMUS:

Yes, I did. I hope you will get a chance to read the material. I help people in the food industry with pension planning as well as with their personal investments and strategies. That's why I am calling.

MR. ACME:

Well, I don't want to cut you short, but we will not reevaluate our pension needs until six months from now. If you want to call back then, I will be happy to set up a meeting with you.

MR. PARAMUS:

In the meantime, would you like to receive other reprints of my published articles on pension planning for the owners of private companies involved in the food industry? I also have several pieces of literature about how you can access America's best independent asset managers. I can send them along as well.

MR. ACME:

Please do. But I thought that big-time money managers only managed eight-figure accounts as a minimum. That leaves us out.

MR. PARAMUS:

I can set you up with top managers if you have at least $100,000 that needs to be managed. Do you have that much in your pension?

MR. ACME:

That much and more. Tell you what. Let's set a meeting with our accountant if you don't mind coming over here. It sounds as if you could help us. But I would not want to make a change right now without consulting our accountant.

MR. PARAMUS:

I will call your accountant and set up the meeting if you would like.

MR. ACME:

Well, before we get off the phone, I will put you back to Mrs. Graham, my secretary. She has my schedule, and she will call our accountant. Just tell her when you're available to come over.

MR. PARAMUS:

That will be fine. I really appreciate the opportunity. But if you have another second, I also do some work with corporate cases. Our corporate money account gives you instant access with the benefits of high yields.

MR. ACME:

Let me stop you right there. I'll be frank with you. We don't have a lot of cash right now. We are putting a whole lot of our resources behind our latest product. It's a great concept, but we can't get shelf space without advertising, and our advertising budget is limited.

MR. PARAMUS:

Sounds as if you could use some good press. Public relations pieces can do wonders for a problem like yours. A few well-placed articles can be more effective than advertising. I can tell you that firsthand.

MR. ACME:

Invoices were the only thing we got from our public relations consultant. That's why I fired him. I'm not too big on PR this week. You understand, don't you?

MR. PARAMUS:

Well, I have to disagree. A good PR consultant can do wonders for your company—especially a PR consultant who specializes in the food industry. Believe me, it works. That's why I'm published.

MR. ACME:

I see your point, Mr. Paramus. Can you suggest someone who might be able to help us?

MR. PARAMUS:

I think of myself as a Talent Scout. Finding top suppliers for you is part of my job description as head of the Food Industry Advisory

Council. We have a list of top-ranked suppliers who provide every-thing from estate planning to vehicle leasing and from commercial site selection to executive stress reduction. It is a part of the service, and all our referrals cost our clients nothing. It is just part of our total service concept.

MR. ACME:

I have stress, but first I need a PR expert who knows how to get our new concept in the press. Do you have someone in mind?

MR. PARAMUS:

Yes, I do. I will get back to you this afternoon or at the very latest tomorrow morning.

MR. ACME:

If this works out, I will send you a case of our new concept.

MR. PARAMUS:

What is your new concept?

MR. ACME:

An entire line of environmentally sensitive all-natural snacks. We have been endorsed by all the nature people and organizations.

MR. PARAMUS:

It's news to me. Great concept, but nobody knows. Did I define your problem correctly?

MR. ACME:

You hit the nail on the head. Nobody knows. We need PR. Can you hook us up with a truly professional PR person?

MR. PARAMUS:

I'll hook you up with the top PR professional in this country. But, Mr. Acme, I have a request. This month I will be talking to more than a hundred owners of food retailing firms and other food distributors. Can you send me some literature and samples of your new snack food line? I'm sure I will like the concept. And I will tell all those distributors about your concept.

MR. ACME:

You would do this for me? Don't say it. It's all part of the service. OK, I'm in your debt.

MR. PARAMUS:

Well, you're right again. I want you as a client. Is there any possibility that you would open an account with me today?

MR. ACME:

Well, I can't do anything about our pension fund today. And also we are real tight for company cash right now.

MR. PARAMUS:

How about opening an account with me for your personal investing? Do you have a favorite category of investments?

MR. ACME:

Tax-frees. Tax-free everything. Bonds and funds.

MR. PARAMUS:

We have several top munis and a top muni fund for residents of your state. But in the meantime, why not open a personal money market fund account. Then, when you receive the information about your tax-free offering, we can just purchase them from your cash fund. Would you like to start with $15,000 or $20,000?

MR. ACME:

I'll send you a check for $15,000.

MR. PARAMUS:

Can you give me your social security number?

MR. ACME:

My secretary, Mrs. Graham, will give you that and all the details. And let her schedule the meeting with our accountant. But don't forget to call back about that PR professional.

MR. PARAMUS:

I will be back to you shortly. It's a pleasure dealing with you, Mr. Acme. I'll talk with you this afternoon. Pass me to Mrs. Graham, please. And send me those samples.

MR. ACME:

Don't forget about the PR professional. So long.

SCOUTING PUBLIC RELATIONS TALENT

Mr. Paramus not only found a public relations professional who suited the needs of Mr. Acme, his new client; he also found a new member of his influence network as well as an affluent prospect.

How did Mr. Paramus find this top public relations professional? In reviewing various trade journals associated with the food industry, he noticed and read a series of articles about how public relations could be used as a proactive/competitive weapon. The author of these articles, Mary Davenport, was the head of a small, but highly successful, public relations firm. Her telephone number was given at the end of each of the articles. Mr. Paramus immediately placed a telephone call to her office. A pro forma dialogue follows.

MRS. WARREN:

Good afternoon. Mrs. Davenport's office.

MR. PARAMUS:

Hello. This is Nelson Paramus. I would like to speak with Mrs. Davenport.

MRS. WARREN:

May I tell her the nature of this call, Mr. Paramus?

MR. PARAMUS:

I just recently completed reading the articles that Mrs. Davenport published in the food industry journals. I write articles for the same journals.

MRS. WARREN:

Are you a public relations professional?

MR. PARAMUS:

Well, part time. I'm the financial writer. And I'm a financial consultant focusing on the members of the food industry.

MRS. WARREN:

Mrs. Davenport does not speak to financial consultants. If you wish to communicate with Mrs. Davenport, please send her your proposal in the form of a letter.

MR. PARAMUS:

Oh, I must apologize. I did not tell you the purpose of my call. I was not calling to discuss the topic of investments. One of my clients is the owner of a food processing and manufacturing company. He is having difficulty getting good press regarding his new snack food line. He desperately needs the services of a high-grade PR professional who understands the food industry. That's why I'm calling. My client asked me to find him a suitable PR firm. I wonder if Mrs. Davenport would be interested in being considered?

MRS. WARREN:

Oh, well, Mr. Paramus. Please hold. I will transfer you.

MRS. DAVENPORT:

Mary Davenport.

MR. PARAMUS:

Mrs. Davenport, Nelson Paramus calling. I have read every one of your articles about using PR as an offensive marketing weapon in the food industry. I am very impressed with your knowledge of both PR and the food industry. I'm also a contributing editor to the same journals.

MRS. DAVENPORT:

You name does sound familiar. What is your field of expertise?

MR. PARAMUS:

I'm the financial contributing editor. I focus on helping the members of the food industry and their suppliers with pension planning and personal financial planning.

MRS. DAVENPORT:

I just bought a rather expensive financial plan, and my brother-in-law is my broker. But I appreciate your call.

MR. PARAMUS:

I'm sorry. Pardon me. I should have made the purpose of my call clear to you. I head up the Food Industry Advisory Council. All the members are suppliers to the food industry. We provide speakers and advice to food industry trade associations and firms that are involved with food distribution and processing. You may want to join the team. But first I wanted to ask you a question. I have read your articles about PR and the marketing of food products. Am I right in assuming that you specialize in this area?

MRS. DAVENPORT:

We have worked in the food industry since 1970. It's one of three industries with which we have considerable experience.

MR. PARAMUS:

I have a client who has developed a wonderful product concept. He calls the new concept "environmentally sensitive all-natural snacks." He has an entire line.

MRS. DAVENPORT:

Sounds like a good concept.

MR. PARAMUS:

Well, it is. But he has a tight advertising budget. So he wants to place more emphasis on getting, as he calls it, good press. He did have someone helping him with his PR. But this consultant knew zip about the food industry.

MRS. DAVENPORT:

Is your client still turned off about public relations?

MR. PARAMUS:

No. Especially if I can introduce him to a PR professional with a winning track record in the food industry. I would very much like to put you two together. He's an entrepreneur. He makes his own decisions about promotions and public relations. So you will not have to dance in front of a selection committee. Would you be interested in helping my client? His company is not a household word yet. But it is a multimillion-dollar operation.

MRS. DAVENPORT:

I would be pleased to discuss our offerings with your client. We know the industry very well, and we have very good relations with the food industry press. We have placed over two dozen articles in the food trades in the past eleven months. In fact, the editors often call us for material. So if your client has a good concept, as you suggest, we can get it exposure.

MR. PARAMUS:

That's what I wanted to hear. My client, Mr. Acme, will be delighted when I tell him about you. In fact, I'm going to fax Mr. Acme your most recent article about proactive PR.

MRS. DAVENPORT:

That is very kind of you, Mr. Paramus. I hope your efforts to find Mr. Acme a PR professional do not cut into your own business. How do you find time to market your investment services and help clients find suppliers?

MR. PARAMUS:

It's all part of the service package. Often, when I call clients or prospects who own food companies, they tell me that their most urgent problem is not investment related (I know—it's hard to believe).

MRS. DAVENPORT:

Ah, what could be more important than investments?

MR. PARAMUS:

Well, some need advice about how to relocate a factory. So I find them a plant relocation expert. Or in one recent case, a client needed to sell his fleet of trucks. He now wants to lease, not own, a trucking company. So I found some buyers for his trucks and hooked him up with a top-ranked leasing company. I'm like a Talent Scout. When a client tells me he needs speakers or consultants, I find him the best—everything from estate planning experts to industrial engineers. By the way, do you give speeches about how to use PR in a proactive manner?

MRS. DAVENPORT:

Why, yes, I do, Mr. Paramus.

MR. PARAMUS:

Well, would you be interested in sending me a dozen copies of your résumé and a one- or two-paragraph concept statement about your topic? And send a dozen of your business cards and your firm's promo kit.

MRS. DAVENPORT:

I will have them in the mail to you today. But why do you want my business cards and promotional package?

MR. PARAMUS:

I talk with hundreds of owners and other top executives in the food industry each month. I'm sure, as in Mr. Acme's case, some of these people will need the advice of a top PR professional like you.

MRS. DAVENPORT:

That is so kind of you, Mr. Paramus.

MR. PARAMUS:

Please call me Nelson if you would like.

MRS. DAVENPORT:

OK, Nelson. And you may call me Mary. But, Nelson, you should be in the public relations business. We are both doing those things that enhance the client's business. But where do you find the time to do all this?

MR. PARAMUS:

I get up early. Actually, I really enjoy helping clients find suppliers and, in some cases, even new clients. I hope I have found you some new business. I'm going to call Mr. Acme right now and tell him that you will contact him.

MRS. DAVENPORT:

I really appreciate your kindness.

MR. PARAMUS:

No problem. I'm sure that your current financial consultants send you new clients all the time. Am I right?

MRS. DAVENPORT:

Not in my lifetime.

MR. PARAMUS:

Well, maybe you're not dealing with the right financial consultants.

MRS. DAVENPORT:

You could be right.

MR. PARAMUS:

What about your other suppliers? Your legal counsel, your accountant, and the like? Do they ever send you new clients?

MRS. DAVENPORT:

Our lawyer has helped us along these lines. But that's about the extent of it.

MR. PARAMUS:

Well, you need to join our advisory group. We all help one another as well as helping the members of the food industry. When we are out there selling for ourselves, we are also prospecting for one another. We are all suppliers to the food industry. And guess what? No one in our group is in the public relations business! We need to fill the void. Are you willing to join?

MRS. DAVENPORT:

Well, here I am taking but not giving. I would like to join. But, Nelson, what can I do for you? It seems that you don't need PR advice and support since you are already in the trades. Am I right?

MR. PARAMUS:

I have been able to publish my ideas in several good trade journals. But there are a few that don't seem too receptive to accepting my manuscripts. And these are some of the really big trades. I can't seem to crack them.

MRS. DAVENPORT:

What trades are we talking about?

MR. PARAMUS:

[*Lists three top food industry trade journals.*]

MRS. DAVENPORT:

I have worked with the editors of all three. In fact, two have called me for articles in the past few months. I know this industry. I will call them on your behalf if you would like me to.

MR. PARAMUS:

Mary, you would do this for me?

MRS. DAVENPORT:

It's all part of the service package.

MR. PARAMUS:

OK, all right. I will call Mr. Acme and tell him about you. Call him first thing tomorrow morning. Cheers.

MRS. DAVENPORT:

And I will call those editors. Give me a day or two to get through to them. Call them Monday. I'll bet they will be receptive to your ideas. Happy holidays!

INFLUENCING INFLUENTIAL NETWORKERS

Most suppliers to affluent business owners do not know how to network. However, Mrs. Davenport, the supplier of public relations services, is skilled in this regard. Like Nelson Paramus, she provides more than a basic service. She established her own influence network long before Mr. Paramus first contacted her. That is why it was so important for Mr. Paramus to align his influence network with Mrs. Davenport's. Their networks certainly overlap. They offer complementary services.

Each industry in America has its own set of influential networkers. These networkers often act as talent scouts for clients, prospective clients, and other influential networkers. Targeting these networkers can be very productive. Mr. Paramus is now networking with networkers. He is enhancing the revenues of influential food industry networkers. They, in turn, are providing him with access via endorsements to the key members of their networks. Some are even opening accounts with him.

IDENTIFYING TOP SUPPLIERS

How did Mr. Paramus identify top food industry suppliers? Remember that the food industry is well served by top suppliers from the fields of accounting, advertising, public relations, marketing, logistics, law, packaging, food sciences, product testing, and, most recently, investments and financial planning.

Mr. Paramus identified top food industry suppliers by scanning articles in food industry trade journals and newsletters, by debriefing writers and editors of key food industry periodicals as well as security analysts who specialized in the food industry and related industries, and by examining the directory entitled *Who's Who in the Food Industry*. But his most productive method was to ask clients and prospects to identify top food industry suppliers.

In the dialogue that follows, Mr. Paramus is turned down when he asks an affluent prospect to open an account. Most sales professionals would feel that nothing positive can be generated in such a situation. Yet significant benefits can be derived even from prospects who say no. Along these lines, reflect on the conversation between Mr. Paramus and Mrs. Sullivan, the CEO of a highly successful food processing company.

MRS. SULLIVAN:

Helen Sullivan. Good morning.

MR. PARAMUS:

Good morning, Mrs. Sullivan. This is Nelson Paramus. I met you at the national convention last month. Hope you remember me. The president, Marv, introduced us. I provided the keynote speaker. The food industry expert from Wall Street.

MRS. SULLIVAN:

I remember you. But let me save you a lot of time. My husband's a security broker, and so is his brother. In fact, half our family works in the investment industry. So the last thing I need is one more financial advisor.

MR. PARAMUS:

Well, I understand and appreciate your frankness. In fact, I was calling to congratulate you for the award you received. I read about you in *Food Industry Today* [*pseudonym*]. How do you feel about being selected as Food Product Innovator of the Year?

MRS. SULLIVAN:

I was delighted to receive the award. But awards don't sell new products. Call me in six months, and ask me the same question.

MR. PARAMUS:

I'm sure your new concepts will be big hits on both the consumer side and the institutional side. Hope you don't mind, but I just sent you a laminated copy of the article with your picture.

MRS. SULLIVAN:

That's nice, Mr. Paramus. What can I do for you—other than opening an account?

MR. PARAMUS:

Well, if you recall, when we chatted at the conference, I mentioned our Advisory Council. All the members, including me, are suppliers to the food industry. We give speeches on various topics. There is never a charge, whether the speaker is addressing a food industry trade conference or a group of employees from one firm.

MRS. SULLIVAN:

Well, Mr. Paramus, that is very kind of you to offer such talent. But we are not in the market for speakers at this moment.

MR. PARAMUS:

I understand exactly. Allow me to ask you another question if I may. In regard to what you buy, are you fully satisfied with the products and services that you are now receiving? Do you think you might need an advisor regarding the marketing, distribution, or advertising, even public relations?

MRS. SULLIVAN:

Mr. Paramus, if we are successful, and many people think we are, there is a reason for it. We have the very best suppliers in this industry.

MR. PARAMUS:

Would you care to nominate any of them for membership in our Food Industry Advisory Council?

MRS. SULLIVAN:

I hate to share them. But they are so good, I feel obligated to helping them. The exposure would certainly enhance their business. How many names do you want?

MR. PARAMUS:

All those that you feel qualify for "Mrs. Sullivan's Top Supplier Award."

MRS. SULLIVAN:

First call Sharon Fana of Fana Design. She's the best package designer in America. Don't tell her I said so. She has not invoiced us yet for the work on our latest concept.

MR. PARAMUS:

That is great. We do not have a package design expert on the council. I will call her today. I'm also thinking aloud. Does Ms. Fana need any advice from the members of the council?

MRS. SULLIVAN:

She's got very low overhead. Works out of her basement. But she is not shy about sending out world-class quality work. She has several major contacts with some top firms. If you're asking about her investments, I would say that she would make a great client for you.

MR. PARAMUS:

I appreciate your thoughtfulness. If you have a bit more time, are there any other suppliers that you would like to acknowledge?

MRS. SULLIVAN:

[*Faxes several dozen copies of a listing of supply sources in the following product/service categories:*

- Wheat flour
- Rice meal
- Corn meal
- Green peas
- Lima beans
- Blueberries
- Raspberries
- Strawberries
- Sweet potatoes
- Almonds
- Pecans
- Pistachios
- Walnuts
- Lemons
- Pork parts
- Sausages
- Milk products
- Eggs
- Cocoa products
- Plumbing, heating, and air-conditioning contractors
- Roofing contractors
- Vegetable oil
- Malt
- Ice
- Computers/ telephones
- Food processing systems
- Laboratory instruments
- Refrigeration specialists
- Refuse systems
- Loan brokers
- Health insurance
- Real estate managers
- Linen suppliers
- Package/graphic designers
- Disinfecting services

- Oranges
- Apples
- Cherries
- Peaches
- Beef parts
- Office furniture

- Printing
- Dust control
- Uniforms
- Conveyors
- Hoists
- Pest control services

- Equipment leasing
- Accounting services
- Legal services
- Warehousing
- Waste management/ Recycling]

MULTIPLE SALES

In some cases, a list of high-quality suppliers is more valuable than just one new client! Always ask clients and prospects to acknowledge their best suppliers. Then ask these suppliers, in turn, to acknowledge their best suppliers. This "Suppliers of Suppliers System" is a productive way to obtain prospects and an excellent foundation for establishing an influence network.

Affluent business owners in growing numbers are now contacting Mr. Paramus because they want access to his list of highgrade suppliers. He has helped many owners of food companies find the suppliers they need. Playing the role of Talent Scout has paid off. Many business owners and suppliers whom Mr. Paramus has helped have reciprocated. They are now his clients.

SUMMARY: KEY STEPS IN BECOMING A TALENT SCOUT

The years that Mr. Paramus spent in prospecting the nonaffluent were not a complete waste. During those years, he proved that he had the basic qualities possessed by most of the great sales professionals—considerable courage, an uncanny ability to withstand the pain of being rejected thousands of times a year, and a good deal of knowledge about the products and services he sold. Given these qualities, he was well equipped to achieve an extraordinary level of success via networking.

Step One: Focus, Focus, Focus
In order to focus, one must understand the anatomy of the wealth within his trade area. How can one determine the composition of the wealth within a trade area? One of the simplest methods is to

consult an encyclopedia. Even the least expensive encyclopedias will tell the reader what industries account for a significant portion of the economy in each of the states.

The food industry, including food processing and distribution, accounted for a significant portion of the economy in the three states in which Nelson operated. Interestingly, the food industry is one of the top five industries in most states.

Step Two: Enhance Your Credibility

What action did Nelson take after discovering the importance of the food industry? He reasoned correctly that this industry comprised thousands of affluent business owners. Nelson contacted one of these owners and asked him what food industry trade journals and newsletters he read.

In this way, Nelson learned the name of the most frequently read food industry trade journal and of its editor. He called the editor and proposed that she publish his article about pension plans for business owners. Why was his proposal accepted? He was the only investment professional who had made such a proposal, and the editor realized that her journal needed to deal with the financial needs of its readers.

Step Three: Target the Flagships within the Affluent Convoy

Nelson identified the heads of several important food industry trade associations. Most trade associations publish a directory of their members. Many also publish a "Who's Who in the Industry" type of directory. Nelson utilized such a directory to target important food industry officials.

He sent a letter to selected officials of food industry trade associations. The letter related to the needs of the officials—offered the officials high-grade speakers free of charge. Accompanying the letter was a reprint of the article Nelson wrote for the top food industry trade journal. This reprint enhanced his credibility among the recipients of the letter.

As a result of the letter, Nelson supplied a speaker for a meeting of an important food industry trade association. Marv, the head of the trade association, felt indebted to Nelson and admired his ability to market himself. Marv not only opened an account with Nelson but also endorsed him to many of the members who attended the trade show, the same trade show at which Nelson heard one of his stable of speakers deliver an important talk on "The Impact of the Financial Market and Wall Street on the Food Industry."

While Nelson was at the trade show, he collected business cards from 320 affluent business owners. These 320 owners constituted his core prospects. On average, he was able to open accounts with one in every five of the core prospects he contacted initially.

Step Four: Offer More than the Core

Despite Nelson's enhanced credibility and demonstrated affinity for the members of the food industry, not all prospects expressed an interest in opening an account with him. However, he rarely ended a telephone conversation with a prospect without obtaining some important information. What types of information?

Nelson reasoned correctly that many prospects who did not need his services needed the services of others. He asked about such needs. And what happened when these prospects had needs that current suppliers were not meeting? Nelson became their Talent Scout. He went out of his way to find top suppliers who would meet their needs.

Furthermore, when Nelson called prospects he often asked them whether they would nominate/acknowledge their most outstanding suppliers of all kinds—everything from specialists in industrial real estate to suppliers of flour and corn meal.

Step Five: Recruit Top Suppliers

As Nelson prospected, he also debriefed members of the food industry. Thus he built up an impressive list of the top industry suppliers. He often called on these suppliers, asking them whether they would be interested in helping his clients/prospects who had needs related to their offerings. In this way, Nelson often gained the endorsements and accounts of important food industry suppliers. These suppliers also referred him to their clients.

In addition to providing food industry suppliers with revenue-enhancing opportunities, Nelson offered them membership in his Food Industry Advisory Council. This membership translated into speaking engagements for many of the suppliers.

Step Six: Target Suppliers of Suppliers

Just as the most productive business owners often deal with the best suppliers, so, too, do these suppliers. Nelson therefore prospected the suppliers to his food industry clients and prospects, and when he began serving such a supplier, he would ask for an endorsement to the supplier's suppliers, and so on. Having followed this practice, he no longer has to call prospects who have no affinity for him and his clients/network members. None of his calls are cold calls because he has something in common with all prospects who are part of the food industry and the industries that supply it. He is not limited to one industry with a finite number of prospects because he has created an endless chain of prospects via his influence network system. Remember that the suppliers to one's clients generally feel that it is important for them to talk to the Nelsons of the world, because the Nelsons of the world have been endorsed by important clients of these suppliers. These suppliers may feel that ignoring the Nelsons could tarnish their relationship with such clients.

Step Seven: Continue to Enhance Your Image as an Expert, Apostle, and Networker

Most sales professionals never reach extraordinary levels of production because they either do not initiate the network strategy or because they abandon it. Most of the sales professionals who initiate the strategy stop networking within the targeted affinity group before the strategy's benefits have been realized. It often takes a full year of networking before this strategy begins to pay dividends.

Networking requires patience, discipline, and a long-range view. It should be a lifetime commitment to helping solve specific problems of the targeted affinity group. That is why it is especially important for the networker to have a genuine affection for the group he chooses to serve.

CHAPTER 3

THE REVENUE ENHANCER

"He sells more remanufactured diesel engines than anyone else. How? He first asks prospects to sell him their worn-out engines. Only after enhancing their revenue in this manner does he ask them to purchase remanufactured replacements."

FATHER FRED MARKETS MORE THAN CONSTRUCTION EQUIPMENT

Fred Peterbaum was the mentor to an extraordinary networker. Dr. J. Conrad Peterbaum, his son, is today a top-ranked dentist as well as an accomplished marketer. Dr. Peterbaum is an advocate of his patients' causes (see Chapter 4). Fred, an independent businessman who owned an equipment distributorship, was in an extremely competitive business. His ability to relate to his customers' needs was therefore critical to his success.

Fred told J. Conrad that construction people could buy or lease their equipment from many different distributors but that few of these distributors offered services going beyond the basic ones related to the equipment business. Fred, on the other hand, often extended credit to customers with "poor credit ratings."

Fred was an excellent judge of character and talent. He realized that many highly talented customers had poor pro forma credit ratings. Such customers were often simply victims of sudden downturns in their industry. They would typically pay their bills, but it would often take them months or even a year to recover from those downturns in the industry. Fred believed that people with talent and character would always pay their bills. That belief is a significant reason why the Peterbaums had a large number of very loyal customers.

This is not to say that Fred indiscriminately extended credit. He did not. He extended credit only to those who he thought had integrity and whom he felt he could "place." What does the term *place* mean? This word hints at the fundamental factor that explained Fred's significant success.

An Information Conduit and a Revenue Enhancer

By the nature of his business, Fred was a conduit of critical information about the construction and contracting business within his market area. He was among the first to know when a major construction job was about to be started. Why? He kept in constant contact with contractors and subcontractors. Every workday he would visit construction sites. While there, he would ask key decision makers about their needs for subcontractors, craftsmen, and, of course, construction equipment. Contractors who anticipated successful bids would place orders with Fred—but not only orders for equipment. These contractors viewed Fred as a "for free" headhunter—as a person who could provide them with the names of the talented craftsmen they needed.

Of course, the size and composition of Fred's orders indicated the types of subcontractors and craftsmen that the general contractors would need on the job. General contractors often regarded Fred as more than an equipment supplier. They regarded him as their apostle and their information conduit. They welcomed and sought his suggestions regarding many types of human resources. In essence, Fred acted as a Revenue Enhancer and an informal employment agent for most of his customers.

So beyond offering a good location, excellent products, and a fine service reputation, Fred offered much more. When a customer, perhaps a mason or foundation contractor, needed work, Fred would refer him to a contractor who was flush with new business. Fred's referral system was based on his genuine desire to help customers and his considerable empathy for their needs. Moreover, he fully realized that those needs often transcended equipment and machinery. Fred's motto was a simple one:

You can't sell equipment to a customer who has no customers. Referrals are among our most important products. People will seek you out if you will help them with their most important need, that is, *enhancing their revenue*. How can people pay their bills if they're out of work? If they owe me money, I won't hassle them; but I will help them get some business. A threat to my client's revenue is a threat to mine. And almost all my customers pay their bills. They are good people, but they also have a very good reason to settle their accounts with me. If they don't, they know that I will no longer campaign for them . . . no more job placements.

Fred would take time to get to know his customers and their businesses. He was particularly sensitive to the needs of highly skilled craftsmen who had recently immigrated to America. He had special empathy for them.

Fred's dad was a highly skilled carpenter who immigrated to America. But when he arrived, he had little marketing or sales experience and no credit rating. Thus he struggled for several years to move from ground zero. What Fred's dad needed when he arrived was a Revenue Enhancer to help him market himself. His dad's experiences helped Fred to conceptualize a marketing plan for establishing an equipment dealership. He concluded that customers would seek him out if he provided them with revenue enhancement services.

Because of their close affinity with Fred, his customers were quick to join his influence network by making referrals and endorsements on his behalf. "Fred is not the lowest-priced distributor," they would tell people, "but he'll earn your business with high-quality, well-serviced equipment and even go out and get you business."

Fred often found that customers who owed him money were willing to barter. Fred's business often offered for sale used automobiles, trucks, and boats that had been given as barter for unpaid bills. Other items that Fred accepted as barter included go-carts, pegged flooring, and a large pig. A master bricklayer paid his bill for the equipment that he borrowed from Fred by constructing two fireplaces and a chimney for Fred's new home.

Fred was successful because he observed the Golden Rule. So, too, did his son, Dr. Peterbaum. Fred and his son wrote their own golden rule for networking. As a result, they both received thousands of word-of-mouth endorsements from influential people. Enhancing the revenue of prospects, customers, and patients brought them endorsements, referrals, and lifelong customers.

WHAT DO FUND-RAISERS REALLY NEED?

Dear Networker:

You are correct in speculating that many professional (for hire) fund-raisers are affluent. So why is it that you have only one of these affluent professionals as a client? Could it be that you only prospected one fund-raiser during your 20-year career? Wake up and smell the java.

There are nearly 1,000 fund-raisers within your self-defined trade area. They are underprospected by the members of your industry. Those who do prospect fund-raisers typically employ the wrong promotional message. Also, they rarely time their solicitations in harmony with the cash flows of these prospects.

Most fund-raisers are paid for performance. For example, the fund-raiser who just fulfilled her obligation to raise $10 million for a nonprofit organization is euphoric. She should be. Ms. Barry just received her compensation ($750,000). But no one from your industry prospected her during this period of cash flow—induced euphoria.

How could you have discovered that Ms. Barry was euphoric? Two weeks ago, your local newspaper reported that Ms. Barry's client (a prominent eleemosynary organization) reached its fund-raising goal. No. The article did not mention Ms. Barry by name. However, I telephoned the organization and asked, "Who is your fund-raiser?" They were kind enough to give me her name and telephone number.

You could have taken this initiative yourself. Assuming you did, what would you say to Ms. Barry when you contacted her? More important, what overall strategy would you employ in addressing the real needs of affluent fund-raisers?

In order to answer these types of questions, consider three levels at which you can relate to this market.

Level I: The Me-Me-Me Orientation

At this level, you identify individual fund-raisers who are euphoric about upswings in their cash flows. You contact these prospects. You congratulate your prospect for succeeding in raising money for a good cause. Then you ask the me-me-me question:

Would you invest your earnings with me?

This is not the most productive way of selling, nor is this high-performance networking.

Level II: The Minor League Revenue Enhancement Operation

At this level, you target successful fund-raisers. More important, you tap their "affluent donor network." Consider adopting the following pro forma dialogue with a prospect.

Ms. Barry, I would like to enhance the productivity of your fund-raising activities.

I'm sure that many of your prospective donors, as well as current patrons, are quite affluent. Also, I venture to guess that many of these people hold large portfolios of publicly traded securities.

I will donate 50 percent of all the commissions I earn in trading securities for these people. I will give these commissions to any nonprofit organization that these donors/prospective donors designate.

These people probably spend considerable amounts of money each year on brokerage fees. Therefore, these types of donations will not really cost them one marginal dollar. They are already paying for these brokerage services anyway.

But perhaps I'm being presumptuous. Has your current financial consultant already proposed giving 50 percent of his commissions? Oh, that's too bad. Perhaps you should fire him. By the way, who is your financial consultant?

If you use this approach, you are likely to convert Ms. Barry from a prospect to a client. Even more important, Ms.

Barry may give you access to the thousands of affluent donors who compose her influence network. Why? Because you are proposing to enhance her revenue.

Level III: The Major League Revenue Enhancement Orientation

There is a drawback to the Level II orientation. At Level II, you target individual fund-raisers, i.e., one at a time.

Remember my lecture on productive targeting. I mentioned the strategy of the top fighter ace in the history of aviation. Why was Major Hartmann so successful? The ace of fighter aces did not target individuals. He targeted clusters/formations/segments. He carefully chose to attack the formation of enemy aircraft that he could most easily conquer. Then he focused all of his energy and weapons on his chosen cluster. Why not learn from Hartmann's record of 352 victories? Target a formation containing thousands of influential opinion leaders. Help stimulate charitable contributions. That is exactly what Ms. Muriel Siebert, a New York City—based stockbroker, recently did. Follow her lead.

What vehicle did Ms. Siebert use in cultivating a network of networkers, a convoy of influential fund-raisers? How did she convey her message to an entire industry of fund-raisers? A recent promotional theme for the vehicle she employed, a trade journal, answered this question.

REACH TOP-LEVEL FUND RAISING PROFESSIONALS!

SUBSCRIBERS TO **THE CHRONICLE OF PHILANTHROPY** ARE THE CEO'S, EXECUTIVE DIRECTORS, DEVELOPMENT OFFICERS, AND OTHER ADMINISTRATORS WHO MANAGE AMERICA'S NONPROFIT ORGANIZATIONS.

THE **CHRONICLE** HAS THE LARGEST PAID CIRCULATION OF ANY PUBLICATION IN THE FIELD—22,970 PAID (SUBSCRIBERS). TO REACH THESE DECISION MAKERS WHO CONTROL THE DYNAMIC AND GROWING **$260 BILLION NONPROFIT MARKET,** CALL (202) 466-1212 TODAY!

Who are among the most influential people in America? The readers of the *Chronicle of Philanthropy* are. When it comes to the affluent market, few professional groups as a whole have more influence than fund-raisers and development officers for nonprofit organizations. Their task is to enhance the revenues of foundations, health care organizations, colleges/universities, religious organizations, the arts, social service causes, and related noble causes.

Successful fund-raisers are almost by definition skilled networkers. Their task is to influence the affluent and their advisors. There are more than 20,000 fund-raisers in this country. Their job has never been an easy one. They must identify and solicit funds from prospective donors/patrons. They must encourage current patrons to keep giving.

Today their task is even more difficult. According to numerous articles in the *Chronicle of Philanthropy,* the affluent are contributing fewer dollars today than they did just two years ago. This is unfortunate in light of the growing needs of various philanthropic associations and their constituents. Also, there are more fund-raisers competing today for these precious dollars.

What do these fund-raisers and the philanthropic organizations they represent need? They need enlightened people like Ms. Siebert to enhance their fund-raising efforts. A networker who could fulfill this need would probably be rewarded. The sense of pride in helping philanthropic organizations is a significant reward in itself. But a skilled networker in this situation will also benefit in terms of his own revenue enhancement. Remember, every successful fund-raiser in America is likely to have networks that contain hundreds, even thousands, of affluent individuals.

A reprint of the article that details how Ms. Siebert enhanced the fund-raising efforts of philanthropic organizations is enclosed. Please read this material.

N.Y. Stock Exchange's First Woman Uses Profits to Underwrite Charities

By Elizabeth Greene

It was going to be a typical birthday for Muriel Siebert, a power-house stocks-and-bonds trader: She would hit tennis balls with a pro and then pamper herself with a massage, a manicure, and a pedicure. Instead, she was asked to appear at a function sponsored by the Manhattan borough president's office in honor of a nonprofit that provides after-school activities for poor kids.

And, as always, she found herself making business deals.

"You must be buying bonds in next week's city deal," she told Robin Farkas, chairman of the now closed Alexander's department store chain. "Give me the order; I'll give the profit to this group."

In the end, she says, "they didn't buy their bonds with me, but the idea stuck."

What started out as a lighthearted attempt to lure Mr. Farkas into doing business on that September day in 1990 has evolved into a full-fledged charitable program run by Ms. Siebert's stockbrokerage, Muriel Siebert & Company. Ms. Siebert, who in 1967 became the first woman to buy a seat on the New York Stock Exchange, is making a new name for herself with an unusual philanthropic program that flies in the face of stereotypical Wall Street greed.

Under the Siebert Entrepreneurial Philanthropic Plan, often referred to as SEPP, Ms. Siebert, 59, gives half of her commission from the new securities she underwrites to charities in the cities where she does business. The only costs that she subtracts from her earnings are what she pays for the paperwork involved in completing a transaction.

"I was raised to believe that when good things happen, you owe," she says. "And it's a good feeling for me to realize that I am able to put together my brain, my heart, and my knowledge of business to create something like this."

Wall Street "a Prejudiced Place"

A lot of good things have been happening to Ms. Siebert lately. As a result of increased interest among federal, state, and local governments in getting more woman- and minority-owned businesses to underwrite new securities, Muriel Siebert & Company is seeing a lot of new business come its way. Corporations, too, are paying women more heed when they look for brokers to sell new issues of their stock.

"Look, I come from Wall Street—it's a prejudiced place," Ms. Siebert says, explaining that she has been excluded from many business opportunities because of her sex. "I've never been in until these deals came around," she adds, referring to the special efforts by securities issuers to get more women involved in selling their stocks and bonds.

Previously, she served mainly as a discount broker for individuals and some institutions, such as insurance companies and those handling pension plans.

In the last three years, the portion of Ms. Siebert's business devoted to underwriting new securities has grown from zero to 20 percent, giving her a whole new pool of money to play with—and donate to charity through the Siebert Entrepreneurial Philanthropic Plan.

Last year, the plan's first, Ms. Siebert donated $300,000. This year, she hopes that contribution will jump to $1 million. Within three years, she anticipates that she will be able to donate $5 million annually.

Ms. Siebert doesn't pretend that her interest in charity is purely altruistic. Part of her reason for designing the philanthropic plan, she says, was to draw new clients to her firm by distinguishing her services from the rest of the pack. Issuers of new securities who choose Ms. Siebert to do their underwriting, as well as the customers who buy those securities through her, do so now with the knowledge that a portion of the money will be used to provide services for their communities—and to improve their image locally.

"See, I'm a competer," Ms. Siebert says. "I realize that this accomplishes many things for me." She adds: "I believe the program is starting to generate business."

Businesses Like Charity Angle

Jeffrey S. Baloutine, vice president for community reinvestments at the United Savings Association of Texas, says traders at his company expressed interest in working with Ms. Siebert because they were attracted to SEPP. Much of the savings and loan's business is lending money to housing developers, so it was no accident that officials there asked that the profits from their transaction with Ms. Siebert go to a charity that develops low-cost housing in Texas and help poor people.

"It reinforces what we are already doing," says Mr. Baloutine. "This enabled us to put a pretty good amount of money out into the community very quickly in response to needs that have been articulated."

An insurance company securities analyst who asked not to be identified says he was attracted to purchasing securities from Muriel Siebert & Company not because it would improve his company's relationship with local groups, but because it would make him feel better about the work he does. It's unusual, he says, to come in contact with a stockbrokerage that isn't interested in getting "every ounce of blood" out of a deal. "It's refreshing," he says.

Depending on the type of deal, charities are selected for the SEPP program either by the issuer of the securities, by the buyer, or by Ms. Siebert herself. Neither the issuer nor the buyer can receive a monetary reward or tax benefit from the donation.

So far, almost 60 charities have received a share of Ms. Siebert's profits. The gifts include $32,804 to City Harvest, a group here that collects food from restaurants and hotels and delivers it to homeless shelters and other programs for the poor; $7,804 to god's love we deliver, a nonprofit that gives meals to homebound aids patients; $5,388 to weave, or women escaping a violent environment, in sacramento, california; and more than $23,000 to para los ninos, a los angeles group that serves homeless and other poor families.

SEPP is also planning to give between $140,000 and $150,000 to Rebuild L.A., the organization that is spearheading the effort to help Los Angeles recover from the recent riots there.

The nonprofits that have received money through SEPP praise the program for providing them with unconditional, easy support. Kay L. Mitchell, acting director of development at God's Love We Deliver, says that because Ms. Siebert's money comes with no strings attached, it has enabled the group to respond to the most urgent needs—to "follow the budget of necessity rather than create an area to fit the funding."

Gail A. Jones, executive director of WEAVE, was delighted when her group received SEPP funds. Ms. Siebert "identified us on her own," says Ms. Jones, "and the first check came in totally out of the blue." Ms. Jones says she has used the SEPP money to help with operating costs for her shelter for battered women and their children and for her counseling center.

Ms. Jones says Ms. Siebert's level of interest in local non-profits is rare. "I really appreciate her sense of stewardship, in giving something back to California or back to the community where she does business," she says. "That is just really unheard of, I think, for a lot of the people who do business across the United States.

Special Emphasis on Women

Ms. Siebert, who seeks out groups that spend little on administration, says she has a special interest in nonprofits that serve women "since a lot of my honors have come because I am the first woman to have done many things." She adds: "I bought my seat [on the New York Stock Exchange] before the women's movement, and yet I've also been a beneficiary of the women's movement."

Her colleagues on Wall Street say that creating the Siebert Entrepreneurial Philanthropic Plan was a wise move for her company.

Glenn P. Evans, a vice president at Pryor, McClendon, Counts & Company, an investment banking firm that competes with Ms. Siebert's, says he views SEPP first and foremost as a "marketing strategy." He agrees with Ms. Siebert that while SEPP serves an important purpose in local communities, it could be highly profitable as well.

"It's certainly something that helps distinguish that firm as one that's interested in being a force in the communities where it has an interest," he says. "It sets them apart and to that extent I see it as part of how the firm is marketed. There's nothing sinister about that at all. I think it's good business."

As for his company, Mr. Evans says, its charity is "driven by the affiliations of the partners."

That sort of charity, Ms. Siebert says, isn't enough for her. "My attitude is that if I just took [my money] and put it into my pet charity, all I would be doing is giving away money to places that I would already give it away to," she says. With SEPP, Ms. Siebert says, she is able to better identify pressing local needs because she is working with people who are closely tied to non-profits in their communities.

She has a separate philanthropy, the Muriel Siebert Foundation, which has $180,000 in assets, for her old favorites—a library, a hospital, and an art museum in Southampton, Long Island, where she has a condominium, for example. In addition, she sits on the boards of the Greater New York Council of the Boy Scouts of America and the World Affairs Council of Long Island, which presents speakers on international topics on the Southampton campus of Long Island University. She is also a trustee of that university and serves on the Metropolitan Museum of Art's Business Committee, which raises funds for operating expenses.

New York State superintendent of banks under Democratic Governor Hugh Carey from 1977 to 1982, when she quit to run unsuccessfully for the Republican nomination for the U.S. Senate, Ms. Siebert has also been heavily involved in politics. She is a founding member of the new WISH List, a Republican group that raises money to get "Women in the Senate and House" and will only support candidates that favor legal abortion.

Ms. Siebert, who came here from Cleveland in 1954 and started her career with no college degree and $500, says she feels a strong pull to give back to a society that has afforded her many luxuries. Looking out her office window onto Madison Avenue, her Chihuahua named Monster (the "love of my life") on her lap, and one leg swung over the side of her chair, she explains how amounts of money that Wall Street considers insignificant can mean a lot to the people who benefit from the small charities she supports.

$5 Million is "Nothing"

"When you talk about these deals, in some cases the contribution comes from a $5 million purchase of a billion-dollar deal," she says. "In the world of boardroom finance, that $5 million purchase is nothing. The big firms spill that off their coffee cups in the morning before they open the door."

Ms. Siebert says she hopes that if SEPP proves successful in bringing her a significant amount of business, the program will set an example for Wall Street firms.

"If I'm lucky," she says, "I'm going to be a leader—and I'm going to show people that sharing is also good business." Not to mention, she says, that writing checks to the various charities on her list breaks up the day. "It's a serious game—a serious, fun game."

Source: Elizabeth Green, "N.Y. Stock Exchange's First Woman Uses Profits to Underwrite Charities," the *Chronicle of Philanthropy,* June 16, 1992, pp. 7, 14. Reprinted with permission of the *Chronicle of Philanthropy.*

Consider the impact of simultaneously telling thousands of fund-raisers how to enhance their productivity. Assume for a moment that you are a fund-raiser who reads this article. What action would you take? You would probably ask Ms. Siebert to assist you and your favorite cause.

Ms. Siebert has enlightened all those who wish to do more for society than just push a core product. Seriously consider employing a similar strategy in your hometown. I look forward to reading about your contributions to our community's noble causes in the local newspaper. Experts write and are written about. They also find that big/affluent schools of fish chase their boat!

Thank you for your continued interest in my work. Best wishes and success.

Sincerely,

Thomas J. Stanley
Chairman
Affluent Market Institute

ENHANCE THE REVENUE OF CLIENTS AND THEIR CHILDREN

Dear Dr. Stanley:

I am 47 years of age and have been a practicing lawyer since 1973. I became a certified public accountant in 1974. I specialize in business transactions, real estate, probate, taxation, and corporate matters.

I have practiced in a town of approximately 15,000 people located in a county of 50,000 people. Our primary market in this area is agriculture, with small automotive-related and manufacturing-related companies.

I market to a narrow segment comprised of owners of small businesses, agricultural businesses, individual farmers, and landowners, as well as local banks and financial institutions. All these people need my services, which include wills and trusts, real estate transactions, tax consultation, general corporate work, and corporate and banking transactions.

I often purchase the livestock offered by my clients' children at our Junior County Fair auction. I also have targeted potential clients in the same way. Their children are often at the fair selling their livestock. To say the least, this strategy has been very successful in retaining clients and attracting new ones.

Very truly yours,

Gary W. James
Attorney-at-Law

BUILD A NETWORK OF NETWORKS

Dear Networker:

You and your partners spend a considerable amount of money each year for subscriptions to newsletters. I am sure that the information contained in these newsletters enhances the productivity of your firm. Why else would you spend between $300 and $900 per year for periodicals that contain fewer than 12 pages of material?

Please note that the newsletter to which you subscribe for $900 per year has over 1,000 subscribers. And the same editor/publisher produces three other successful periodicals. It is estimated that the gross annual revenue generated from these periodicals is more than $2 million. Given the relatively low cost of publishing newsletters, especially out of one's converted garage, one might think that the editor/publisher is a wealthy man. Also note that his "office" is within ten minutes' driving distance from your office.

Given the facts as outlined, I would like to ask you a very simple question. Why have you failed ever to prospect the editor/publisher of the newsletter to which you subscribe for $900 per year?

Perhaps you did not see the opportunity that regularly crosses your desk. Or perhaps you feel that there are little or no profits to be made from the newsletter industry. Open your eyes.

Call the editor/publisher today. Tell him you're a sub-scriber. Acknowledge his achievement in having produced the top newsletter in the industry. Then make an appointment to see him. By the way, there is a way that would ensure that he will say yes to your request for an in-person meeting. It would also enhance the probability of the editor/publisher becoming your client. Ask him to have several hundred copies of this month's newsletter and subscription forms waiting for you when you arrive at his office for your meeting.

The editor/publisher surely will ask what you intend to do with several hundred copies of his newsletter and subscription forms. Your answer is very important in establishing yourself as his **Revenue Enhancer.** What you say can also help you establish the foundation for networking among affluent editors/publishers/owners of successful newsletters.

What will you do with this material? Distribute copies at the next monthly meeting of your state's chapter. I understand that several hundred planners, estate attorneys, insurance underwriters, and securities brokers usually attend. Distributing promotional information in this manner is much less costly than using direct mail methods. Tell your prospect that you're sure that many of your colleagues who attend the meeting are excellent prospective subscribers. I understand that this is one of his targeted groups.

When you do meet your prospect in person, spend at least 80 percent of your time asking and listening. Ask him about the problems that he is facing in the industry and his goals for his newsletter and his company in general. Also discuss the two or three major production and marketing issues that he is facing.

Production is often a problem for people in the publishing industry. They are in constant search of quality suppliers. Suppliers of what? Everything from paper and printing to office supplies. Often, the top-performing newsletter publishers patronize the best suppliers. So don't forget to ask your prospect for his list of the best suppliers. Also ask his permission to mention to the suppliers the following: "Your client, Mr. ————, told me you're one of the top suppliers of software, printing, direct mail services, etc." He should be willing to direct you toward his best suppliers because he is in your debt. You're going to distribute hundreds of his promotional pieces to potential subscribers. You will endorse his product.

Like almost all great networkers, you are enhancing the revenues of your prospects, clients, suppliers, and other members of your network. Remember that suppliers most likely will give you an audience if you tell them that their client endorsed them.

Start to construct your network system today. Begin to target owners of successful newsletters and their suppliers. You're going to beat your competitors. Why? Because you will offer prospects much more than estate planning, life insurance, and mutual funds. You will offer enhanced revenue and related services.

Now it is time to target owners of other successful and potentially successful newsletters. But how can you identify your targets, all those thousands of owners of successful newsletters? Go to your local library and ask your reference librarian to direct you to *Newsletters in Print.* This directory is published by Gale Research, Inc., P. O. Box 33477, Detroit, MI 48232-5478 (1-800-877-GALE).

You may even wish to purchase a copy of the directory for $175. It is an outstanding tool for identifying successful newsletters. It provides a description of more than 10,000 newsletters. It includes several key pieces of information, such as the newsletter title, editors' names, publisher address, topical issues, frequency of publication, telephone number, fax number, and features illustrations.

But even more important, *Newsletters in Print* provides information on the sales revenue of many of the newsletters listed; the price (cost of annual subscription) and circulation are key elements. This information was employed by yours truly in estimating the sales revenue for the newsletter to which you subscribe for $900 per year. Now you can make the same estimates, and, correspondingly, target the editors/publishers/owners of those newsletters that are successful.

Moreover, with the information from *Newsletters in Print* you will be able to determine which newsletters will accept articles/letters to the editor, etc. List those newsletters that have a policy of accepting outside articles and editorials and also have an affluent audience. Editors of these types of newsletters may welcome your proposal to write a monthly column on estate planning. Remember, newsletter editors are typically looking for low-cost sources of high-quality manuscripts. You could conceivably write one monthly article and publish it in 100 noncompeting newsletters. Many of the newsletters listed in the directory are read by affluent business owners, senior corporate executives, as well as other successful people with a common interest in the environment, history, or collectibles, just to name a few.

I hope this information will prove useful to you.

Regards,

Thomas J. Stanley, Ph.D.
Chairman
Affluent Market Institute

NOT IN FATHER'S FOOTSTEPS

John is the son of a highly successful life insurance general agent. From his earliest recollection, however, he was determined not to work for his father. He wanted to go his own way. In fact, even the liberal arts college that he chose to attend was a thousand miles away from his father's business operations. When he graduated with honors from the college, he worked for three years as a management executive in a major corporation.

Recently, he decided to further his education. His goal after completing his education is to provide estate planning and related services to wealthy people. He's currently pursuing both a master's degree in finance/insurance and a law degree.

John expressed his interest in practicing law in the town in which the university he attends is located. He made it very evident that he didn't want to return home and essentially walk in his father's footsteps. He wondered how he should market himself after completing his degrees. "Dr. Stanley," he asked, "do you have any suggestions for me?"

An Independent Study

John is in an excellent position to take advantage of his knowledge of finance and insurance as well as the legal aspects of estate planning. I suggested that he seek a mentor in either the business school or the law school. This mentor would act as his advisor for the independent study course that he should pursue.

Most colleges and universities grant three to six hours of credit for an independent study course. A research paper is required for a course of this type. John's mentor would act as a senior faculty advisor for the proposed research.

What research should John propose? He should propose to interview 100 senior officers, that is, the owners of small- and medium-sized companies within the town where he is pursuing his graduate studies. His proposal should contain a simple questionnaire that addresses his interviewees' estate planning needs, including trusts, wills, insurance, and related types of services. A study of this type would open John's eyes to the opportunities afforded by the market segment he is interviewing.

John should orient himself toward this market segment. He should ask for a personal audience with the affluent business owners he proposes to interview, making it very clear that his primary goal is to research their estate planning needs. However, he should also make it very clear that they are likely to hear from him after he obtains his degrees. Why? Because he will then be providing estate planning and insurance services to business owners and other affluent individuals. One way to encourage these business owners to respond is to promise them a summary of the study results.

John should consult several key advisors as he develops his proposal and questionnaire. He should discuss his proposal with such key informants as top lawyers, trust officers, fund-raisers, and insurance providers in his community. In this way, he will gain exposure to some of the community's most prestigious law firms, banks, eleemosynary organizations, and insurance providers. He may also wish to consult several certified public accountants who cater to the needs of affluent business owners. Often, amazing things have happened to people who have taken my advice and conducted surveys of this type. Respondents have offered several of them jobs, and many enlightened key informants have offered to underwrite the cost of their research.

John should have his résumé and proposal handy when he visits his respondents and key informants. He will find that asking questions is a form of flattery. Respondents will be impressed by his effort to understand their needs and will appreciate his ability to position himself as a future expert in relating to affluent business owners.

John can develop his own influence network even before he finishes his graduate studies. While interviewing affluent business owners, he can ask classic networking questions:

- What do you sell?
- What do you buy?
- What types of customers do you want?
- What types of suppliers do you seek?
- What types of products and services that you need have you been unable to obtain in the marketplace?

John can also direct similar revenue-enhancing questions to selected attorneys, accountants, trust officers, and investment and insurance professionals. Next, he can list the needs of each respondent and key contact. Armed with this information, he can begin to act as an intermediary between potential sellers and prospective buyers/clients/customers.

John, in essence, can position himself as a Revenue Enhancer for many successful business owners and professionals. This is an excellent way for him to build a foundation for his estate planning practice.

THIS AUTHOR'S SUPPLIERS/REVENUE ENHANCERS

Shortly after publishing the *Selling to the Affluent* tape album, I sent copies to clients, suppliers, and associates. The response I received from several of my suppliers was unexpected. My accountant, Mr. Joseph (also known as "Joe"), listened to the three-hour tape while he was flying out to Colorado. The day he returned to his office, he called me. Allow me to paraphrase parts of our discussion.

DR. STANLEY:

Hello, this is Tom Stanley.

MR. JOSEPH:

Hello, Tom. It's Joe. Hey, I wanted to get back to you after I had a chance to listen to your audiotape.

DR. STANLEY:

Did you have a chance to review all the material?

MR. JOSEPH:

Yes, did it on my way out to the ski slopes. You really have something. Let me tell you this is really beneficial to people in my business. Most accountants don't know how to network. They really don't know what to say when they are in front of a prospect. Our industry needs this kind of material. But let me tell you why I called. I would like you to get involved with a marketing and sales organization here in town. I already spoke with one of the officials about having you join and also having you as a speaker. In fact, many sales and marketing managers are members. You speak and they will listen. I'm sure you could sell a lot of your material to them.

DR. STANLEY:

Joe, I really appreciate your endorsement.

MR. JOSEPH:

Well, I was listening to your tape about how to become an apostle to clients, and that's what I have always tried to do. But, you know, we all need to be reminded of this time and time again. It is too easy to forget the principles that contributed to our success.

DR. STANLEY:

Well, Joe, you wrote the book on how to be an apostle in the field of accounting.

MR. JOSEPH:

We appreciate your business and endorsement. Oh, Tom, by the way, you need to get over here soon so that we can do your end-of-the-year taxes.

DR. STANLEY:

How about Wednesday morning next week? Set a time.

MR. JOSEPH:

How about 10 A.M.?

DR. STANLEY:

OK, 10 A.M. it is.

Why did Mr. Joseph endorse me as a speaker and potential member of a prestigious sales and marketing organization? He listened to the message on the tape. In essence, the message (see the following transcribed extraction from the *Selling to the Affluent* tape album) stated that marketers of products and services who don't offer clients benefits that go beyond their core offerings may lose business to marketers who do provide clients with more than the conventional product or service.

A Provocative Message to a Supplier

[Telephone rings.]

DR. STANLEY:

Tom Stanley.

MR. READ:

Hello, Tom. Bob Read calling.

DR. STANLEY:

Hey, Bob.

MR. READ:

Just called to see if anything new was going on at your house.

DR. STANLEY:

Gee, Bob, yes. I just got my first royalty check.

MR. READ:

Well, Tom, what a coincidence that I called today. What are you going to do with all that money?

DR. STANLEY:

Well, I'm going to invest it.

MR. READ:

With me, I hope.

DR. STANLEY:

Well, to tell you the truth, Bob, I've got four other guys who are helping me right now, and I'm sort of spread too thin.

MR. READ:

Well, how many of these folks that you're working with right now sent you a walnut laminate plaque of the jacket cover of your book in recognition of its being selected as a finalist for the Ben Franklin book of the year?

DR. STANLEY:

Ah, nobody sent me a plaque.

MR. READ:

What a coincidence. What do you think about maybe opening an account with me?

DR. STANLEY:

Wait a minute. You have a plaque of my book in recognition of the Ben Franklin Award?

MR. READ:

Yeah. I think it would be suitable for hanging on the library wall in the house there.

DR. STANLEY:

Are you serious?

MR. READ:

Yeah. I was very impressed with your accomplishments.

DR. STANLEY:

Well, you know, it's very interesting to me that not one of my current providers, including my accountant, my attorney, and the other people, none of them even sent me a note to say congratulations.

MR. READ:

Makes you wonder about reciprocity, doesn't it?

DR. STANLEY:

Well, I guess so, Bob, because you bought the book and I sent them all free ones.

MR. READ:

Well, no price paid, no value perceived. But really, what do you think about opening an account?

DR. STANLEY:

It's a done deal. What do I have to do?

MR. READ:

We'll send out some forms . . .

MODERATOR:

Well, Tom, it looks to me like he's switched from defensive to a little bit of offensive here.

DR. STANLEY:

Yeah, he did. And if we talk step five, "Recontact prospect when he is expected to be euphoric because he has forecasted changes in his cash flow," Robert Read called just 22 hours after this target received his first royalty check.

MODERATOR:

Which wasn't a coincidence, not an accident.

DR. STANLEY:

Not an accident at all. But realistically, when you think about this, Robert Read is an apostle to affluent prospects and clients. Think about the things that he offered me, and he was quite sincere. If you want to be a speaker, you'll be a speaker. If you want to do autograph parties in seven of the bookstores that my clients own, you will do autographs. If you would like to join an exclusive literary society, you must be nominated. He will nominate me. What he brings to my party is purchase of my products, increased revenue, a very important need for most affluent people. He's recognized at least some achievement on my part, which is important, and he is going to give me the opportunity to associate and affiliate with people in my league, and it may help my career. That's why anybody in my position would want to deal with this person. Because essentially he's going way beyond the core product. He is providing me with all the basic characteristics that the affluent person is all about.

MODERATOR:

And his other clients too. If you had been amenable to autograph parties, if you had the type of book that lent itself to that, he'd be serving the clients that own those bookstores, giving them a top-name author ready to autograph books.

DR. STANLEY:

Absolutely.

MODERATOR:

He's giving them more than just the core product that he gives them.

DR. STANLEY:

Absolutely. And I think it's very important to point out that this young man is not an antagonist. He in fact is providing all of his clients and prospects with some networking system, with a chance to enhance their reputations, their self-concepts, their revenue, their careers. And that's how he operates so very, very effectively. And I might point out that 95 percent of all his discussions and solicitations are done by phone. He has no problem with calling people in my business or related businesses and talking to them intelligently about their basic and fundamental problems. He is clearly what I call an apostle or an advocate of the needs of affluent authors.

MODERATOR:

And that's the study of Robert Read, an extraordinary sales professional who targets affluent authors, or at least those who appear to be affluent. Did you enjoy his conditioning techniques? Did you notice how he caters to the needs of the prospect and is willing to provide much more than just his core product? That, says Dr. Stanley, is one of the essential virtues of ESPs, extraordinary sales professionals.

Beyond the Core

The very marketers of accounting services offer clients first-rate accounting and much more. They provide referrals on behalf of clients with something to sell to prospects with a significant potential to buy. In other words, enlightened accountants are not doing only accounting for clients. They are also constantly seeking ways in which clients can tap into a referral/endorsement network. All else being equal, would you prefer to patronize an accounting firm that provides only high-caliber accounting or one that provides high-caliber accounting and also enhances your revenue?

Yes, Mr. Joseph is my apostle and an apostle to more than 700 other appreciative clients. There are many thousands of accounting firms in this country and hundreds in my town alone. Why did Mr. Joseph's firm grow from a three-person organization 15 years ago to a top 10 firm in my metro area? The firm does an excellent job with the nuts and bolts of accounting—for example, accuracy, rapid response, and excellent advice. But many of the local accounting firms deliver high-quality core accounting service. Mr. Joseph's firm, I believe, has grown rapidly for reasons beyond the mundane. It has grown rapidly because it recognizes clients' achievements in letters, conversations, and its own newsletter because, and as the following scenario illustrates, Mr. Joseph will even act as a sales professional in behalf of its clients.

When I did show up for my 10:00 A.M. appointment, Mr. Joseph offered me more than coffee and tax forms. And clearly, the message of the *Selling to the Affluent* tape album had an impact on his orientation toward me.

DR. STANLEY:

Hello, Joe. End-of-the-year tax returns have you up all night?

MR. JOSEPH:

Busy, busy, busy. How about a cup of coffee? Cream, no sugar?

DR. STANLEY:

Yes. I need it. Well, I have all the papers and everything else for you to do the taxes.

MR. JOSEPH:

Well, before that, I wanted to ask you about a possible opportunity for you. One of my clients owns an equipment company. The company is having its annual sales meeting in July. It asked me to be a speaker.

DR. STANLEY:

I'm sure you will do a great job. Let me know if I can help you with some ideas.

MR. JOSEPH:

Let me tell you what I'm thinking. There will be 200 top sales professionals in the audience. I think they should all buy your books and tapes. They all need to learn how to network in a more productive way.

DR. STANLEY:

They would definitely benefit from reviewing our material, especially if they are going to succeed in selling to professionals and successful business owners.

MR. JOSEPH:

That is exactly what I'm thinking. Tom, I'm wondering if you could supply me with 200 fliers that describe your material. I will also need a few samples to display at the meeting. What do you think?

DR. STANLEY:

That's a fabulous idea.

MR. JOSEPH:

I don't mind at all carrying your material out to the meeting. I would like to display it and quote some of the ideas from your books. Then, while I'm at the podium, I'm going to tell them that they all need to have this material. They can fill out the order forms and send the orders to you.

DR. STANLEY:

That's a great idea.

MR. JOSEPH:

I could even sell the stuff out of the box right after my speech.

DR. STANLEY:

Won't that be a lot of trouble for you? I want you to enjoy your trip out there.

MR. JOSEPH:

It's not a problem at all. My client's equipment firm will benefit from your material. And I hope I can sell a bunch of your stuff.

DR. STANLEY:

Well, I can supply you with as much as you can load on the plane. But I don't want to impose on you.

MR. JOSEPH:

> Look, Tom, it's my pleasure. I want to help push your material. I'm glad to do so, believe me. No problem. Just make sure you get me the material a week or two before I leave for the meeting. It's the least I can do for a client.

A Letter to an Apostle

Dear Joe:

Enclosed are copies of the offerings of the Affluent Market Institute. Also enclosed are fliers and order forms that detail our offerings. I really appreciate your interest in my business and your willingness to endorse my books and tapes.

I'm sure you will be a major hit as a speaker to those 200 top-producing sales professionals. Your message about how to accumulate wealth should be very helpful to the members of your audience. Of course, on a more selfish note, I am delighted that you will be hawking my materials to the audience. I really do believe that the members of your audience will also benefit from my ideas.

Joe, you are my Revenue Enhancer. Actually, one of the most important things that people in business want from their suppliers is assistance in increasing revenue. This is even more important to me than the first-rate accounting services you have always delivered. But it is so nice, so reassuring that our accountant is outside batting for the Affluent Market Institute. Far too few professional service providers ever demonstrate true and deep understanding of all the goals of their clients. "Empathy for My Goals" is the number one dimension/characteristic that affluent business owners want from their service providers. And these goals include recognition of achievement. You get an *A* on this one. Featuring my work on the front cover of your newsletter was an unexpected pleasure. But even more significant is your help in achieving my goal of having a book in the best-seller category.

I am in your debt and will try my very best to reciprocate. Even when I'm not asked about the best CPA firm to patronize,

I always recommend Mr. Joseph. It's my pleasure. I hope you think of me as your apostle.

Thanks,

Tom Stanley

Innoculate Your Clients against Competitors

Mr. Joseph is a Revenue Enhancer for his clients. This is a major reason why his clients regularly turn down other accounting firms that attempt to solicit their business. Yes, Mr. Joseph has inoculated his clients against foreign antibodies (promotional messages from competing accounting firms). And his inoculum is an extremely powerful serum. A serum that is not unidimensional. Its strength is based on high-quality traditional service and a powerful referral/endorsement network. That is why his clients go out of their way to tell all the business owners and professionals with whom they come into contact to patronize Mr. Joseph's firm. Those who sell to the affluent will find that a referral from their accountant to successful business owners and professionals is extremely important. Why not patronize an accountant who does more than tax preparation and payroll?

A Letter from Number One

Not long after Mr. Joseph made his magnanimous offer, one of my other suppliers sent me a note. Attached to the note was a copy of a letter that he had sent to a senior partner of one of the largest law firms in the United States.

Mr. Steven S. Edwards
Smith, Edwards, and Associates

Dear Steven:

It was great to be with you last week. I'm delighted to hear about your recognition by your firm. Hello, senior partner! You deserve everything you get, and your hard work is really paying off now. All you need is a few more $1 million clients as you described them to me, and you will set the world on fire!

It occurred to me that you and other members of your firm might be interested in how to attract new clients. While an insurance agent can call on anyone he wishes to call, an attorney has to find a way to "get the fish to chase the boat." Dr. Thomas Stanley has developed a way to do this, and it might profit you and the other members of your firm to have a copy of his tape. Please accept this copy as a complimentary gift.

I would recommend that, if you approve, the firm consider purchasing these tapes for all of the attorneys in the firm who wish to make themselves more valuable to the firm, and that's all of them! Thank you for your business and your friendship.

Sincerely yours,

D. F., CLU
Chartered Financial Consultant

The author of the note and letter is the fine fellow who supplies me with life insurance. He is not just an ordinary sales professional. He is the top life insurance agent for a firm that employs more than 10,000 agents.

He realized that clients of his who offered legal services could benefit from sales and marketing information. So he inserted me into his referral/endorsement network. He sent a complimentary copy of my tape album to a client, a client always interested in learning how to attract more new clients. At the same time, he endorsed a client's product. Thus he enhanced the probability of increased revenue for that client. Yes, the very best sellers and marketers offer clients much more than a core and often mundane product. They also enhance the productivity of their clients' practices.

Are your suppliers just suppliers? Why not convert them into revenue enhancers? Most suppliers can be trained to play the Revenue Enhancer role. Ask your suppliers to enhance your revenue by making referrals on your behalf. Ask them to read the material in this chapter. You may be pleased by the subsequent change in their orientation toward you. They may never again take you for granted.

CHAPTER 4

THE ADVOCATE

"An advocate is a person who speaks and/or writes in support of another's cause. Many high-grade networkers are ardent supporters of their clients' causes. These causes are usually more important to clients than any product or service."

AN EXAMPLE OF DOING MORE: THE LETTER OF LETTERS

Of your top 10 clients, 3 are luxury automobile dealers. But apart from selling them insurance products and sending them "Season's Greetings" calendars, what have you ever done for them? Remember, if you are a top-producing sales professional, you should share your skills, your sales and marketing genius, with your clients and prospects. You should aggressively support their causes. You should serve before being served. To do these things, consider becoming an Advocate like Mr. Wood, the author of the following letters. A sales professional recently sent out similar letters to 11 auto dealers. On the very day that they received the letters, 3 of the 11 called him. They said thank you and "What can we do for you, Mr. Advocate?" All of the others immediately took his call when he contacted them by phone. At the time of this writing, 3 of the 11 had purchased large life insurance policies from this extraordinary networker.

If you sent the following letter to the head of the Automobile Dealers Association in your state, he would probably be very appreciative. He might even publish it in the association's newsletter.

Thousands of affluent automobile dealers would then be exposed to you and your role as their Advocate. Many of these dealers might wish to reciprocate by purchasing your products or services.

A LETTER FROM AN ADVOCATE TO U.S. SENATORS AND SELECTED NEWSPAPER EDITORS

Dear Senator Smith:

Ten years ago, my son played Little League baseball. Life then was less complex, more relaxed than it is today. As I think back to those days and the games, I remember that the uniforms were provided by local car dealers. They supported our teams because it was good for business, good for the community, and good for the kids.

Today the same businessmen are not buying uniforms for the kids. They are in a very different position. Because competition is keener than ever, their profit margins have narrowed. Because of current problems in their industry, banks have become very difficult "partners." Manufacturers are undermining these traditional dealers by selling cars below wholesale to rental companies, which in turn remarket the cars to the consumers. Good employees are harder than ever to find and more expensive than ever to keep. And now our own government has passed a so-called luxury car tax that is driving customers away.

It is not the high-line foreign car manufacturer that is being hurt by this tax. It is the local American businessman. He is your neighbor who lives down the street. His kids play with your kids. His family sits next to your family in church. Many of my best customers are car dealers. Our government's tax policies threaten their livelihood as well as mine. I cannot sell my product to car dealers if they are bankrupt. Car dealers are part of the backbone of the free enterprise system and of America. They risk their capital in the hope of making a profit. They provide jobs and leadership in your town and mine. We need to do all we can to preserve them. Any tax that restricts the free market is bad for business and bad for America. We need to repeal the 10 percent luxury tax.

As I think about it, there are no independent car dealers in Russia. And there is no Little League either. Nor is a Russian-type economy one in which my business would survive.

W. G. Wood
President
The Wood Agency

A LETTER TO CONSITUENTS, AKA CLIENTS AND PROSPECTS

Mr. Robert S. Arnold
President
Arnold's Automobiles
3036 West Way
Midtown, IL 60777

Dear Mr. Arnold:

Enclosed is a copy of a letter that I wrote to our U.S. senators and the editors of six local and national newspapers. Please review the letter. Did I fail to address any of the major points concerning the so-called luxury car tax?

Originally, I was going to write you a letter about the insurance policies related pension products offered by my agency. I was anticipating that you might be interested in obtaining new or additional coverage. However, given all the other issues you must currently contend with, I am going to postpone my invitation.

In the meantime, if I can be of any help to you or your industry, please let me know. I would be delighted to ask all of my customers to sign postcards that petition the government to repeal its recently enacted tax on automobiles.

I feel obligated to help your industry and its members. Car dealers account for a large portion of my industry's customer base. When your industry is threatened, so is mine. I hope your current suppliers, especially your insurance professionals, are aggressively supporting your cause. Let's work together to repeal unfair tax burdens.

Sincerely,

W. G. Wood
President
The Wood Agency

DR. J. CONRAD PETERBAUM IS AN ADVOCATE OF MORE THAN FILLINGS AND EXTRACTIONS

Dr. J. Conrad Peterbaum is the oldest child of Fred and Gloria Peterbaum. From the time he was in the fifth grade, he showed significant aptitude for constructing various types of models, such as model airplanes, model rockets, and model boats. He constructed his models from very basic components—clay and balsa wood. Yes, Dr. Peterbaum excelled as a model builder.

At the same time that he developed an affinity for model building, he also showed considerable interest in dentistry. His choice of profession had a great deal to do with the opportunities it offered for carving, drilling, reshaping, molding. He reasoned that if he became a dentist, he would be able to exploit his talents, aptitudes, and avocational experiences within a well-paid profession.

But Dr. Peterbaum's background in model building is not the only factor that explains his current success as a dentist. Dr. Peterbaum's family operated a highly productive construction equipment company. This company sold and leased construction equipment, machinery, and tools to small and medium-sized contracting firms and to craftsmen of all types. It distributed everything from hammers, shovels, chain saws, and jackhammers to large air compressors, hoists, cement and mortar mixers, and cranes.

Even as a young boy, Dr. Peterbaum was always in the shop helping out with the family business. Through this experience, he learned a great deal about relating to people, a knowledge that he has applied to his patient relationships.

Dr. Peterbaum today places the highest value on his patients' needs. Unlike most people of high status, such as a dentist, he gives accolades to people who occupy low-status positions. He thinks nothing of asking patients whether he can write letters of recommendation enabling their sons and daughters to get into high-quality schools. He also has empathy for the cash flow of his patients, especially those who are employed in industries that are undergoing adversity; he does not press patients for payments. Moreover, he attempts to enhance his patient's revenue. Many of the people with whom he deals are independent business owners, and many others are self-employed professionals. Dr. Peterbaum makes recommendations to patients on their behalf. He often acts as an industrial matchmaker by introducing business owners who sell to persons who seek new sources of supply.

Dr. Peterbaum's dental practice has succeeded where the dental practices of others have failed because he understands and empathizes with the basic needs of his patients. Yes, he did attend a top five dental school. However, half of his classmates are now contract employees, and many of the others are not generating even average profits in their practices. The revenue generated by most, if not all, of his former classmates has never reached the level generated by Dr. Peterbaum. Last year the revenue generated by his dental practice exceeded $4 million!

Explaining Dr. Peterbaum's Success

Despite his competitors' high grades in college and dental school and despite their perhaps superior education, they still do not measure up to Dr. Peterbaum in terms of revenue generated. Some might contend that Dr. Peterbaum works harder than his competitors. He does work hard, but so do his competitors. Others might contend that Dr. Peterbaum is better qualified and has greater aptitude for dental work than his competitors.

While this may be true, it is not a complete explanation of his success. Yes, he is well educated; he does have exceptional aptitude for his work; he does have a good personality. But most important, he is an Advocate for his patients. He goes beyond the mundane, dane, beyond fillings, extractions, and other standard dental services. He provides his patients with other kinds of services. To illustrate his relationships with his patients, a case scenario is given below.

Upon completing his degree in dentistry, Dr. Peterbaum worked as an apprentice for a group of top-notch dentists, several of whom were professors at the prestigious dental school that he attended. Then he became a junior partner in a highly productive dental practice. In that capacity, he learned a great deal about the business and about the proactive marketing of professional services. The senior partners of this practice were not only skilled dentists but also very good entrepreneurs. They knew how to make money in a profession not known for producing millionaires. Later, Dr. Peterbaum opened his own independent practice, the practice he currently operates in a major metropolitan area.

One of Dr. Peterbaum's most important patient segments was attracted to his independent practice because of services that went beyond outstanding dental services. This relationship developed because of a favor that Dr. Peterbaum had rendered a patient while he was still a junior partner. From the very earliest stages of his dental career, Dr. Peterbaum established rapport with patients. Many of his patients in the practice where he was a junior partner were members of major labor unions. Others were staff employees and executives of the firms whose employees the unions represented.

In the course of time, Dr. Peterbaum attracted an increasing number of patients who requested that he, rather than any of the other partners, provide them with the dental services they required. He was personable, empathetic, and always took time to ask patients about their needs, activities, and interests. He became aware early in his career that many of his patients were employees of a major airline headquartered near his office. Knowing this, he was especially attentive to news items about the airline and its employees.

One Monday morning, Dr. Peterbaum read a newspaper article in which it was reported that the airline contemplated repairing its planes in "a Third World country" and thereby saving "considerable money." This change would threaten the careers of patients who worked for the airline. Not long after Dr. Peterbaum read the article, the president of the machinists union was sitting in his dental chair. The first thing Dr. Peterbaum asked him was how he felt about the airline's contemplated shift. The president admitted that he and his constituents were frightened by the prospect.

Dr. Peterbaum stated that he would very likely refuse to fly on any plane that was not repaired at a domestic location. However, the union president responded that it was unclear what could be done to prevent the airline from taking this action. Dr. Peterbaum immediately took 25 minutes of nonbillable professional time to discuss several possible solutions to the problem that faced the union.

Dr. Peterbaum suggested that a letter and petition campaign would probably encourage Congress to prevent domestic airlines having their planes repaired by nonunion labor in foreign countries. Dr. Peterbaum, the Advocate, also offered to write letters in the union's behalf and to have all of his patients address to their respective congressmen petition cards requesting that the government do something about the union's problem.

Dr. Peterbaum's suggestions were followed to the letter, and the campaign succeeded. The airline backed down from its contemplated change.

Obviously, the president of the machinists union felt indebted to Dr. Peterbaum. When he again appeared at the dental office in which Dr. Peterbaum was a junior partner, he requested that Dr. Peterbaum serve him. The receptionist informed him that Dr. Peterbaum no longer worked there. He then asked the receptionist for Dr. Peterbaum's new address. The receptionist replied that no one knew where Dr. Peterbaum had gone.

Actually, this reply, programmed by the senior partners of the practice, was untrue. The senior partners were fearful that Dr. Peterbaum would take patients with him to his new office. In reality, Dr. Peterbaum had told none of the practice's current patients that he was opening a new practice, because he felt that it would be improper to do so.

However, the union president was determined to find Dr. Peterbaum. He took it upon himself to ask the state dental society for Dr. Peterbaum's new address. The dental society gave him the address. But the president did not immediately make an appointment to see Dr. Peterbaum.

What he did first was to take out a large advertisement in the monthly trade magazine distributed to all of the airline's employees. The advertisement said that Dr. J. Conrad Peterbaum, D.D.S., had opened his own dental practice. The advertisement also listed the address and phone number of the practice. Upon reading the advertisement in their trade magazine, large numbers of airline employees, machinists, stewardesses, pilots, executives, and administrators, sought out Dr. Peterbaum and his unique brand of service. The union president had made them fully aware that they owed Dr. Peterbaum a debt beyond that typical of a relationship with a dental professional.

In essence, Dr. Peterbaum is an Advocate for his patients' causes. And in at least one instance, an important patient, the union president, reciprocated by endorsing Dr. Peterbaum. The president enhanced Dr. Peterbaum's revenue by giving him access to the airline's employee influence network. Today, Dr. Peterbaum has more of the airline's employees as patients than does any other dental practice.

Dr. Peterbaum's attitude and business philosophy reflect his need to serve his patients. He has a unique way of defining *service*. For him, *service* means relating to the critical problems of patients and becoming part of patients' affinity groups. Dr. Peterbaum excels in playing the role of Advocate. That's why he is now among the top-performing revenue generators in the dental profession.

But where were all the other so-called professional service providers? Certainly, the airline's employees were clients of many attorneys, CPAs, insurance agents, and security brokers. However, no one from these groups came to the help of the union president and members. The same can be said of bankers and a myriad of other types of so-called service providers. They failed to help the union president and members because they were insensitive to the broader definition of *service*. Like most marketers, they viewed the core product or service as their only offering. However, the best marketers of professional services, such as Dr. Peterbaum, realize that service has multiple dimensions.

Implications for Followers of Dr. Peterbaum

Both Dr. Peterbaum and his father, Fred, do more for their clientele than offer just a core product or service. But neither of them could have succeeded without asking their patients/customers these basic questions:

1. What do you do for a living? What's your speciality?
2. What do you buy?
3. What do you sell?
4. Do you (if self-employed) need more customers/clients?
5. If you own a business, are you in need of new sources of supply?
6. What concerns you about your employer or your industry?
7. Are you interested in sending your children to college?
8. How can I help you beyond providing you with equipment or fillings and extractions?

Not every professional will have the president of an important labor union as a client or patient. And only a few professionals will ever be endorsed by such an important center of influence. However, you can create your own influence network. Ask all of the clients, patients, and prospects with whom you have contact about endorsing you and your offering to other members of their affinity groups. Also consider sponsoring advertisements in the publications of these affinity groups. Mention in your promotional themes that you're committed to supporting the key decisions that benefit their industry. But what affinity publications should you choose? Why not find out by asking all of your clients/patients what affinity publications they read?

THE IMPORTANT CONCERNS OF AFFINITY GROUPS

What major concerns face affinity groups in America? Members of our seminar audiences often ask this broad question. Broad issues, almost by definition, are rarely the most important concerns facing particular affinity groups. The most important concerns of such groups are generally industry/profession specific. For example, manufacturers of snack foods are very concerned about the possibility that certain states will reclassify their products as "nonfood" items. States such as New York do not place a sales tax on food items. But if New York State classifies snack foods as nonfood items, then it will tax them.

Snack food manufacturers are fearful that such a sales tax

would raise the prices of their offerings enough to significantly reduce the demand for snack foods.

Do you want to become a networking Advocate of owners of snack food companies, employees of and suppliers to the snack food industry, and distributors of snack foods. If so, why not take an active role in petitioning selected state governments to reclassify snack foods as food items, as nontaxable food products.

Affinity groups other than snack food manufacturers are also threatened by governmental bodies. For example, if the EPA has its way, dry cleaners may be forbidden to use a now widely used cleaning solution. This change might force many dry cleaners to buy new equipment.

Some forest farmers feel threatened by the increasingly aggressive support that the federal government has been giving to the rights of owls and woodpeckers. Because of that support, forest farmers in some states will not be allowed to harvest their own trees. Doing so, according to the EPA, would endanger the natural habitat of some species of wildlife.

Is there a significant issue on which any marketing professional can capitalize? Almost without exception, business-related affinity groups in this country are concerned about government policies, proposed policies, mandates, injunctions, paperwork, taxes, and red tape. Most affinity group spokepersons/executives can fill you in on the details. Also, most trade journals and industry newsletters describe the issues that concern their readers. But often neither the local nor national press will relate to these issues. Do you want to find out about what your clients and prospects really need? Of course you do. Why not ask them to identify the key issues of concern to their industry and begin to read what their affinity literature has to say about these issues. Knowledge of these issues will help you become a networking Advocate of their important causes.

SEEDS OF SUPPORT

The importance of understanding your client's needs and problems cannot be overstated. Most sales professionals appreciate the value of matching product and service offerings with the client's needs. However, only a minority of those professionals fully comprehend those needs from the client's point of view.

Those sales professionals who do appreciate the depth and complexity of their clients' needs are typically found in larger concentrations among the top-producing sales and marketing professionals in this country. Dan is certainly among these elite marketers.

Dan is a certified life underwriter and chartered financial consultant employed by a top five insurance firm that employs more than 14,000 agents. He is the firm's top-producing life agent. How did Dan attain his number one ranking? How do his marketing and selling strategies differ from the marketing and selling strategies of those who never attained his level of production? Can Dan's strategies be applied to accounting, law, engineering, architecture, investment services, banking, health care, and the like?

In a nutshell, Dan's strategies can be applied to business areas other than insurance. Dan is now number one because he approaches the market differently. Oh, yes, he offers quality products and is employed by a top-rated company. But so do thousands of other agents.

Unlike many of his competitors, Dan is very disciplined in targeting his prospects. He targets and succeeds in selling to very affluent business owners and professionals. Moreover, he has an uncanny ability not only to retain these clients but also to obtain business from them via their endorsements and referrals to other affluent business owners and professionals.

Dan also has a unique market orientation. He is clearly an Advocate of his clients. His clients' problems are his problems. He spends considerable time and energy in developing an understanding of the clients themselves, their businesses and professions, their products and services, and their problems.

Most of Dan's clients market something. Some are auto dealers with too many automobiles to sell. Others are attorneys in search of new clients. Dan makes important referrals among members of his growing network of clients. His referral network is one of his more important assets and competitive weapons.

Many top-performing marketing professionals like Dan have a well-established referral network. However, Dan goes beyond helping clients increase their revenue. He is one of a kind when it comes to protecting their interests. Especially noteworthy is a recent episode in his career in which he let an important client know that his insurance agent was also his Advocate.

Any professional who is truly extraordinary in selling his own product or service should be able to help solve marketing- and sales-related problems for a variety of clients. This holds especially true for extraordinary sales professionals who sell such intangibles as insurance, legal services, health care services, and investment services. Dan provides his marketing intellect to his clients free of charge. Dan when he visited a local nursery to pick up a special brand of grass seed, he was on a mission. He wanted to buy a large bag of grass seed produced by one of his clients. But when he requested the Egan brand, the salesclerk aggressively tried to switch him to brand X.

Since the nursery Dan was patronizing was only one of more than 30 in a chain, Dan quickly concluded that this switch tactic was a potentially serious threat to his client's livelihood. Sales professionals less sensitive than Dan would probably have walked out of the nursery without their client's product or might even have bought brand X.

Dan not only refused to be switched; he also gave the salesclerk a lecture on the variations in quality among grass seed brands. As an extraordinarily gifted marketer, Dan realized that his client, Mr. Egan, would be at a serious competitive disadvantage if his product did not receive dealer support. Typically, variations in the support offered by retail distributors are the key cause of variations in market share among companies in the seed industry. Dan took this threat to his client's business very personally. He immediately sent a letter to the owner of Rivers Nurseries (see below). He strongly suggested that the salesclerks at Rivers Nurseries outlets give better support to the Egan brand of grass seed. Dan sent a copy of this letter to Mr. Egan.

AN ADVOCATE'S LETTER PROTECTING AND DEFENDING A CLIENT'S FLANKS

Mr. Paul J. Rivers
Rivers Nurseries, Inc.
5395 Forde Highway, N.E.

Dear Mr. Rivers:

Forest Egan has spent a lot of money, effort, and time to truly differentiate his product and service. Through his research and testing with our state university and his commitment to quality and service, his total market offering is second to none. In addition, through advertising and customer loyalty, he has built a business that brings customers to you and your stores.

Yet when I went into your Rivers (Williams Center) store and asked for a bag of Egan grass seed, the salesman immediately tried to get me to buy a different brand of seed instead.

It seems to me that business is built on relationships, quality products, and service. Inasmuch as Forest Egan delivers in all three of these areas in a way second to none, and brings customers into your stores with his good name, I believe he deserves and has earned your support. I hope you will communicate this to your sales staff. I look forward to continuing to be one of Forest Egan's customers through you. Thank you.

Sincerely yours,

Dan
Chartered Financial Consultant

cc: Forest Egan

The Advocate's Evidence

What did Dan accomplish with one simple letter and one first-class postage stamp? He provided evidence that he was an Advocate of a client's cause. Clients appreciate the support that suppliers like Dan provide. All too often, suppliers view their client's needs and offerings in terms of their own needs and offerings. However, truly gifted marketers like Dan understand that clients' problems encompass more than selling and delivering core products and services and that it is therefore essential to understand the other major problems that clients face.

Too many prospects and clients view most sellers as antagonists. Antagonists live by the creed that what is good for me-me-me must be good for my prospects and clients. But antagonists find it difficult to attract clients and even more difficult to retain them. If you were a successful entrepreneur or professional, whom would you patronize, Dan the Advocate or just another antagonist? You would probably patronize Dan.

Through his excellent level of service delivery and his position as an Advocate, Dan has inoculated his clients against foreign (competitive) organisms. In other words, he is so very good at what he does that competitors find it impossible to gain new business from his clients.

AN INTERVIEW WITH AN ADVOCATE IN THE MAKING

Jim Weck is a sales manager of one of this nation's top-performing insurance agencies. His agency focuses on affluent business owners and self-employed professionals. His agents are specialists in satisfying the particular needs of particular affluent affinity groups. Jim himself is a top-producing life insurance agent as well as a sales manager. He is an excellent role model and mentor. He employs a highly disciplined and focused approach to prospecting, and he helps others to adopt this system.

DR. STANLEY:

> I recall your telling me recently about an experience you had in selling to a very wealthy business owner. As I recall, this business owner was involved somehow in the poultry industry. Could you reflect on that experience?

MR. WECK:

> Yes. Recently, I was traveling with one of our young agents. We made an appointment to see a current client. This was essentially a courtesy call. While we stood in the foyer of our client's office, I noticed several trade and related periodicals on many of the tables in the outer office. The trade journals ranged from something called *Poultry Times* to *Turkey World*. After seeing these periodicals, I remembered that we were sitting in the middle of a town that was a major center for poultry production in America. I then asked our client if he would mind if I took several copies of the trade periodicals displayed in his outer office. He graciously agreed.

DR. STANLEY:

> What did you do with these periodicals?

MR. WECK:

We took them outside and began to page through them. I was especially impressed with *Turkey World*. As I paged through *Turkey World,* I noticed a full-page advertisement with headlines that said something to this effect: "Our competitors say that our deboning machine is the most expensive one on the market today. Our competition is correct. And our machine is the very best on the market." Included in the full-page advertisement was a large picture of the author of the ad copy, the business owner.

DR. STANLEY:

What did you do after you reviewed this advertisement?

MR. WECK:

I noticed immediately that the featured company had offices just a few blocks from where we stood. I convinced my young colleague that it would be worthwhile for us to visit with the author of the advertisement. We walked into his office, and we were met by a receptionist. From the look on her face, this receptionist gave us the impression that she had seen other types of cold callers before. She asked, "What can we do for you?" And I responded that I wanted to see the fellow whose picture appeared in *Turkey World,* and I showed her the advertisement. I asked, "Is he here?"

DR. STANLEY:

What happened after you showed the receptionist the picture of her employer in *Turkey World* and made your request to see him?

MR. WECK:

She immediately accompanied us into his office.

DR. STANLEY:

What did you say to the prospect?

MR. WECK:

I said, "My name is Jim Weck, and this is David. We are with a financial services organization, and we'd like to discuss some of the things that we may be able to do for you." Then our prospect asked why we had chosen to visit with him.

DR. STANLEY:

How did you respond to that question?

MR. WECK:

We told him we were there because we noticed his picture and advertisement in *Turkey World*. The fellow looked like he was in shock.
And then he said, "You saw me in *Turkey World*?" I replied in the
affirmative.

DR. STANLEY:

What did he say after that?

MR. WECK:

He asked us an interesting question. He said, "What are a couple
of fellows from a financial services company doing reading *Turkey
World*?"

DR. STANLEY:

Mr. Weck, how did you respond to that question?

MR. WECK:

I told him that those suppliers who are really interested in serving the
important people in this industry read *Turkey World*.

DR. STANLEY:

What did your prospect say in response to that statement?

MR. WECK:

He told us that he was impressed. So I took the opportunity to ask
about his background, his business, his product, and eventually about
his disability and life insurance policies and needs. We had a very
interesting conversation for approximately 30 minutes. We did not
attempt to make a sale at that time. We left our prospect, but before
we did, we told him that we would be in touch. In the meantime, we
would send him some literature and other things about what we do.
He agreed to visit with us again in a week or two.

DR. STANLEY:

What did you do after you left the prospect's office?

MR. WECK:

When I returned to the office, I immediately made a laminate of
the advertisement that had contained his statement, his product, his
picture, and the logo of *Turkey World*. On the following day, we

mailed this material to him along with collateral material about our products and our corporation. Later that week, we called and set up an appointment.

DR. STANLEY:

What took place during the second appointment?

MR. WECK:

The second appointment took place two weeks after the first visit with our prospect. Within 20 minutes of our arrival, the prospect purchased a large-denomination life policy as well as a disability policy. Most of the 20 minutes were spent listening to the prospect talk about his needs, and during that time he was especially appreciative of the lamination that we provided him of his advertisement and picture and dialogue in *Turkey World*.

DR. STANLEY:

Mr. Weck, how important is the concept of achievement recognition through your lamination method in prospecting affluent business owners?

MR. WECK:

I think it was the single most important reason why we were able to gain an audience with the prospect. I think he was impressed with our ability to find the winners in his industry. He was also impressed with our sensitivity to his achievements and to his need for recognition. After that, of course, the quality of our products and our people becomes paramount in closing a prospect and a sale.

DR. STANLEY:

Mr. Weck, have you had any other experiences recently in terms of prospecting people via *Turkey World?*

MR. WECK:

Yes, we have. In fact, there was an interesting profile published in *Turkey World*. This feature article was about an innovative character, a young entrepreneur who was providing turkey products to fast-food restaurants. We also visited this young entrepreneur, and during our visit we presented him with a laminate of the article and the logo of *Turkey World*. He, too, was appreciative and he, too, bought a sizable policy from us.

The *Turkey World* case study is one more example of the importance of understanding what we call the anatomy of the wealth in one's community. It is particularly interesting that only Mr. Weck and his agency employed the trade journal method of prospecting "Mr. Deboning Machine" since the area in which Mr. Weck operates is one of the top three U.S. market areas for poultry production and for affluent business owners who serve the poultry industry.

Mr. Weck has discovered the value of recognizing the achievements of wealthy entrepreneurs. Affluent prospects are vulnerable to solicitation when they are euphoric. They are especially euphoric when their achievements are featured in the trade journals of their industries. Achievement recognition is a highly productive way of capturing the business of wealthy entrepreneurs.

What market segments hold the greatest promise for Jim Weck and his agency? Should he spend more time prospecting via affluent industry affinity groups? Clearly, the market potential of industry affinity groups is considerable. The really big opportunity at hand is among the wealthy poultry producers and the suppliers to the poultry industry.

Members of industry-specific affinity groups by definition have much in common. For example, poultry producers all have the same concerns regarding increased government regulation. They are all fearful that the government's proposed sanitary and safety standards will drive their profits down to zero. This presents Jim with an opportunity to play the role of Advocate.

Logic dictates that Jim focus his energy on the industry or industries that will generate the greatest revenue for him. The poultry industry within his trade area, including producers and suppliers, contains more than a thousand very affluent prospects. These prospects actively communicate with one another via word of mouth and trade media. And all of them can be approached in the same manner and with the same central theme.

Jim can rapidly capitalize on the intraindustry communication system that already exists. His reputation as a quality supplier and Advocate can be and will be diffused rapidly through the poultry industry. This is not to say that Jim's reputation will be diffused to 1,000 members of this affinity group overnight. Within one or two years, however, his name can be known to 1,000 or more members of the poultry industry. Conversely, it often takes 20 years for an unfocused sales professional in Jim's industry to be recognized by 1,000 prospects. Moreover, these prospects typically represent hundreds of industry groups!

Jim and his agents have already made a commitment to the poultry industry. They now tell prospects that they respect this industry and that they're going to spend more and more and more time understanding the needs of their prospects and clients in this industry. They spend time learning about Occupational Safety and Health Administration regulations that are encroaching on the industry. They spend time learning about pollution concerns. Then they can write letters advocating legislative action friendly to the poultry industry to people in Congress and the Senate.

But Are They Your Advocates?

Think about it. Does your life underwriter write letters to Congress lobbying for legislation positive to your industry? Does your CPA or your attorney? How about your other suppliers? If not, maybe you should ask your current service providers to read this material. Wake them up and sensitize them to networking.

BE AN ADVOCATE FOR A BETTER WORLD

Dear Manager:

The organization of your sales force should be based on two important affluent market concepts. First, each geographic area in this nation has a unique economic infrastructure. Analyze the areas where products and services are produced in high concentrations. What are you likely to find? Affluent wine producers in the Napa Valley of California; affluent cattle ranchers in Colorado, Nebraska, and Florida; affluent coal producers in Kentucky; affluent science professors in and around Boston; affluent timberland owners in Georgia; affluent apparel producers and printers in New York City; affluent attorneys, fund-raisers, and lobbyists in Washington, D.C.; and affluent environmental engineers in California, Florida, and Texas.

Knowledge of the industries that create wealth within
various market areas is a critical foundation stone for the
sales professional. Interestingly, economic geography is
overlooked not only by many sales professionals who target the affluent but even by many strategic planners at
the largest financial institutions. Few marketers in this
industry have an accurate assessment of the various
industries of the affluent even within their trade area.
(Thomas J. Stanley, <u>Marketing to the Affluent</u> [Home-
wood, Ill.: Irwin, 1988], p. 48)

Second, most successful sales professionals who market to the
affluent are specialists in regard to both product offering and
targeted segments. The productivity of this deep and narrow
approach is reflected in the following statement:

Most extraordinary sales professionals (ESPs) are more
knowledgeable than other sales professionals about the
products or services that they market. ESPs are also more
likely to have superior knowledge of the market segments
that they target. This superior knowledge of offerings and
targets results not only from dedication in learning but
from the proclivity of ESPs to focus on a relatively narrow
product line and on a well-defined target base. (Ibid.,
p. 30)

As a sales manager, you must resolve two basic issues that
relate to the concepts of the anatomy of wealth in terms of
geography and the strategy of the deep and narrow. The majority of your branches, agencies, and even district sales offices
are staffed with scores of sales professionals who work inde-
pendently in terms of both target selection and product selection. You often find that at one branch or agency many professionals are targeting the same prospects, the same industries
or other affinity groups with identical products. At the same
time, some of the affinity groups that produce a disproportionate number of affluent prospects are all but ignored.

You must become more sensitive to the importance of
matching the specific strengths of each of your sales professionals with the unique anatomy of wealth within a given

market area. Build a portfolio of sales professionals, each with a unique focus that reflects the particular needs and interests of each affluent affinity group.

There are several advantages of organizing and managing a sales force in this manner. These include:

1. Placing one's greatest effort in the direction of the most lucrative targeted opportunities.
2. Focusing on an analysis of affluent market segments.
3. Placing each ambitious sales force member in areas of opportunities congruent with his background, aptitudes, and motives.
4. Helping managers in recruiting sales professionals based on strategic needs and market opportunities.
5. Increasing the productivity of both experienced top producers and younger achievement-oriented types.
6. Reducing competitive threats by dominating key targeted affluent segments.
7. Accessing critical information about major league concentrations of wealth and changes in wealth.
8. Developing a reputation of superior expertise for the firm as well as its sales professionals.
9. Creating an image that will encourage the affluent to initiate contact with the sales professionals.

To enable you to appreciate fully how you should reorient your marketing efforts, allow me to provide some specific recommendations. These recommendations relate to a market segment that should be of special interest to you. Use this example as a pro forma for other market segments. Your firm has a significant presence (retail distribution system) in many affluent geographic areas. One of these areas contains the highest concentration of organizations related to the environment industry. Members of this industrial category include environmental consulting/engineering firms, law firms that specialize in environmentally related litigation, distributors of products and services to the environment industry, research organizations that study the environment industry and related industries, and trade/professional associations that represent suppliers to the environmental marketplace.

The owners/heads of most of these types of organizations are affluent. Nevertheless, not one of your branches, not one of your sales professionals has ever focused on the needs of the affluent environment industry! Not one. At least two of your sales professionals hold degrees in environmental engineering. But neither of them has ever called on members of the environment industry.

I suggest that today you reorient your selected branches and sales professionals. At least one branch should support an effort to penetrate the environmental affluent segment. What products/services should you attempt to sell to this segment? No, you should not suggest generic investment products. That is much too broad despite the fact that you're in the business of marketing investment products and services.

You wish to succeed in reorienting your efforts. Start by asking yourself to have empathy for the investment needs of your prospects. Affluent prospects who own businesses that are part of the environment industry have similar investment needs. They have a clear commitment to caring for the environment. They want to invest money in environmentally sensitive firms. They want to deal with a financial consultant who is environmentally sensitive.

To implement a focused approach in relating to his segment these questions need to be answered:

- What corporations are the most environmentally sensitive?
- What firms are members of the environmental marketplace?

The information needed to answer the first question can be found in Shopping for a Better World, published by the Council on Economic Priorities (CEP), 30 Irving Place, New York, NY 10003. Also be sure to request a copy of CEP's Socially Responsible Investing. CEP rates the environmental programs of large corporations. The top-rated firms are categorized as having substantial positive programs. Firms in this category, according to the Council on Economic Priorities, use and encourage recycling, alternative energy sources, reduced waste production, green products, and reduced packaging. Firms in this category also have "a record relatively clear of major regulatory violations."

Less than 20 percent of the corporations listed were classified in the substantial positive programs category. Included on the list were Abbott Laboratories, Clorox Company, Colgate-Palmolive, Johnson & Johnson, and Marcal Paper Mills, Inc.

In regard to the second question, it is not difficult to identify affluent prospects that are part of the environment industry. The most useful source for this purpose is Environmental Industries Marketplace, published by Gale Research, Inc., Detroit, Michigan. This annual publication identifies more than 10,000 companies that are part of America's environment industry. It contains critical information about environment industry organizations, including their names, their addresses, and their phone, fax, and toll-free numbers. Subcategories include consultants and attorneys, engineering firms, surveyors, manufacturers and distributors, research facilities, retailers and wholesalers, transportation and disposal firms, and analysis and treatment facilities. Mutual funds that manage green funds (securities of environmentally sensitive corporations) are also listed. Environmental Industries Marketplace is arranged alphabetically by company name to make locating and contacting a known company a one-step process. By means of the indexes, users will be able to locate specific companies in such subject areas as

- Air pollution
- Asbestos
- Financial services
- Hazardous waste
- Landfills
- Noise pollution

- Recycling information providers
- Soils
- Spills
- Trash
- Wastewater and sludge
- Water pollution

Shopping for a Better World also contains a list of large corporations that make substantial contributions to charitable causes. Corporations in the top-ranked category donate 2 percent or more of their annual domestic pretax earnings. Corporations in this group include Anheuser-Busch, Avon Products, Campbell Soup, General Mills, Polaroid Corporation, Scott Paper, Upjohn, and Warner-Lambert Company. Who in your firm focuses on the investment needs of fund-raisers? Not one person! This is not the way to target. After all, your Alpha Branch is located in the fund-raising capital of America. Perhaps affluent fund-raisers would be very interested in buying shares in firms that have a high propensity to give.

Many other market opportunities are afforded to those who read Shopping for a Better World. CEP also rates many large corporations along several other dimensions. These include women's advancement, minority advancement, animal testing, disclosure of information (the company provides current and substantive materials on its social programs and policies), community outreach, South Africa, family benefits, and workplace issues.

Don't you think that successful/self-made affluent women are prone to purchase the securities of a firm that has an excellent track record in promoting women to top-level positions? But who in your firm is targeting self-made affluent women? Would affluent members of minority groups tend to buy shares in corporations that are sensitive to their causes?

> CEP looks at representation of minorities on a company's board of directors as well as among the company's top officers (vice presidential level or higher at corporate headquarters or president/chief executive officer of a subsidiary or division). . . . These ratings are adjusted up or down according to equal employment opportunity commission reports on percentages of minorities among officials and managers, company size and industry, purchasing from minority-owned firms, banking with minority-owned banks, and representation of minorities among the top 25 salaried officers of the company.

To date, no one in your organization is targeting affluent members of minority groups via CEP's rankings of corporations. It's time for a change. You, your firm, and several of its selected sales professionals should become "special members"

($35 per year) of Shopping for a Better World. Special members receive free copies of The Better World Investment Guide (Prentice-Hall, 528 pp.) in addition to Shopping for a Better World (the address of CEP, the publisher, is given above). You may also wish to purchase bulk orders of this book. Distribute the book to clients and prospects. This will benefit you and your target audience. The book will sensitize your prospects to benefits extending beyond the core dimension of your offerings (return on investments). They will view your sales professionals as being enlightened. Enlightened sales professionals market the securities of firms that fulfill the needs of the affluent who are sensitive to environmental issues, the advancement of women, and minority rights.

Remember that many affluent members of this society are strongly committed to these and related issues. Issues of this type are often more important to many affluent prospects than maximizing the return on money invested.

Thank you for your continued interest in our offerings. I hope that this material will be useful in reorienting the members of your sales force.

Regards,

Thomas J. Stanley, Ph.D.
Chairman
Affluent Market Institute

An Ecologically Sensitive Sales Professional

MR. MICHAEL:

What about your own interests and hobbies? Do they ever relate to networking?

DR. STANLEY:

Absolutely. I've met many people, for example, who are involved with ecological issues and have capitalized on networking very, very well. One character whom I met, an extraordinary sales professional, deeply believes in enhancing the environment. He started to prospect environmental engineers. With what? With an ecologically sensitive mutual fund, a fund of the equities of companies that are on the top 20 list of people who are most sensitive to the ecology. And he also happened to have his picture taken while picketing a major nuclear plant to be shut down. This picture was published in a major newspaper.

MR. MICHAEL:

So this showed that he was part of ecologically sensitive causes.

DR. STANLEY:

Absolutely. But make no mistake about it. It's not a gimmick. It's not a show. He has paid his dues.

MR. MICHAEL:

He really is concerned about the environment.

DR. STANLEY:

He really and genuinely is concerned. There's nothing worse than people who pretend to be concerned about the issues of an affinity group just to exploit it in terms of money. They won't be happy, and their constituents won't be happy. And eventually they, in fact, will be exposed.

TEST TIME: ARE YOU AN ADVOCATE OF CLIENTS?

Take a simple test. Determine whether you are an Advocate of your clients or whether you are an antagonist of your clients. The results may amaze you. For I never have met even one professional service provider, one sales professional, one new business development officer who self-designated himself or herself as an antagonist of clients. However, my research shows that there are a lot more antagonists than there are advocates.

Multiple-Choice Exam—Circle the Correct Answer(s)

1. You're driving to work, and you notice a stalled car in the emergency lane. You also notice that the fellow opening the hood of the stalled car is one of your clients/patients/ customers. How would you respond to this problem?

a. You pull over and see if you can help get the car started.
b. You pull over and offer the driver a ride to the shop of the local mechanic.
c. You pull over and call a tow truck via your mobile phone.
d. You turn your head to the left and increase your speed so that the driver, your client, cannot possibly see your face as you pass by at 83 miles per hour.

This question is not difficult to answer. Most service and product marketers who target the affluent answer it correctly. Few selected *d* as an answer. Most circle *a* and/or *b,* and/or *c.* But this way of responding does not necessarily make you a true Advocate of your clients' causes.

How about another simple question?

2. You're having lunch at a fine downtown restaurant. Halfway through your main course, you notice that one of your clients is seated at a nearby table on your right. Apparently, he is looking for his wallet. A waiter with an impatient demeanor stands beside him, and he is obviously flustered. He must have lost his wallet. The waiter is looking at your client suspiciously. How would you respond to this problem?
a. You immediately walk over to the waiter and tell him to place your client's tab on your bill.
b. You summon the waiter and tell him in a very loud tone that your client is one of the most respected people in the state.
c. You walk over to your client's table and hand him $300 in cash, telling him that you stopped by to pay him back that $300 you borrowed from him last week.
d. You turn your head to the left so that your client in need can't see your face, finish your meal hurriedly, and rapidly exit the restaurant.

This question is also not difficult to answer. Few service and product marketers who target the affluent indicate *d* as a possible answer. Since nearly all of these people answer the two questions correctly, you may rightly ask yet another question: Why are there so few advocates among them?

You must remember that the opportunities for helping affluent clients with car problems on the road or with bill-paying problems at a restaurant are rare. Such problems are not of major concern among affluent clients. While embarrassing, they typically do not threaten the goals and dreams of these clients.

Analyze the questions and answers given above in the context of the real needs of your affluent clients. You will then see how shallow we all are when it comes to becoming a true Advocate of clients' really important needs and causes. In the questions given above, you responded correctly for several reasons. First, you have a real need to serve your clients. Second, your client has a problem that you feel competent to address. Third, you are aware of the problem. To prove to a client that you are his or her supporter, all of these conditions must exist.

Few Are Advocates

Why do clients and prospects view so few marketers as being advocates? It's not because of the first condition. Most marketers truly wish to serve their clients. In regard to the second condition, however, clients may have a variety of serious problems that marketers do not feel competent to solve. In regard to the third condition, most marketers do not know what major problems confront their clients.

To demonstrate how one may become an Advocate, let us review yet another question from the "Advocate examination."

3. More than 20 of your customers, clients, or patients are business owners in the boat/yacht industry. Some are boat/yacht builders; others are dealers; four are suppliers to this industry. All of them own private businesses. Today, on an inside page of the business section of your local newspaper, you notice an interesting article. Its headline reads as follows: "Boat and yacht manufacturers and dealers going broke in record number." The article does not go into detail about the causes of this downturn in the industry. It merely gives statistics about the number of industry members who have gone bankrupt in the past six months.

How would you respond to this problem? Possible responses of those who "serve" clients in the boat/yacht industry include the following:

a. You begin immediately to find new clients in another industry.

b. You call your people in accounts receivable to determine how much credit you have extended to your clients in the troubled industry.

c. You send letters to your clients in the troubled industry requesting updated information about their ability to pay for your products/services.

d. You immediately place a stop on all requests for your offerings that have been made by your clients in the troubled industry.

e. You intensify your selling activity in the troubled industry. When the going gets tough in an industry, it's time to turn up the heat on clients and prospects in that industry. This is the only way to beat the competition.

f. All of the above.

g. None of the above. (*Note*: If you selected *g*, please state the action you would take in dealing with this problem.)

Far too many marketers antagonize their clients in an industry that they are supposed to be serving when there is a downturn in that industry. However, abandonment is not the way of the Advocate (review responses *a, b, c,* and *d*). In the long run, the troubled industry will probably bounce back and those who acted as its advocates will then be rewarded. Also, clients in a troubled industry may view "turning up the heat" as grossly insensitive (review answer *e*).

The Pro Forma Answer from an Advocate

Don't abandon clients who are facing an industry downturn. Don't hit them with a marketing/selling sledgehammer. Do act as an Advocate. How should you respond to this situation? Examine the response given by an Advocate. This specialist in new business development responded to the last multiple-choice question by circling *g* ("None of the above"). He then went on to provide his own approach, the Advocate's orientation toward the situation.

I would first find out what caused the downturn in the industry. Since several of my clients are actually in the boat and yacht manufacturing industries, I guess I have an advantage over some of the other respondents. The greatest advantage that I have, however, relates to the fact that I read the trade journals of the industries that I serve. My organization is an accounting firm that employs 43 certified public accountants. I'm one of the three senior partners. Our firm decided long ago that it would be more appropriate to target several selected industries to focus on rather than have several hundred clients in several hundred industries.

More than half of our clients are in several targeted industries, which include automobile dealerships and related service providers, physicians, attorneys, and engineers/architects. Also, because we felt that boat manufacturing and dealerships would prosper in our region of the country, we decided about six years ago to involve ourselves in providing accounting and related services to the boat industry.

I read many months ago that the government was proposing to place a so-called luxury tax on the products that many of our clients produce and/or sell. Several of our clients sell top-of-the-line boats and yachts that would be included in the luxury tax.

After learning about the proposed tax, I contacted all of our boat industry clients and discussed the tax with them. Actually, some of them were not directly affected by the tax, because they sell smaller craft, which do not come under the heading of luxury products. However, some of our best clients were affected, not only those who manufacture yachts but also those who supply yachts and those who are yacht dealers.

Even those who were not directly affected felt somewhat threatened by the government's position of placing a tax on "nonessential durable goods" at the high-priced level. They rationalize or suggest, however, that if the government can tax expensive boats, perhaps next it will tax inexpensive boats. All of the clients in this industry whom we contacted felt the same—that they were genuinely concerned about and threatened by this legislation but that they were not really certain about what action they could take. They did feel that their own trade association would devise some ideas about dealing with these issues. However, they were somewhat frustrated because they realized that it takes time to put forces together that might change the mind of certain legislators.

As an accountant, I believe not only that this tax is unfair but also that it is probably ineffective. In fact, the cost of collecting the tax would probably be greater than the revenue that the tax would generate. I told several of my clients this in lengthy conversations. I also called all of our clients in the boat industry and followed up with a letter saying our firm was on their side and that if the tax law were passed, which in fact it was, we would stand beside them, we would give them a little extra time to pay some of the bills they had accumulated with us. I also promised that we would help them as much as we could in terms of downsizing their inventories and giving them some advice about dealing with a decline in demand for their products.

Our firm has not only accounting ability but also management consulting ability that relates directly to some of these issues. But perhaps most important from our point of view, and I think from our clients' point of view, I wrote a letter to each of our state's two U.S. senators and also to all of our state's U.S. congressmen. Very simply, the letter blasted the so-called luxury tax legislation. I indicated very strongly that not all boat owners are in fact wealthy, yet the tax was supposed to be a tax on wealthy people.

I pointed out that some people genuinely fond of boats do not think of them as a luxury product. I also outlined how unfair it was to pick out just a few industries to target, how ineffective and insensitive some of the lawmakers were in this regard. I sent copies of this letter to all of our clients in the boat industry and to several clients in other industries. I accompanied the copies with a personal note saying that we do support the needs of people in the boat industry.

The need, in this case, was to petition the government to change its mind about the proposed legislation. Letters were also sent to all boat manufacturers in the state, all boat dealers, and all suppliers of boat manufacturers and dealers. Most of these people were not our clients. However, I wanted to let them know that we were on their side. The response was excellent. Our purpose in writing the letters to the congressmen and senators was to show that we are advocates of our clients' causes and of the industries that our clients represent. The letters were not designed as a gimmick or as a short-lived type of commercial message. However, I must tell you that we have gotten dozens of letters that said thank you. Also, several boat manufacturers and boat dealers have told us that they would like to do business with us.

Even suppliers who count on the boat industry for only a small portion of their revenue were very complimentary about the effort that we made. In fact, I received one letter from a major supplier of the boat industry who is not currently a client saying that he received letters from two accounting firms in the same week. One was our letter, to which he responded by saying that he would like to meet with our firm to discuss the possibility of our doing his accounting work. The other letter, from his accounting firm, suggested that he speed up his payment of the bills that had been sent to him for accounting services.

The letter he sent me went on to say that he was most excited that a firm in the accounting industry, a firm that supplies the boat industry, was taking it upon itself to play the role of an advocate for the causes of the industries that it serves. On the other hand, he was quite perturbed about the fact that an accounting firm that he had dealt with for over 15 years and had provided with hundreds of thousands of dollars in business had sent him a rather cold letter indicating that his firm should speed up the payment of its accounting bills.

I will guarantee you that this firm will do everything in its power to continue to support the industries and the members of the industries that we serve. I also sent copies of the letters that were originally sent to the members of Congress and our U.S. senators to newspaper editors in every major city in the state. Interestingly enough, several of these editors were kind enough to publish our letters. Because of that fact, we've discovered that some of the heaviest readers of editorials and letters to the editor are writers and reporters.

Since the publication of our first letter, more than six writers/ reporters have contacted us and asked our opinions about this and related issues. We've gotten some very positive press in the local periodicals, and we were also fortunate enough to have a writer for one of the boating trade journals pick up on our story. It is more than likely that we will be given some excellent coverage on the role that we have played and continue to play in helping our clients in the boat industry and related industries to fight the unfair tax.

I then asked this respondent why so few suppliers to industries play the role of Advocate for their clients. His reply was quite interesting. It shows how perceptive this senior partner of a major regional accounting firm was with regard to his clients' needs. First, he pointed out that

most of the people against whom our firm has competed provide little else other than traditional accounting services. Most accounting firms do provide a high level of service in terms of the fundamentals of their profession. However, most clients greatly appreciate receiving more than core services. They genuinely appreciate accountants who take to heart the real problems that clients and their industries face.

As a case in point, when the federal government levies what we consider to be an unfair tax on some of our most important clients, we view that not only as a threat to our clients but also as a threat to our own livelihood. And we put our money where our mouth is. We took the time from our own word processing facilities to send hundreds of letters to newspaper editors, to congressmen and senators, and to others who we thought could influence the repeal of the so-called luxury tax legislation.

I believe we are probably the only firm in this region that played such an active role. But we have done this for other industries as well. In fact, not too long ago we asked all of our clients to complete a petition/postcard write-in to their congressmen that took exception to proposed legislation that would adversely affect one of our other industry client groups. The main reason that we can respond so quickly is that we are members of seven trade/professional affiliation groups that represent our clients and their industries.

We find that this is vitally important in terms of appreciating and understanding their needs and that they feel better about us because they know we are a part of their affiliation group. In addition, we religiously read the trade journals that are produced by the industries we target. This, too, is indispensable in terms of understanding the problems that crop up as well as some of the opportunities. It is not unusual for us to bring to the attention of our clients some of the trends that are taking place in their industry before our clients are even aware of them. They appreciate that interest, and they tell us that many many times in letters, in phone calls, and, of course, by important referrals they make on our behalf. In fact, we have quite a high level, and a professional level, of reciprocity in terms of referring clients to clients, customers to customers. We are a firm that is in the accounting industry, but we are also a firm that is in the service industry. And we consider service to be our number one product.

Only Part-Time Networkers and Advocates

I find it valuable to review the responses to the exam question regarding the client's stalled car. Most members of my audiences indicated that they would pull over and attempt to repair the car. Yet these same respondents indicated that they had never acted as an Advocate for the important causes of their clients. Why? Because they felt that they were not skilled or trained in the Advocate role.

Interestingly, most of the people who indicated a readiness to help repair a client's car had no mechanical experience. On the other hand, most of the same people had a proven ability to write letters, to make phone calls, to negotiate, and so on. Many of them probably mailed out thousands or even tens of thousands of letters each year to clients and prospects.

What could be more important than writing a letter on behalf of a client's cause? Many of the people in my audiences recognized that a client was in distress if his car stalled or if he was unable to pay a restaurant bill. But most of these people were much less sensitive to the critical needs of their clients, such as the need to avert a tax that threatened their clients' very livelihood.

A Published Letter from an Advocate

On April 23, 1991, *The Wall Street Journal* published James W. Taylor's "Luxury Tax Sinks U.S. Boating Industry." In this letter to the editor, Mr. Taylor recommended that the tax on luxury products, including some boats, be repealed. While Mr. Taylor does not manufacture boats, he is nonetheless an Advocate of boat manufacturers and their causes. He is also president of Nelson A. Taylor Company, a supplier to boat builders, and chairman of the 1,700-member National Marine Manufacturers Association.

Luxury Tax Sinks U.S. Boating Industry

By James W. Taylor

A simple ceremony during the Miami Boat Show this winter illustrates why the Bahamian government has a better grasp of simple economic theory than does our own. Prime Minister Sir Lynden Pindling used the backdrop of the world's largest boat show to announce that the Bahamas would be reducing boat taxes to less than 1 percent of a vessel's value and accelerating marina development. Sir Lynden's motive was straightforward: to lure American boaters, draw boat sales and service to the islands, and, in turn, create jobs.

Sir Lynden's action came less than two months after imposition in the United States of a 10 percent excise tax on that part of a new pleasure boat's price tag that exceeds $100,000. While that will make it better in the Bahamas for those who wish to buy and slip their boats there—and for people looking for work there—it will further eliminate jobs in the U.S. boating industry.

In fact, the blood is already running here. Because of local labor sensitivities and fear that their names in the media will further jeopardize sales, many boat builders won't go on record to explain how hurtful the tax is. But one major builder confides he has cut $100,000-plus production to custom orders only and given more than 450 workers layoff notices. A household name in sport-fishing yachts has closed its Southern plant, forcing 600 people out of work. The tax is cited regularly by those entering bankruptcy proceedings.

In Florida, the nation's top boat-building state, the Labor Department estimates that builders alone laid off 5,000 of 18,800 workers by the end of 1990. Marine retailers, original equipment manufacturers, and services allied to boating, such as lending, insurance, and publishing, are feeling the ripple effects. Are all of these job losses directly the result of the excise tax? No. But the new tax deepens our industry's woes.

The boat tax and other so-called luxury taxes on jewelry, furs, private aircraft, and high-ticket autos were originally included in the budget reconciliation game as a swap for the capital gains tax cut for the "rich" that never happened. Worse for all taxpayers, the Joint Committee of Taxation of the U.S. Congress has released an estimate of collections showing only $3 million attributable to boats in 1991.

In an interview, Peter K. Scott, a partner at Coopers & Lybrand and former general counsel to the IRS, stated: "The revenue gains from the luxury tax are illusory; businesses and the IRS will spend two or three times more to comply with and collect it than the small amount of revenue it raises. This is the ultimate in bad tax policy." Fred Goldberg, Jr., commissioner of internal revenue, has been quoted as saying he has no estimate of the cost of collecting the new taxes and questions whether the revenues collected are worth the burden to the IRS and the taxpayer.

Before you dismiss this issue as parochial, consider what consequences an arbitrary 10 percent price hike on shoreside condominiums, backyard pools, European travel, wide-screen televisions, season pro football tickets, or a host of other "luxury" goods and services might have. The excise tax on boats sets a dangerous precedent.

Price points affect boat sales, just as they affect refrigerator and clothing sales. Pleasure boats are affected by a price elasticity of two, according to industry pricing and marketing studies and as illustrated by the experience of two European nations. Lawmakers in Britain and Italy found that boat sales decreased by double the percentage amount of the excise taxes they levied and tax revenues decreased. Subsequently, Britain withdrew the tax and Italy reduced it significantly. In the United States, this means we could expect sales of affected boats to be depressed 20 percent.

The National Marine Manufacturers Association estimates that 10,000 to 15,000 boats will be affected by the tax and that 6,000 to 8,000 workers will lose their jobs this year. Those workers pay more than $30 million in federal income taxes annually.

America's boating industry is one of a few U.S. manufacturing industries that maintain a net trade surplus—$239.4 million in 1989, the latest year available. U.S.-built recreational boats are highly regarded in all world markets and in demand in countries, such as Japan and Germany, where insistence on quality is high. The new excise tax, while not collected on exported goods, lowers domestic demand and volume, thus reducing American boatbuilder productivity. It will directly jeopardize our competitiveness with trading partners and could ultimately sacrifice the boating trade surplus, which is an economic benefit shared by all Americans.

The boating industry has found members in Congress who recognize the folly of the boat tax. Senators John Breaux (D., La.), John Chafee (R., R.I.), and Claiborne Pell (D.,R.I.) and Representatives Clay Shaw (R., Fla.) and David Bonior (D., Mich.) have cosponsored bills in their respective chambers to repeal the excise tax on boats.

For businessmen now unaffected by an excise tax burden, helping these bills succeed might be the best insurance to keep matters that way.

Source: *The Wall Street Journal*, April 3, 1991, p. 22. Published with permission of *The Wall Street Journal*.

If you were a boat manufacturer, all else being equal, would you prefer to patronize Mr. Taylor's firm or some other organization? All else being equal, most boat manufacturers would probably select Mr. Taylor's firm. Why? Because Mr. Taylor understands that marketing is much broader than merely delivering products and services. Buyers prefer to deal with suppliers who understand all of their important problems and needs.

Problems and needs transcend product and service specifications. Thus the truly gifted supplier places a priority on becoming an Advocate of prospects and clients. Less enlightened suppliers focus on their own need to sell core offerings to prospects and clients in spite of serious industry downturns and threats. But not Mr. Taylor. He focuses on the most urgent problems of prospects and clients. He realizes that in the long run he and his firm will benefit from helping to eliminate threats to the industry that he so nobly serves. Conversely, most suppliers across a wide spectrum of professions and industries respond to the threats facing their clients' industries as antagonists.

Mr. Taylor provides strong evidence that he is an Advocate. His letter to the editor in *The Wall Street Journal* tells his clients that he has their interests at heart. He clearly uses his marketing and selling skills in a manner that will make them most productive, that is, by communicating to clients, the press, the public, the lawmakers that the newly enacted tax on so-called luxury boats must be repealed.

Moreover, Mr. Taylor has done his homework regarding the key issues of the luxury tax debate. Thus he is again able to demonstrate his marketing genius, this time by focusing on the needs of the reader rather than solely on the needs of his clients. First, he provides evidence that America will lose jobs and business to foreign boat builders and foreign organizations that service boats. He provides statistics regarding the number of American workers who have been laid off because of the downturn in demand for "luxury boats." He attributes this downturn to the tax on boats.

He quotes a senior partner at a major accounting firm and former general counsel to the IRS who stated: "The revenue gains from the luxury tax are illusory; businesses and the IRS will spend two or three times more to comply with and collect it than the small amount of revenue it raises."

He also points out that the luxury tax threatens an industry that generates a net trade surplus of over $200 million. And he alludes to the fact that taxing products is a potent threat to other industries. He contends that the luxury tax sets a dangerous precedent that could eventually be applied to a wide variety of products and industries.

Mr. Taylor's marketing instincts and his empathy for client needs are exemplary. His contribution to the marketing discipline is, in reality, a case study on how to serve the real needs of clients. However, surprisingly few advocates exist in today's marketplace. Where are the letters to the editor that should be forthcoming from all the other sales and marketing professionals who "serve" an endangered industry?

Never in an entire lifetime do these professionals act as advocates with regard to the really important issues that confront their best clients and customers.

It does not take much time or effort to demonstrate your willingness and ability to be an Advocate. Take the letter to the editor that Mr. Taylor wrote as an example. It contained approximately 875 words. That is the equivalent of a 1½–2-page single-spaced letter. Think about how many letters of this length sales professionals write each year. How difficult would it be to write just one more? It is likely that a letter matching the quality of Mr. Taylor's contribution could provide the sales professional who writes it with considerable long-term benefits.

The Probability of Being Published

Some sales professionals whom I confront with the issue of becoming advocates of clients respond with this shopworn objection: "I'll never get my letter published." I quickly counter that objection with this quote:

> On January 23, 1987, *The Wall Street Journal* (pp. 12–13) placed an interesting letter in its own publication. The letter bore this title: "A Word of Thanks to 10,000 Men and Women of Letters." Praising the people who wrote letters to the editor of *The Wall Street Journal*, it stated that 10,000 people wrote such letters during 1986, of which about one in six was published (1,671). Thus, if one were to write six letters to the editor of *The Wall Street Journal*, the chances are that one of them would be published.

> Thomas J. Stanley, *Marketing to the Affluent*, (Homewood, Ill.: Business One Irwin, 1988, p. 217.

Think of all the suppliers, the sales professionals, and the marketing professionals from such industries as insurance, accounting, law, investments, and engineering, who never see the big picture and never fully leverage their marketing skills. How long would it take to write an 875-word letter to the editor that supports a client's cause? What better use of an hour or two is there? Tell your clients and prospects that you are an enlightened supplier. Tell them by sending them a copy of your letter. They will appreciate your support and recognize your value as a supplier. Also send copies to the editors of selected newspapers, lawmakers, industry-specific opinion leaders, and trade association officers. And be sure to inform your clients and prospects that you are willing and able to share your marketing resources in furthering their causes.

Most professionals who are successful in marketing their own products and services are typically much more skilled in this discipline than their clients. Why not occasionally share your marketing and selling skills with those who need an Advocate? What is the most valuable product or service you could supply a client whose industry and business are threatened by ruinous taxes and government regulations? You are that product or service, because you will act as an Advocate for clients who need support at their time of critical need.

Why So Few Advocates?

Examine hundreds of letters to the editor in scores of popular newspapers and related print media. What will you notice? In fewer than one in four hundred editorial sections will advocacy messages from suppliers to an industry appear. Why are there so few advocates among the population of sales, marketing, and new business development professionals in America? Are they all uncaring about and insensitive to the most pressing needs of their clients and prospects?

Most of these professionals are truly interested in furthering the causes of those they serve. However, several factors explain why so few actually become advocates. These factors include:

   1. *Narrowly Defined Training Curriculums*. Few, if any, training programs teach new business development officers/sales professionals how to network with affinity groups by becoming their advocates. This applies both to in-house training programs and to seminars offered outside the organization.

   2. *Narrowly Defined Job Descriptions*. Most of the professionals responsible for generating business are told to find prospects,

condition prospects, and close prospects. Their job description is very narrow. It views serving the client in the context of product/ service quality, rapid response, fast delivery of the product, service of the product, and perhaps lunch and dinner. But rarely, if ever, does the job description of the sales professional specify becoming an Advocate for the client's causes.

3. *Generic Targeting.* Too few sales professionals target effectively. Many merely ask prospects from dozens, even hundreds, of industries to do business with them. Thus they end up with a wide assortment of clients who represent a wide variety of industries. In such cases, sales professionals never really have the opportunity to develop a deep understanding of the people, companies, and industries they serve. Most affluent business owners and self-employed professionals are better served by sales professionals who focus, that is, specialize in servicing a narrowly defined set of industries that produce opportunities to deal with affluent clients and prospects.

CHAPTER 5

THE MENTOR

"Influential people go out of their way to endorse him. Why? Because he teaches them how to fish for new clients."

NETWORKING VIA THE "TEACH THEM TO FISH" METHOD

Affluent auto dealers and authors are members of Mr. Gregory's influence network. In fact, Mr. Gregory actually recruited me to that network. He called me one morning and followed up the call with an interesting letter that he uses to network with affluent auto dealers.

Mr. Gregory is a very creative fellow. He provides free seminars, books, and tapes to auto dealers in order to help them sell expensive vehicles to the affluent. He teaches clients and prospects how to fish for buyers. His message is quite simple: "I will teach you how to enhance your revenue before you enhance mine."

The Indirect Approach Produces Excellent Results

Mr. Gregory calls on the owners of luxury automobile dealerships. He introduces himself as a senior vice president of a brokerage firm. In that capacity, part of his responsibility is to train brokers and to help brokers find wealthy prospects. While training brokers in selling to the affluent, the idea of doing the same thing for sales professionals in a noncompeting industry occurred to him. Thus he could simultaneously enhance his own revenue and the revenue of prospects and clients. That's exactly what he did.

When Mr. Gregory contacts an auto dealer by phone, by letter, or in person, he points out that his responsibilities include helping his own sales force find affluent people, especially when those people are coming into money. Mr. Gregory used this sales theme in the following pro forma letter:

Mr. W. B. Gregory, Jr.
First Vice President
Acme Securities, Inc.
October 11, 19___

Mr. Mike Jones
Jones Imports
401 South Midway Boulevard
Center City, Texas

Dear Mike:

It is said that time is money. During my most recent visit to your showroom, you and members of your sales staff invested a significant amount of time for my benefit. Since I did not purchase one of your imports, you may feel that your time generated very little return.

As thanks for your efforts, please accept this autographed copy of *Selling to the Affluent* by Dr. Thomas J. Stanley. This book and a companion tape album will help you and your sales professionals identify, condition, and close prospects who are in the mood to buy.

The financial advisors at our firm, Acme Securities, Inc., target individuals in the top income and net worth brackets. One of my jobs as first vice president is to help our brokers find these same affluent prospects and become comfortable marketing investments to them. Many of these people are difficult to identify and even harder to meet. To help me understand this complex and elusive market segment, I enlisted the help of Dr. Stanley. During the last several years, he has given me many hours of personal and classroom instruction. His information and enthusiasm, combined with my efforts, have resulted in a marked increase in our sales.

It occurred to me that both your company and mine are seeking to do business with the same types of high-income groups. Perhaps the sales training information I have would be helpful to your sales professionals. If you have any interest in exploring that idea, let me know. It would be a pleasure to present my favorite seminar topic, "How to Sell to the Affluent," to your sales force.

Thanks again for your help.

Sincerely,

Mr. W. B. Gregory, Jr.
First Vice President

cc: Dr. Thomas J. Stanley

Synergy in Selling

If you were an auto dealer, you might say: "OK, Mr. Gregory, I appreciate it. But why do you want to help my sales force? Aren't you busy enough helping your own sales force?"

His answer to that question is very clear: "There are a hundred thousand sales professionals out there selling investment products to people, and that's all they're selling. They only care about their need, the need to shove the investment of the day down your throat."

That is why some auto dealers are initially skeptical about Mr. Gregory's approach. Such auto dealers often ask: "What do you want from me, Mr. Gregory, for helping us in this way?" His response is very simple. He asks two questions: "With whom are you currently dealing?" and "What types of things is that person doing for you?" A typical answer is: "Mr. Bob Common, who locks in on service delivery and provides the ABC fundamental plain vanilla investment account. Nothing spectacular."

Then Mr. Gregory asks the question of questions: "How many of the people with whom you're currently investing have offered you the opportunity to enhance the production of your sales force?" And the answer comes back, typically after a long pause: "None." In sharp contrast, Mr. Gregory is offering an investment package that is at least as good as, and probably better than, the investment package offered by the current provider, but in addition he's saying, "I will help you where you really need help." And clearly, the number one need of auto dealers today is to increase the productivity of their sales force. Mr. Gregory provides this as a free service.

In his initial attempt at this novel sales method, Mr. Gregory did not have his presentation perfected. Therefore, the dealer was a little skittish about accepting Mr. Gregory's concept, though he's still a prospect. However, the next dealership that Mr. Gregory approached responded very positively. Within two days, Mr. Gregory received a $150,000 IRA account from the dealership owner, who said, "Even basic quality service is rare, but enhancing the selling skills of my people is a divine form of service."

Intrafranchise Referrals

After successfully prospecting the dealership owner, Mr. Gregory began to prospect other affluent owners of automobile dealerships. What owners? Those who sold the same make of automobile as that sold by his client.

Mr. Gregory's pro forma prospecting dialogue is as follows:

You know Mike Jones. His dealership is 50 miles away. You remember playing golf with him at the national dealers' meeting in Palm Springs. He suggested that I call you. Let me tell you what I do.

It's rather interesting that when Mr. Gregory recently called me, he said, "I still don't feel comfortable doing seminars." I answered, "Well, you've read more of my research than anybody." And we talked at length about his knowledge. I then said, "If it will make you feel better, I'll certify you." In essence, I gave him my blessing and I certified him. In fact, I'm currently putting together some certificates that say Mr. Gregory has been certified to teach *Selling to the Affluent* and *Marketing to the Affluent*. Why not?

Mr. Gregory is a scholar with high integrity and a very bright fellow. Like many other extraordinary sales professionals, he's a great Mentor. He reads a lot and is genuinely interested in helping people. For these reasons, he's going to succeed.

Mr. Gregory can go to any state in this country and talk to people in the automobile business using their language. He can prospect dealers all day. They'll never hang up on him. They'll return his calls. Why? Because their colleagues have endorsed him as a trusted Mentor. The increase in sales productivity generated by Mr. Gregory's seminars more than offsets the fees he charges for financial services.

A MENTOR TO DOCTORS, DEANS, AND EDITORS

Early one morning, I received a telephone call from Mr. Gordon, a financial consultant for a premier regional brokerage house. He told me that he had just finished reading *Marketing to the Affluent*. He was particularly interested in my discussion of hawkers and talkers. In the book I point out that prospects often perceive talkers as hawkers. Conversely, they usually perceive writers as experts.

Following this thinking, Mr. Gordon indicated that he wanted to write articles and conduct seminars. He wanted several affluent affinity groups to perceive him as an expert.

There was a large teaching hospital in Mr. Gordon's trade area. In order to target the staff of this hospital, he requested my permission to reprint a part of *Marketing to the Affluent*. He said, "Dr. Stanley, I'm calling you today to see if I could reprint, with your permission, a portion of *Marketing to the Affluent*. I'd like to reprint the letter you wrote about doctors, the letter in which you suggest that most doctors have big incomes and relatively small levels of wealth."

Of course, I asked Mr. Gordon why he wanted to reprint this letter. His reply was very direct. "I want to send a copy of it along with my own letter to the dean of the large teaching hospital in my trade area telling him that his young doctors, as well as his middle-aged ones, his teaching professionals, and even his medical students, need to be educated about the high consumption propensity and the low investment propensity of doctors. I want to offer my services, my investment advice, my training, and my ideas about discipline as it relates to the accumulation of wealth."

My response was simple. "Mr. Gordon, all the readers of my books can receive upon request a copy of my latest article on the relationship between high income producing occupations, including doctors, and wealth accumulation. Just send a self-addressed, stamped envelope to my attention at the Affluent Market Institute, 325 Crosstree Lane, Atlanta, Georgia, 30328.''

Of course, a good sales professional who gets his or her foot in the door will make additional requests. Mr. Gordon was no exception to this rule. He asked rather casually, ''By the way, while I have you on the phone, who is helping you with your pension money?'' I quipped that it was someone who didn't know how to invest money.

On a less whimsical note, I followed up with this brief question: ''Mr. Gordon, what industries do you want to target?'' He replied that he wanted to target construction contractors and other business owners involved in the construction industry. I asked him another brief question about his current client group and learned that one of his best clients was in the construction business. Then I asked him, ''Mr. Gordon, tell me. How did you first come into contact with this owner of a major construction contracting firm?'' His answer was very intriguing. He said:

> I saw the trucks of a construction firm. Every time I saw them on the road, I noticed that they were extremely clean and very well kept. So I called the owner and said to him, ''You and the United Parcel Service have the cleanest trucks in the country. Tell me about your company.'' I could sense that he was most appreciative of my comment. I told him that I wanted to put my cross hairs on him. I wanted to deal with winners, and I knew that he was a winner. I knew that his desk was clean too. I wanted to focus on him and his industry. And I asked if he was a member of an association. He replied that he was a member of two associations, both related to construction. One had to do with people who provide construction products and services for the utility industry, and the other was the association of the heavy construction industry.

It seems that Mr. Gordon wisely spent several hundred dollars to become an associate member of one of these trade associations. Which one? The one with the high concentration of very wealthy business owners and executives. What does Mr. Gordon get for his money? Among other things, he gets the association's newsletter, its journal, and its directory of who's who in construction contracting. Because Mr. Gordon paid his association dues by the deadline, he also received a free membership orientation, during which he met many new "big-league members as well as many up-and-comers." As a bonus, many current members of the association were also present at the orientation.

Perhaps the most interesting comment that Mr. Gordon made to me concerned his role as Mentor to the editor of the trade association's newsletter. This biweekly publication is distributed to all of its members. Mr. Gordon persuaded its editor to add a "Winner's Profile" section featuring people who had recently won major contracting bids.

Mr. Gordon interviews these winners about their achievements and then writes profiles based on the interviews. These profiles are published in the association's newsletter. What a splendid way to meet winners of multimillion-dollar contracts. In addition to meeting these winners, Mr. Gordon will, of course, be recognized as a person with high credibility because of the fact that he is "a noted industry columnist"! Since his section recognizes the achievements of successful association members, he will be a welcome guest at any of their offices and, perhaps, even at their homes.

The newsletter also publishes the specifications of winning bids, the amounts that will be paid, and the names of the winning bidders. These are the people, the doers, the movers and the shakers, the winners with whom Mr. Gordon will come into contact.

Mr. Gordon will also provide seminars for the members of the trade association. He will not be paid for this service. However, he will be able to teach the association's members how to market to business owners. In this way, he will use his knowledge, his intellect, and his ideas in fulfilling his role as Mentor. Again, he will be recognized, not as a hawker, not as a talker, but as a writer, an expert, and a Mentor.

Finding and Prospecting Capital Ships and Convoys

Mr. Gordon also mentioned that he had asked the conference coordinator of the largest hotel in his trade area for a list of all the affinity groups that would be holding meetings at the hotel in the next two years and of the key contacts that represented these groups. He was given this information. Thereupon, he wrote to all of the people on this list, informing them that he was locally based and that he would be delighted to speak free of charge to their groups. Many of them indicated that they had selected speakers and that their programs had already been solidified. To these people, Mr. Gordon replied, "I would be honored to act as a substitute in cases where speakers aren't able or are unwilling to attend the meeting." And in the spirit of a true Mentor he told them that "it is more than likely that down the road you will have some cancellations. If this is the case, I would be delighted to help you out. Moreover, I have no problem with sharing my wisdom at night, on weekends, or even holidays!"

Questions Often Asked

How did Mr. Gordon get the assignment to write the section on successful construction contractors in the first place? He called the editor and asked for the job. In other words, he was the only one who proposed such a section to the editor. He was the only one who acted as a Mentor to the editor. He was the only one who called.

MR. RICHARD: A TARGET AND NETWORKER OF NETWORKS

Early one morning, I received a telephone call from a most extraordinary networker. Mr. Richard is one of this country's premier marketers of quality collectibles. His firm sells everything from rare documents to original paintings. Are you seeking a document signed by one or more members of America's First Continental Congress? Mr. Richard probably has several dozen in stock!

Why was Mr. Richard calling me? Was I a target for his offerings? No, he called to introduce himself and to order several offerings of the Affluent Market Institute. One week later, his secretary called our offices. She stated that he was leaving on vacation the next day and wanted copies of the books *Marketing to the Affluent* and *Selling to the Affluent* delivered immediately so that he could read them while vacationing. We informed her that it would be impossible to provide "same day delivery" for books. "Mr. Richard must have the books today," she repeated. How could we accommodate him? After all, serving clients is the basic orientation of all productive businesses.

Near the end of this conversation, Mr. Richard's secretary was promised that "the books will be in your offices within 10 minutes." She seemed to be shocked by this promise, but the promise was kept. Copies of both books were on Mr. Richard's desk less than 10 minutes.

How did we accomplish this? Do we have an electrobeam that sends solid materials to distant cities at the speed of light? No. However, our organization does have a highly efficient network of extraordinary sales and marketing professionals.

Directly across the street from Mr. Richard's office is the Alpha branch of another client of ours. This client markets investment and investment-related products and services. We examined shipping records and collateral information at our institute and quickly determined that at least two dozen of the financial consultants housed in the Alpha branch had copies of both *Marketing to the Affluent* and *Selling to the Affluent!* I then called the Alpha branch administrator and had this conversation with her.

MS. BAKER:

Good morning. This is Susan Baker.

DR. STANLEY:

Good morning, Susan. This is Tom Stanley. Thanks for buying our materials. I have a special offer for you today.

MS. BAKER:

Oh . . . should I sit down for this one?

DR. STANLEY:

Yes. Strap on your safety belt. I just received an urgent call. Are you familiar with a company in your neighborhood called Jamestown Galleries?

MS. BAKER:

Oh, yes. They are right across the street from us.

DR. STANLEY:

Well, the owner, Mr. Richard, besides being a millionaire, is in desperate need of a favor from one of your financial consultants.

MS. BAKER:

You have my undivided attention.

DR. STANLEY:

Mr. Richard is leaving on a vacation trip tomorrow. He wants a copy of my books today, and I mean today. I cannot get the books there until tomorrow.

MS. BAKER:

What do you suggest?

DR. STANLEY:

I suggest that many of your financial consultants would like to become fast friends with a millionaire. Can you get one of your financial consultants to walk himself or herself across the street with a copy of the books? Don't you think Mr. Richard would be indebted to any financial consultant who would solve this problem for him?

MS. BAKER:

I'll take care of this immediately.

DR. STANLEY:

I knew I could count on you. Good-bye.

Following our conversation, Ms. Baker turned on the Alpha branch's public announcement system and said:

The owner of Jamestown Galleries, located across the street from us, needs our help. He would like to borrow a copy of *Marketing to the Affluent* and *Selling to the Affluent* while he is on vacation for a week. He has to have the books today. I emphasize *today*. Or sooner! Is there anyone in this office who would like to make friends with a millionaire today? I emphasize *today*. Start your own lending library for millionaires today. Walk your copy of the books over there immediately.

Was Mr. Richard's wish fulfilled? Were these books made available to him at the time and place he wanted them? Affirmative. In fact, Mr. Richard was offered the books by the equivalent of a "bookmobile" filled with financial consultants. Interestingly, Mr. Richard now does his financial investing with the lender of the books. This financial consultant was smart enough and fast enough to be first in the line that formed to offer Mr. Richard the loan of the two books.

Let us analyze why Mr. Richard opened an account with the "lender of books." Before Mr. Richard was willing to discuss his investment needs, he wanted to learn how to enhance his revenue. In other words, Mr. Richard places more importance on learning how to enhance the productivity of his business than on selecting a financial advisor. Therefore, those who target the Mr. Richards of America, take note: Offer to act as Mentor to a prospect before offering the prospect your products and services.

Mr. Richard's Mentor provided him with tools to enhance his revenue. Only after Mr. Richard accepted this favor did the financial consultant address his own needs. Mr. Richard opened an account with the financial consultant because he felt indebted to him and because he felt strong empathy for a person who, like himself, targeted and networked with the affluent. Mr. Richard and the financial consultant have much in common. They can share information about marketing and selling to the affluent and networking with the affluent. Moreover, they can refer clients and prospects to each other.

There are nearly 90 financial consultants in the Alpha branch. Why is it that not one of these sales professionals ever made a personal call on Mr. Richards prior to my suggestion? Those who prospected him did so via telephone and failed to gain his business. Why? Because when they called, each and every one of them employed the shopworn me-me-me theme of "I have some wonderful investment ideas for you." This message does not reflect any empathy for the prospect. It suggests that these sales professionals were never trained in the art of relationship building.

Mr. Richard Develops an Influence Network

The financial consultant in this case may eventually learn more about networking with the affluent and their advisors from Mr. Richard than he ever imagined possible. Mr. Richard is one of the very best networkers I have ever encountered.

He telephoned me shortly after returning from his vacation. He thanked me for having the books personally delivered to him by an extraordinary financial consultant. During our conversation, he was kind enough to share some of his ideas about building an influence network. Mr. Richard's "rules of networking" are as follows.

1. If you wish to sell to the affluent, first gain the endorsement of their affinity groups.
2. Once you have gained such endorsements, display your offering at the trade shows and professional society meetings of these affinity groups. Promote your offering in their trade and professional periodicals.
3. Donate part of the revenues you generate from affinity groups to their respective associations.
4. Telephone the headquarters of every affluent affinity group you wish to target. Ask each of these organizations the *fundamental questions of influence networking:*
   a. What *public relations firm* represents your organization?
   b. What *law firm?*
   c. What *accounting firm?*
5. Hire the top-quality public relations professional who already represents the most important affluent affinity group that you have targeted. This professional will place important news items and articles about you in the publications of affluent affinity groups and will help you gain the endorsements of these groups.
6. Consider hiring the law firm and the accounting firm that represent the affinity groups you wish to target. Part of the professional duties of these firms should be to help you gain the endorsements of the affinity groups they represent.
7. Target networks of networks if possible. Can you imagine the advantage of being endorsed by an affinity group that represents thousands of affinity groups? Are there such groups in America? Yes. Take as an example the American Society of Association Executives (ASAE). It is the professional society of paid executives of national, state, and local trade, professional, technical, and business associations. Its monthly publication, *The Magazine for Association Executives,* is read by 20,000 executives who manage thousands of affinity groups!

8. Deal with service providers who have more than basic skills, who will network for you. Why deal with a public relations professional who can only do public relations, with a financial consultant who can only hawk investments, with a law firm that only gives legal advice, with an accounting firm that can only prepare tax returns? Do your current providers of professional services aggressively network on your behalf? If not, insist that they do so, train them to do so. Or else consider changing your habits of professional service patronage.

9. If you wish to succeed in developing your own influence network, associate with, patronize, relate to the best networkers within your market domain.

10. Once you have mastered the art of networking, train others in this art. Be sure to share your networking with networks skills and part of your revenues with eleemosynary organizations and affinity groups.

AN INTERVIEW WITH THE CREATOR OF THE INFLUENCE "WOLFE" PACK

DR. STANLEY:

You mentioned that several of your most important clients are in the education industry. Tell me, please, how did you attract so many affluent clients from this field.

MR. WOLFE:

There are three top-notch universities within our metropolitan area. It occurred to me to target affluent faculty members. I wanted to do something in the context of networking. That's why I always wanted to have good visibility among successful attorneys.

DR. STANLEY:

How does the legal industry relate to the educational field?

MR. WOLFE:

Let me back up. As I stated, I wanted to target affluent professors who write or will write top-selling books. Sure, I could go knock on their doors, especially around the time that they receive their royalty checks. But I assumed that this would take a lot of time. People who operate the on-campus bookstores told me that more than 400 books have been written by locally based faculty members. Four hundred equates in my mind to a whole lot of door knocking and appointment making.

DR. STANLEY:

You still have not told me how this target relates to the legal profession.

MR. WOLFE:

I interviewed several top authors. They have one big thing in common. All of them feel a need to do a better job negotiating a more lucrative deal with their publishers. They will all tell you that they did poorly in negotiating contract terms. Even the seasoned authors feel that they do not know how to negotiate with publishers. That's when it hit me. These people would be responsive to a seminar that focused on their need to improve their negotiating skills.

DR. STANLEY:

How does this relate to your profession, the profession of financial planning? Are you also a literary agent with skills as a negotiator?

MR. WOLFE:

No. None of the above. That's where my contacts from the legal profession bore fruit. Have you ever prospected partners in top law firms? They, or more commonly their secretaries, will tell you: "Mr. Adams does not talk to financial planners." I have heard that in many cases myself.

DR. STANLEY:

So what is the point?

MR. WOLFE:

The point is that one of my very best clients and source of referrals for new business is the most senior partner at a very prestigious law firm.

DR. STANLEY:

You still have not told me how this relates to professors and seminars on how to negotiate with publishers.

MR. WOLFE:

I wrote a letter to the "most senior partner." The letter spelled out my ideas for a seminar. It also asked the most senior partner whether he or any of his colleagues would like to participate in the seminar.

DR. STANLEY:

When you say "participate," do you really mean "speak at a seminar"?

MR. WOLFE:

Of course. I asked the question or, as you call it, the "question of questions": "Would you or one of your colleagues like to speak to a large audience of outstanding professors? Many in that audience have written highly successful books. Others in the audience aspire to become authors of best-sellers. Your topic will be 'Publishing Contracts: Factors That Favor the Author.' "

DR. STANLEY:

How did the most senior partner respond to your question?

MR. WOLFE:

He agreed to speak. Why should he speak? As you say, it will enhance his revenue. Some of these authors are well into the six figures in annual royalties. Many of them are business owners. They are the business.

DR. STANLEY:

How did you translate this seminar into financial planning revenue?

MR. WOLFE:

The seminar theme was not limited to contract law. I also had a literary agent speak. His topic was "Negotiating with Publishers." He was the really big draw. In addition, I had a well-known textbook writer talk about "The Problems and Opportunities of Publishing Textbooks."

DR. STANLEY:

How much did you have to pay these speakers to address the audience?

MR. WOLFE:

The most senior partner spoke for free. Actually, he paid me for his participation in a way. He bought a financial plan from me. But even more important, he referred me to his colleagues. I have done several plans inside his firm to date. The literary agent did not charge me for his time. He will also have me do planning for him. But I mainly want his referral to his clients. This is in the works.

DR. STANLEY:

And what about the author who spoke? How much did you have to pay him?

MR. WOLFE:

He agreed to do it for a barter deal. You know, a complimentary financial plan. I agreed since he is a big draw. Plus, he agreed to allow me to tell prospects in the education field that he is my client.

DR. STANLEY:

Mr. Wolfe, did you do any speaking yourself?

MR. WOLFE:

Oh, yes. And I made this quite clear when we promoted the seminar.

DR. STANLEY:

Made what clear?

MR. WOLFE:

That I was the sponsor of the program and that I would discuss ways of investing royalty dollars.

DR. STANLEY:

How did you promote the program?

MR. WOLFE:

I placed a few cheap advertisements in the university newspapers. The ads contained a registration form. I can't believe that no one else in my business ever did this! I'm now toying with the idea of various faculty associations to cosponsor these events at other universities in my region. I now have lawyers and many successful authors, who are complete strangers to me, calling me up and asking for my advice about how to reach their goals.

MR. TODD PENETRATES INFLUENCE NETWORKS

Several factors explain Mr. Todd's high performance as a financial consultant. One of those factors is his ability to find affluent prospects precisely when they are experiencing euphoria based on socioeconomic successes.

But Mr. Todd does not do all the looking himself. Important allies provide him with information on and even referrals to affluent prospects. Who are these allies? They come from a number of industries and professions, but the two main categories are accountants and business brokers. In fact, Mr. Todd is president of his market area's CPA Club. Hundreds of CPAs are members. No, Mr. Todd is not a CPA. But he is an important member of the CPAs' influence network, and many CPAs perceive him as their Mentor.

Mr. Todd's CPA Club is akin to a business college/speakers bureau. It provides monthly educational seminars for CPAs who operate within the four counties comprised by Mr. Todd's trade area. Mr. Todd does not give all the seminars himself. His primary task as president is to recruit important speakers and seminar leaders. By asking these individuals to speak, he acknowledges their achievements. These speakers are typically experts in their respective fields. Top-rated, affluent attorneys, business executives, and successful entrepreneurs are often featured speakers.

Mr. Todd's system is a productive and innovative method of networking with the winners in his market area. And what a great way to introduce yourself to such people: "I'm Mr. Todd. As president of the CPA Club, I would like to invite you to speak to a group of several hundred CPAs."

Keep in mind that CPAs, especially those who service owners of small and medium-sized businesses, are important patronage opinion leaders. In other words, they very often influence the patronage decisions that affluent business owners make with regard to service and product providers. In fact, the results of both our survey research and our focus group interviews suggest that as a group CPAs are the single most important source of referrals and endorsements that a financial consultant can cultivate.

CPAs are among the first to know when their affluent clients are euphoric because of positive changes in their cash flow. They are among the first to know when their clients are going to change from a sole proprietorship or a partnership to a corporation with a formal pension plan. They also have complete access to all or most of their clients' financial statements, including revenue and profitability figures.

Accountants are often asked the following question by their affluent clients: Whom do you recommend as a qualified financial consultant to help us with investments? Accountants also exert a strong influence on the patronage habits that their clients establish with regard to attorneys, bankers, life insurance agents, and even physicians, architects, and auto dealers.

Many CPAs view Mr. Todd as their networking Mentor. And many reciprocate. They see Mr. Todd not only as a high-caliber financial consultant who supplies excellent products but as a financial consultant who goes beyond merely delivering core products and services. (After all, many of his competitors are equally bright and have identical or at least similar products and services.) CPAs in his market area are required to take several hours of continuing education courses each year. And Mr. Todd, the Mentor, supplies these types of courses each year. Moreover, he supplies them on a not-for-profit basis.

For these reasons, many of the CPAs who belong to Mr. Todd's club do favors for him. Many have hired him as their financial consultant. He often serves CPAs as a financial advisor with regard to their personal and business investments. But perhaps even more important, members of "Club Todd" give him access and endorsements to their own clients.

Inside the CPA Network

Mr. Todd is also a master at leveraging relationships. Once he gains a new client who owns a business, he goes that extra mile. He writes to the trade association representing the client's industry. In the letter, Mr. Todd mentions that "one of my clients is a member of your association. In an effort to better serve my client, it would be important to learn more about your association, industry trends, problems, and issues." Most of the associations provide him with the materials he requests. Then he decides whether it would be productive to join the group as an associate member or to subscribe to the group's trade journals and newsletters.

Buyers/Sellers of Businesses

Mr. Todd also has considerable affinity with business brokers, another important group. Many businesses brokers within his market area regard him as their Mentor. Business brokers help owners of small and medium-sized businesses find buyers who are interested in acquiring businesses. They also help potential buyers find suitable businesses.

Business brokers are an excellent group with which to network. Consider the following scenario. You're a professional looking for prospects who are highly liquid because they just cashed in their business chips. Then why not follow Mr. Todd's lead? Why not recruit business brokers to your influence network?

An increasing number of professionals of various types have been prospecting business brokers. These brokers are often themselves affluent. But more important, they are information conduits, as well as opinion leaders, for many business owners who are in transition—that is, about to sell and retire. Can you imagine the benefits of gaining the endorsement of business brokers? You would be among the first to know who is going to sell out. And you would be recommended as someone who can help the seller through a transitional period.

How did Mr. Todd become a Mentor to business brokers? He did so by focusing on their needs before he presented his own. You must realize that business brokers need to find buyers for clients who are selling and sellers for clients who are buying. These are not easy tasks. Business brokers also need access and exposure to people with businesses to sell and prospects with enough money to buy those businesses.

Before I give specifics about how to prospect business brokers, let me comment on how not to prospect them. Many professionals from a variety of disciplines never succeed in obtaining business from these prospects. Attorneys typically pitch their own needs. In other words, they want to write buyer/seller contracts for the business broker's clients. So they tell the business broker how well they can write contracts. This approach does not focus on the business broker's needs. Hundreds of thousands of attorneys are capable of writing contracts of this type.

And who else hits on business brokers with the me-me-me

theme? Some of the more aggressive CPAs knock on their doors, again with the wrong message: accounting, accounting, superior accounting. It is the dull-dull-dull theme once again. These CPAs are pushing accounting services such as business valuation, tax, and payroll systems. Dullsville! Most CPAs can provide these services. And the same wrong message is conveyed by most of the life insurance professionals who call on the business broker: "That prospect who just bought a business needs my special whole life or keyman policy. It will be really good for your client to be associated with me and my products." How dull. How self-centered. How totally lacking in originality.

Mr. Todd penetrated the affluent convoy called business brokers because he knew what they really needed and gave it to them. What is the number one need of the typical business broker? You can rule out accounting services, investment advice, legal services, and life insurance. But do business brokers really need a financial consultant? No, what they need is a Mentor who can get them inside the information and influence network. Mr. Todd had the insight to leverage his affinity with the CPAs who attended the CPA Club's seminars. This close relationship paid off in his prospecting of business brokers. It enabled him to offer business brokers access to CPAs and ultimately to their respective clients and their respective influence networks.

During his initial approach, what did Mr. Todd say to prospects in the business broker category?

- "I'm Mr. Todd, a financial consultant and president of the area's CPA Club. More than a hundred private practice CPAs are members. As part of our educational program, we have a monthly news bulletin. I wonder if you wish to list any of the businesses you have for sale. Many of our CPAs are very influential with wealthy clients who might be interested in purchasing a business."
- "I understand that several of the CPAs in our club have clients who are likely to be interested in learning about how you could help them buy or sell their businesses."
- "What I'm proposing is for you to list all current and newly listed businesses for sale in our bulletin. And if you have a

client seeking to purchase a particular type of business, you may wish to list a description of this type of business as well."

- "It costs nothing to place your listing in our bulletin."
- "Please send me several of your business cards and brochures."
- "What's in it for me? Well, I hope you would not object to my calling on the sellers of businesses. They may benefit from the advice and products we can offer people who are about to cash in their chips. I did not think you would object."
- "Do you ever give speeches to accountants?"

Mr. Todd focused on the needs of his influence network before focusing on his own needs. Perhaps that's why so many CPAs and business brokers now seek him out.

Mr. Todd Does Not Have Macho Needs

Doesn't Mr. Todd feel left out if he has others act as seminar leaders? Not at all. He is in charge. It's his program. Speakers are just guests. Mr. Todd plays a role akin to that of a talk show host. Actually, his credibility is greatly enhanced because he lets others do the speaking.

Mr. Todd's Topics

Each year Mr. Todd presents his ideas at only 1 of the CPA Club's 12 monthly meetings. His topic areas include:

- Low-risk investments.
- How to survive in today's economy.
- How to select a professional money manager.

This list may look complete, but it's not. Not quite. He missed one. Mr. Todd is obviously an expert in selling and marketing via networking. He should offer his skills in these areas in seminar form to prospects and clients who need to enhance the productivity of their sales forces.

A LETTER TO THE PRESIDENT OF A
TRADE ASSOCIATION

March 30

Dear Mr. Edwards:

Managing an association such as yours can be very difficult. Organizing all the events along with meeting publishing
deadlines can add up to much more work than your members
realize. One challenge that occasionally arises is locating a
professional to speak to your group on a subject relevant to
your members. Most important, the presentation must be from
an educational perspective.

I can provide such a seminar, entitled

"How to Survive in Today's Economy."

This seminar is one hour in length, with time allowed for
questions. The topics include an overview of economic jar-
gon—what it means and how it affects your members. Asset
allocation and estate planning are also examined briefly.

Enclosed is a copy of a reference letter from the Tire Dealers Association (TDA). I spoke to over 100 business owners at
the TDA convention. Afterward, the executive director received
several positive comments from his colleagues for organizing
the seminar. They especially liked the way in which I involved
the group in the presentation. My presentation is not a lecture.

I believe your members would also appreciate this seminar. I would like to discuss this with you in more detail. Please
call me with any questions at 1-800-111-1111.

Sincerely,

W. G. Todd
Senior Financial Consultant

AN ENDORSEMENT FROM A CREDIBLE SOURCE

February 20

Mr. W. G. Todd

Dear Mr. Todd:

Our Convention and Trade Show is over, and the scorecards have been marked. Your program, "Survival in Today's Economy," got a lot of "10s," some "9.7s" and "9.8s." This clearly shows that your presentation hit an area of great concern and that you provided our members with an insight into financial matters that shows your professional ability.

As a meeting planner, I am always pleased when the chairs are full at the start of a program, more pleased when we have to add chairs during the program, and delighted when all of those chairs are still full and the walls are lined at the end of the program. You did a great job in presenting your subject without commercial content, yet it was clear that you know your field.

Would I recommend you for another session? You bet! Winners are easy to bet on! Thanks for helping us make our program the success it was.

Sincerely,

R. K. Smith
Executive Director

Mr. Todd Reads the Trades

I have often stated that those who aspire to become extraordinary networkers should read the trade and professional journals and newsletters that their targeted affluent audiences read. For most sales situations, the trades have much to offer. But what trade journals should the networker read? Mr. Todd recently shared some of his ideas in this regard. He has found it useful not to rely fully on others to help him find prospects.

I had spoken to him earlier and recommended that he first identify the affluent affinity groups in his trade area. And how did he accomplish the task? I suggested that he list all of affluent affinity groups in his trade area given in Gale's *Encyclopedia of Associations: Regional, State, and Local Organizations*.

Alternatively, he could have accessed similar information from the Chambers of Commerce of the towns in his trade area. Mr. Todd also found that the yellow page directories of the telephone company in his trade area listed many important affinity groups under the heading of *Associations*.

So *step one* is to identify and list local affinity groups. And that's exactly what Mr. Todd did. But remember, not all affinity groups contain high concentrations of affluent prospects. And don't necessarily limit yourself to targeting trade and professional affinity groups. Remember that Roger Thomas, as mentioned in *Selling to the Affluent*, found that the highest concentration of millionaires in his trade area was inside the convoy called Garden Club!

Can you tell beforehand whether millionaires are hiding inside, say, the Garden Club or the Scrap Metal Dealers Association? That's the question that makes life interesting. The answer often depends on a gut feeling. There is no perfect predictor of the level or concentration of wealth. You may have to sample the population to obtain reliable information on this score.

What does the term *sample* mean? As suggested in Mr. Todd's *step two*, he telephoned the offices of each locally based affinity group. He requested back issues of each group's trade journals and newsletters. Not one group charged him a cent for these issues. Then what did he do?

In *step three*, Mr. Todd examined and weighed the value of the information contained in each of the periodicals he received. He subscribed only to those that contained critical intelligence about people/prospects/money. He found about one half of the periodicals he reviewed to be useful in prospecting.

His most favored trade publications are monthly newsletters produced by local affinity groups. For example, he reads *The Auto Bulletin* (*TAB*), a newsletter for people in the fuel distribution business. Each issue contains critical information about "businesses for sale by owner."

Does Mr. Todd exploit these opportunities? Yes, and this brings us to his *step four*. He reacts immediately to information about euphoric prospects. In fact, the first business for sale listed in the very first newsletter he reviewed was a retail filling station that eventually sold for $350,000. Mr. Todd made a personal call on the seller. The seller told him that the station had been listed for three months in the newsletter but that *only Mr. Todd had attempted to prospect the seller.* Despite being 70 years of age and affluent, the seller had never before used the services of a financial consultant. Mr. Todd gained a client who was euphoric because of a $350,000 windfall.

Although it may seem amazing that only Mr. Todd called on the seller, you will realize that it is not amazing once you know how few sales professionals prospect via trade news. Unlike Mr. Todd, few of the sales professionals who target the affluent subscribe to *TAB* or any of the other 20,000-plus affinity publications.

Having called on the prospect, what did Mr. Todd say? His approach was *step five* of his networking via affiliation marketing. He simply said:

- "I read about you and your business in *TAB*."
- "You have been in business for over 30 years. How did you succeed for so long?"
- "Several of my current clients have recently sold their businesses."
- "How are you going to deal with being retired, not going to work each day?"
- "You may want to talk with some of my clients who have recently sold their businesses. It may help you. Several told me it's a bit depressing to walk away from a business."

In this step, Mr. Todd emphasized the networking dimensions of his prospect's affiliation need. He also demonstrated considerable empathy for the prospect's problems. For $30, Mr. Todd joined the prospect's local trade association. He received its monthly newsletter, *TAB,* and obtained a new client within a week after he read the first issue. Not a bad investment.

What else does Mr. Todd read? More than a dozen trade journals and newsletters, all produced by local affinity groups. Two of the more interesting are *Auto Glass Monthly* and *Construction Data*. I asked Mr. Todd why he read *Auto Glass Monthly*. His answer: "Well, the first fellow I encountered via *Auto Glass Monthly* had a net worth of over $5 million."

Construction Data is a weekly local publication. Like many other local periodicals of its type, it is distributed within just the few counties that make up Mr. Todd's trade area. Unlike most of the other local periodicals, however, it is quite expensive. The material it contains is very worthwhile. It lists the award winners, or the so-called low bidders, on construction projects. Yes, *it identifies all the current winners of construction contracts, and it gives the dollar amounts of the awards*. It is geographically specific—that is, it reports on the winners within Mr. Todd's trade area. Each area in this country has periodicals of this type. How can you identify the periodicals of this type that relate to your trade area? Call the new business development officers at several locally based construction contracting firms. They will tell you what publications they read to identify winners of construction contracts. They may give you the current issues of these publications. They may even do business with you someday!

When Mr. Todd found out that it would cost $600 per year to subscribe to *Construction Data,* he balked. So he called a relative who just happened to own a construction contracting firm, discovered that the firm subscribed, and now gets this information for free. *Yes, I mean to tell you that Mr. Todd never before asked his relative about who the bid winners were in his trade area.* And perhaps you're now starting to understand that networking by affiliation and affinity is so obvious, so simple that most people overlook these types of opportunities.

Before Mr. Todd read *Construction Data* did he ever prospect the construction industry winners and losers? No! Why? Perhaps because he had too much in common with the prospects to see these wonderful opportunities, because he was too close to the trees to see the forest. But Mr. Todd has changed his orientation. He now calls prospects when, through his access to their trade periodicals, he knows they have need for his services, that is, when they are euphoric because of upswings in their cash flow. And because of his association with selected local area affinity groups, he is able to present himself as a colleague. He has tapped into his prospects' networks. He is part of their information networks.

A Single Source?

Is there a single source that lists all of the trade journals and related periodicals that are published in this country? *No.* However, you can find several directories of business periodicals in any major league library. These directories typically list only trade journals that carry paid advertisements, most of which are national or regional in scope. Few local trade journals and related periodicals are listed in these directories.

Thus sales professionals who really want a list of such periodicals must assemble one. This takes time, but it's time well spent. Such a list provides the sales professional with a strategic advantage.

I agree that time is money. But how long would it take to make 50 telephone calls to the headquarters of selected local trade associations? Even a part-time work-study student could knock this out in a day or two. How about the time it would take to sift through each of the relevant trade journals? From your 50 calls, you will probably receive at least 40 good responses—that is, you will be sent at least 40 trade journals or newsletters.

You then have to pick out the good ones. You can tell whether a trade journal contains critical information about affluent prospects in less than 30 seconds! So what is your next objection? You will still have to page through each one. How else can you pick out your prospects? I have trained college sophomores in a few hours to do this task effectively. Just buy them an Xacto knife and turn them loose. A good work-study student can identify, cut, and paste up 50 leads in less than two hours. And at $8.50 per hour or $17.00 for two hours, the labor cost will not break your bank. Fifty leads at $17 translates into 34 cents per lead. Yes, 34 cents per lead. Add in the subscription cost, and you're still under 60 cents per lead. And keep in mind that many trade journals are free for the asking. Can you afford 34 or 60 cents for the identity of a euphoric millionaire?

TIM GOODNOW IS A MENTOR TO AFFLUENT ALIENS

MR. MICHAEL:

Talkers are often perceived as hawkers, whereas writers are looked upon as experts, says Tom Stanley. Write an article and enhance your credibility.

Take the case of Tim Goodnow, an enterprising life underwriter, who wrote an article aimed at affluent noncitizens. It was entitled "Noncitizens Should Review Estate Plans."

DR. STANLEY:

Let's look at the first sentence: "Legislation known as TAMRA has quietly but quite effectively eliminated the estate and gift tax marital deductions for property passing to a spouse who is not a citizen of the United States." A little bit farther on—"although property transfer still can occur on a tax-free or deferred basis, these changes have caused problems that can be solved only through estate planning and the use of life insurance. This planning should be accomplished through professionals familiar with this tax law and who are practiced in this area."

MR. MICHAEL:

Why do you think this particular article was so effective?

DR. STANLEY:

First of all, it's geared toward a highly targeted audience. It's not generic. Hundreds of thousands of people sell insurance today, and they target what we call "the generic audience." This is not a generic audience. If I go back and look at the hundreds and hundreds of case studies that we have, what I find is that most of the extraordinary sales professionals in America who target the affluent are specialists. And this young man is a specialist. He has clearly demonstrated his speciality and his expertise. His specialty is understanding the needs and the problems of affluent aliens. He has the ability to meet those needs and solve those problems by working in concert with skilled estate attorneys. I will wager you that dozens of these high-grade estate attorneys will be calling Tim. They will want to network with him, providing him with their clients, and vice versa.

MR. MICHAEL:

Can't affluent aliens pass on their rich estates to their spouses?

DR. STANLEY:

They can to some extent if in fact they use proper trust planning, estate planning, and insurance products. And this article is excellent because it provides clear access to the expert, in this case the author. It tells you where he can be found. It also sensitizes readers to seek more information.

MR. MICHAEL:

Yes, it's true that people responding to the article could call another life underwriter. But Tim wrote the article. He's the expert. He took the time to research the problem and offer a solution. Don't you think that those who read the article are more than likely to call him?

GREAT SCOTT IS A MASTER MENTOR

MR. MICHAEL:

You had another letter, Tom, that you considered a prime example of enhancing credibility when one writes an article.

DR. STANLEY:

Yes. In fact, I titled this "Great Scott: The Master Mentor." Scott's article generated more response than any other article I've come across in my career.

MR. MICHAEL:

Well, you've certainly got my interest there, Tom. Where did the article appear?

DR. STANLEY:

Scott published this wonderful article in the *Jewish Journal of Greater Los Angeles*.

MR. MICHAEL:

That's a specific audience.

DR. STANLEY:

Yes, it is. And you asked about the response. According to Scott, he received about 40 unsolicited telephone calls inquiring about the availability of these investments.

MR. MICHAEL:

What was the article about?

DR. STANLEY:

Scott is a Mentor to people with a common cause, as demonstrated in this article. The title—"An Easy Way to Support Israel: Israeli Government Trust Certificates Offer an Attractive Alternative to U.S. Treasuries."

MR. MICHAEL:

So it's as simple as that. He's saying if you're going to invest anyway, why not invest in Israeli bonds?

DR. STANLEY:

He compared both investment vehicles. He talked about the fact that both have relatively low risk, fairly high yields. In fact, he was suggesting that in this case they call their own brokers. He said, "You don't have to call me." What he's saying is "Look, I will get something out of this by contributing to a cause." It's amazing how much response he received and how many people copied this article and sent it to friends. He's still getting a lot of response from it.

MR. MICHAEL:

Analyze the article for me, Tom. What do you consider the better portions of it? Why was it so effective?

DR. STANLEY:

First of all, I think there are a lot of people out there who are heavily invested in U.S. Treasuries, and they may feel they have enough money in that area. They would like something equivalent in terms of risk. They also have an affinity for Israel and the causes related to that country. And Scott is saying, "I'm informing you; I'm your Mentor; I'm making a contribution to a common cause; and I'm part of your affinity group." At the age of 30, he's a high-grade Mentor. Along these lines, he is also currently president of his temple.

HELP THE NOBLEST CAUSES FISH FOR AFFLUENT DONORS

Assume for a moment that you have now mastered the Mentor networking system called "Teach Them to Fish." What should be the next step in your development as a true marketing and sales professional? You should consider donating your marketing skills and intellect to charitable causes.

Most charitable organizations are finding it increasingly difficult to meet their financial goals and commitments. Thus they would probably welcome any advice about how to enhance the productivity of their fund-raising activities.

The material in this section contains several suggestions about how marketing and sales professionals can assist noble causes. The committees of charitable organizations are often composed exclusively of very affluent people. What should you do if your initial request to be on a committee is turned down because you're not a multimillionaire? Do not take no for an answer. Counter by offering more than your own monetary wealth. Become the Mentor of such committees. Offer them your genius in finding and networking with large numbers of very affluent donors. And share the knowledge that you will obtain from the material contained herein.

Networking at a Higher Level

A minister recently wrote to me, stating:

> Dr. Stanley, I agree with your hypothesis that many people who have money don't appear to be affluent. So how can I identify them, as you say, especially when they are euphoric because of big upswings in their net worths? I am even having trouble identifying the members of our church who are affluent, let alone euphoric.

I am receiving an increasing number of similar inquiries from religious organizations. Their leaders and fund-raisers are often frustrated. They know that some members are wealthy. However, it is frequently difficult to distinguish the truly affluent from the pseudoaffluent.

Many affluent people deliberately "dress down," "drive down," and "house down" to disguise themselves as ordinary people. Why? One reason is that many affluent people are achievement oriented and therefore have a low propensity to spend money on status products. Conversely, many people, even those with high incomes, never accumulate wealth because they are status oriented and because they define their status via pseudoaffluent products and related artifacts.

The truly affluent also make themselves hard to identify because they do not want to be gouged. They often feel that product and service providers love to charge them high prices. They believe that everyone from the dentist to the lawn care specialist adjusts prices according to the patient's/client's/customer's/prospect's ability to pay. So they contend that if you "dress poor," "drive poor," and "dwell poor," you will be given invoices for products and services that the poor can afford.

Many service providers have told me that they do, in fact, charge the affluent (or those who appear to be affluent) more, much more, than they charge the nonaffluent. One of them, a dentist, described his system of price discrimination. His office overlooked his parking lot. From his office, he could see every patient who drove into the lot. "I charge to the max," he told me, "anybody who pulls into our lot driving a luxury automobile." This dentist based his pricing system on a proxy to wealth. He firmly believes that affluent people drive expensive automobiles. He is wrong. Most of the people who drive expensive automobiles are not affluent.

Fund-raisers often make the same mistake as that made by the dentist. But how is this discussion going to help our minister? Stated simply,

Most affluent people are self-employed business owners.

Look for the wealthy among owners of businesses, not owners of status symbols. Because of marked improvements in their socioeconomic/cash flow situations, most self-employed business owners have their moments of euphoria. So, Mr. Minister, if you can't easily identify them (especially when they are euphoric), move in the opposite direction. Let them identify themselves.

Will these people call up the minister and say, "Impale me/ prospect me. I'm euphoric because my company just went public/ my patent was just sold." They will if you encourage them to do so. Remember, affluent people *need* to have their *achievements recognized.* And they *need to affiliate.* They are more likely to donate to their house of worship if the timing of the solicitation is right. Timing is a critical issue.

You have to provide prospective donors with a vehicle for communicating their euphoria. I am recommending that the minister and his associates periodically ask all the members of his congregation whether they are euphoric. All the houses of worship with which we have been associated produce a newsletter or a weekly flier. I will wager that this minister's church distributes such a publication to its members. A publication of this type is ideal for allowing euphoric members of the church to communicate their successes.

Once, again, the affluent are much more interested in having their achievements acknowledged than in their status. I am proposing that the church's publication have a special section that reports on the achievements of members. And in each issue there should be a form for members to report on their achievements. Let's look at a pro forma example:

MEMBERS, WHAT'S YOUR NEWS?

Promotions? New contracts received? Bids awarded? Career milestones? Achievement recognized? We want to publish your news in the *First Church's Chronicle.* Just fill out the following form and submit it to Ms. Rose Lowe, Director of Membership Relations, The First Church, 100 Smith Street, Proformaville, NY 10710. Or just drop your completed form in any of the "Information Please" boxes located throughout the church and the recreation walk. Photos, news releases, news articles, and transcripts of award citations would be greatly appreciated. Let all of our members take joy in your success.

Name: _____ Name used/nickname_____

Business Title:_____
_____

Name of business/organization:_____
_____

Type of business/organization:_____

Home address:_____
_____

Business address:_____
_____

Telephone number:(Home)_____
           (Business)_____

My news is:_____

_____

_____

_____

_____

                                                    Thank you!

Proactivity at a Higher Level

Will members of the minister's church fill out the form? Some will
and some won't. However, the issue of response rate is too often
an excuse for not being proactive. Even in regard to collecting news
about euphoric members of his church, the minister and his team
must be proactive. The minister should have a staff of volunteers
who periodically call members and encourage them to "tell their
stories."

But is it feasible to call all the members? After all, there may
be hundreds, even thousands, of them. No, you don't have to call
them all. But you should call those who are business owners and
self-employed professionals. They are the members most likely to
encounter significant upswings in their cash flow. To maximize the
effect of the calls, the volunteers should always ask the respondents
whether they know of any other church members with good news
to report.

Once a member's good news has been reported in the church's
publication, what then? Someone has to ask the member for a
donation. Do not just call and say, "Give us some of your euphoria
dollars." You do not have to be that obtrusive. In fact, the best
way to initiate communication with the member is to contact the
member by letter. Let's review a pro forma letter of this type:

Mr. Hughes J. Anover
Chief Executive Officer
Walburn Supply Company
8300 Douglas Avenue
Atlanta, GA 30303

Dear Hughes:

I was absolutely delighted to learn that your firm has gone public. The news in *The First Church's Chronicle* mentioned that shares in your firm are selling like hotcakes. I am not at all surprised. The market always responds positively to quality issues such as yours.

No doubt you are extremely busy at the moment with your public offering and your other duties. However, I was wondering whether you would take a moment from your hectic schedule to consider a special request. As you are probably aware, our annual fund drive is about to begin. We all have high expectations for its success. However, given the current economic conditions, success is not likely to come easily this year.

I suspect that you feel especially fortunate to have the market respond so strongly to your offering. You may feel the need to help those who have been much less fortunate. The members of our foundation league would like you to accept our offer to join its ranks. Enclosed is a brief description of the foundation league's goals and objectives.

I will telephone you next week. Your consideration of our proposal is greatly appreciated. Once again, congratulations on your success.

Sincerely,

Robert "Bob" McDougal
Senior Pastor

Will Mr. Anover respond positively to Mr. McDougal's request? Mr. Anover is much more likely to respond positively to such solicitations during periods of euphoria. The probability of a positive response has also increased significantly because Mr. Anover has designated himself as being euphoric. Thus he cannot easily say: "I can't give because I have no money." He realizes that his minister knows not only that he is a millionaire but also that he is in a highly liquid position. Thus there is significant social pressure on Mr. Anover to respond. Call it what you wish. But it is psychologically incongruent for a person whose enormous economic success has been disclosed in a church bulletin to reject his minister's suggestion that he make a modest donation.

Some would argue that a $100,000 donation is more than a modest donation. But what is $100,000 as a percentage of $55 million. You're right—a very small percentage (0.18 percent). Or stated in another way, the donation represents only 1 in every 550 euphoria dollars. These are actual amounts taken from a recent case study. Yes, the prospective donor in this case did become a member of the foundation league.

The Other Side of Euphoria

But look at the other side of the euphoria continuum. Don't people often give considerable donations to a house of worship in commemoration of a parent who has recently passed away? They do. They are often kind and thoughtful enough to give part of their inheritance to a house of worship. But in a low-key manner memorials of this type must be reported to the membership. Doing this in the house of worship's publication fits the parameters of effective and unobtrusive communication.

Share Your Interest at a Higher Level

I receive many calls and letters each year from nonprofit organizations. They seek advice about how they can be more productive in targeting the affluent. On this score, nonprofit organizations need as much help as for-profit organizations. In every city, in every town where nonprofit organizations operate, there are dozens, even hundreds, of highly skilled marketing and sales professionals who target the affluent. But all too few of these professionals ever offer their skills, their marketing genius, for higher needs—the need, for example, to build a new wing on a children's hospital, to increase the funds available for scholarships for minorities, to give the homeless food.

Why is it that most marketing and sales professionals do not help such noble causes? Most likely, because nobody ever asked them to help. This is a serious oversight of those who manage charitable causes. The marketing and selling instincts and aptitudes for targeting the affluent possessed by top-producing new business development officers from the fields of accounting, law, life insurance, and investment are second to none. However, these professionals have to take part of the blame for not "aggressively contributing" their services.

What should they do to help the noble causes in their market areas? First, they should not wait to be asked to join the team. They should be proactive. They should contact the charitable organizations in their market areas that need help. They should not be discouraged from asking to be placed on a fund-raising committee simply because the present members of the committee have pedigree names and titles. Too often, volunteer groups are overstaffed with so-called celebrities who are more interested in self-promotion than in the promotion of noble causes. What the noble causes in this country need are skilled marketing and sales professionals who know how to identify the affluent and solicit business from them.

Of course, some of these professionals ultimately benefit from their association with noble causes. And they should benefit from donating their time and their genius. This goes with the total professional package. But their basic motive should be to serve noble causes. Psychologically, they will find this very rewarding. It will enhance their self-image and their self-esteem. If it also enhances their visibility and their credibility, that's icing on the cake. After all, this is networking at its highest level.

A Mentor for Noble Causes

What can sales and marketing professionals do to help noble causes? First, they can read the following case study. Second, they can contact selected noble causes in their communities and offer to help them raise funds. Third, they can reorient these noble causes.

What is meant by *reorient?* As a start, convince these organizations that the timing of their fund drives should be restructured. This change would in itself help raise significantly more dollars from the affluent segment of the population. Advise these noble causes to time their solicitations in harmony with the economic euphoria of potential donors.

Are there any sales professionals who are regarded as mentors to noble causes? There are quite a few. However, one in particular comes to mind. I consider Mr. Samuel to be one of the premier private bankers in America. He is an absolute master at finding affluent prospects precisely when they need his credit and investment products and services. However, he is a Mentor not only to clients but also to a number of noble causes in and around the Chicago area. As a result, he has a network not only of grateful clients who make referrals on his behalf but also of admirers from the community of noble causes.

Mr. Samuel tells the leaders of various charities that he is always available to help raise funds, provide advice and consultation, sit on advisory boards, and sponsor seats at benefit luncheons and dinners. In these ways, he lends his marketing genius and his tremendous energy and enthusiasm to the noblest of causes. He teaches people involved with these causes how to fish. He also does considerable fishing himself on behalf of these causes.

Did Mr. Samuel ever receive any business as a direct result of his contribution to noble causes? Yes. Quite a lot of business. For example, his offer to become a committee member of an important charity was recently accepted. As a committee member, he was asked to market/sponsor seats for a hospital construction fund luncheon. He performed this service and attended the affair. As a result of his work on the committee, he obtained one of the biggest accounts of his career.

Most of the committee members were very wealthy. The very first committee meeting was attended by Mr. Samuel, three priests, seven sisters of charity, and 16 multimillionaires. One of the sisters seated Mr. Samuel next to a very wealthy fellow who asked him, "What kind of business are you in, Mr. Samuel?" When the fellow found out that Mr. Samuel was a private banker for a high-quality commercial bank, he asked, "Mr. Samuel, do you offer certificates of deposit for seven?" Mr. Samuel responded with his own question: "Seven what?" The fellow then stated confidently, "Seven million, eight hundred thousand dollars!"

Was the prospect for real? Yes. How did Mr. Samuel succeed in attracting a $7.8 million account? In general terms, affluent prospects see you at your best when you're helping others. Mr. Samuel was viewed as a person who cared a great deal about noble causes. This certainly enhanced his image as a man of integrity. Of course, the institution for which he works has considerable credibility as well.

An important part of this equation was the fact that Mr. Samuel served on the same committee as did the fellow who needed a $7.8 million certificate of deposit. Mr. Samuel is in the middle of many such affluent convoys.

Is there a noble cause in your neighborhood that desperately needs talented human resources. Why not volunteer your own? Do it today. Disseminate your knowledge on behalf of a higher calling.

Timing, Relating, Targeting, and Prospecting for Noble Causes

Most charities have an annual drive of some sort. Each year at a predesignated period, your favorite charity asks for your contribution. But is this the best time for you to give in terms of your economic position? Like most of the other prospective donors, you probably don't exactly love the concept of the annual drive. Too often, the timing of the drive is set, not for the convenience of the people who are being targeted, but for the convenience of the fundraisers themselves.

Despite noble intentions, many charitable organizations arbitrarily pick the time of year when they're going to collect money. I know of major charities that ask people for money during the worst time of the year. For example, they may ask wealthy people to donate at the same time that the tuition of their children is due at the private schools these children attend.

If you're a skilled sales professional who targets the affluent, take it upon yourself to assist the noble causes in your community. Share your wisdom and your wealth. Help these causes improve the timing of their solicitations. Also assist them in solving these problems:

1. Identifying affluent targets.
2. Relating to affluent minorities.
3. Prospecting affluent opinion leaders.

The information given in the following letter should be useful to you in your work as a Mentor to noble causes. Share your intellectual wealth as well as your financial wealth. Are you ready to become a Mentor to all the people and affinity groups that need you?

Mr. Bobby A. Glover
Group Vice President
Omnibus Giving of Gotham
P.O. Box 99
Gotham, U.S.A.

Dear Bobby:

Thank you for seeking my opinions concerning the affluent donor market. I very much enjoyed sharing my ideas with
you and your colleagues at Omnibus Giving of Gotham. Enclosed within this letter are the details of my recommendations. It is important to begin implementation of these recommendations immediately. Too often, organizations spend an
inordinate amount of time in planning and too little time in
asking people for donations. Many of the ideas I have outlined
can be exploited today. I am sure that many potential donors
who live within the Gotham area will be encountering major
positive changes in income/wealth/status this week. Why wait
until your fall campaign to capitalize on their euphoria?

The Issue of Timing

One of the major problems that charities experience in
targeting the affluent relates to the issue of timing. Often,
charities are apostles to beneficiaries but antagonists to donors and prospective donors. Many affluent respondents in
our studies have expressed outrage about solicitors who ask
them for money when they are at the depths of their economic
wealth and cash flow.

Once-a-year solicitations are convenient for many charities but do not reflect the wide variations in the mood of the
target audience. Most affluent prospects are vulnerable/euphoric for only two weeks a year. Some are euphoric only once
in their lifetime, that is, when they sell their businesses and
retire as millionaires. This type of euphoria is not being capitalized on, given the timing parameters of your current campaign. The timing oversight is particularly serious in situations where you are targeting individuals who are able to
contribute in the four-, five-, six-, and even seven-figure ranges.

I am not suggesting that you completely abandon your conventional campaign methods. However, you should certainly consider having an "affluent strategy" that will focus on donors' need to give when they are euphoric.

Perhaps this point can be best illustrated by a recent case study. A senior officer at a client's organization was recently asked to volunteer some of his "oceans of spare time." He agreed to head up the annual fund-raising program for the Fawn Brook School. Fawn Brook is a private school providing education for grades 1 through 12.

How successful was the campaign? According to the committee chairman, "not very successful. . . . Just as ineffective as in past years." More recently, the same committee chairman was present at one of our seminars entitled "Identifying, Conditioning, and Closing Affluent Prospects *when* They Are Most Vulnerable to Solicitations." I wondered why he kept shaking his head throughout the seminar. Afterward, he informed me that the Fawn Brook campaign never took into account the issue of timing requests for donations with the ever-changing financial mood of the target donor audience. Never once did the requests for donations parallel the announcements reported in the local press about increases in the corporate earnings of area-based corporations. Nor did these solicitations ever reach the senior executives of these corporations at the precise time when they sold substantial shares in their respective companies, when bonuses were announced, when stock prices increased significantly, or when increases in quarterly earnings were announced.

When did Fawn Brook ask for donations? Its first request was made on September 15. This coincided with the date on which two thirds of the tuition was due at the school. Many of the targeted donors were not only senior corporate executives; they also had children who attended the school. Tuition at the school is *very* expensive. Fawn Brook's next request was made during the second week of December. This coincided with expensive vacations and the purchase of Christmas gifts. Finally, Fawn Brook sent letters of solicitations to targeted donors during the second week of April. Obviously, the school failed to recognize the lack of enthusiasm among potential donors faced with the impending April 15 deadline for personal tax payments!

However, it is likely that next year the Fawn Brook School campaign will be successful. Fawn Brook will now campaign at the pleasure of the target donor audience. It will solicit when various segments feel euphoria because of positive socio-economic changes. Omnibus Giving should consider making the same changes. Think about how much more productive your campaigning can be if you follow Fawn Brook's lead. Also follow its lead in developing an affluent intelligence system.

Fawn Brook is located within a large metropolitan area. The number one target for its campaign, in terms of occupational category, is the corporate executive. More than 100 large corporations are headquartered within the school's "trade area."

Gotham is not as densely populated with corporate head-quarters. Still, the corporate segment is an important one for Omnibus Giving. I suggest that selected volunteers be assigned the task of monitoring the socioeconomic changes that will take place within the large corporations headquartered within the Gotham metropolitan area.

Omnibus Giving should have at least one volunteer who is knowledgeable about the economic changes that take place within targeted corporations. It may be useful to recruit (for volunteer intelligence work) a securities analyst from a bro-kerage company. This "intelligence officer" should be able to provide you with a list of corporations that are likely to en-counter significant increases in earnings. These earnings, in turn, will probably translate into substantial increases in ex-ecutive bonuses and profit sharing. Stock prices should also be monitored. Remember that many area-based executives hold substantial stock in the targeted corporations. Income does not have to be realized for a prospect to feel euphoric. Signifi-cant increases in the value of corporate stock held by targeted executives translate into a "wealth effect," a euphoria based on an increase in net worth. Here, too, your securities analysts/intelligence officers should be able to provide you with the (public) information about the numbers of shares of common stock that selected executives own.

Omnibus Giving should focus its resources on those corporations that are forecasted to have appreciable earnings. Selected volunteers should target and time their solicitations accordingly. In other words, they should prospect among executives who are likely to be euphoric, given contemplated positive changes in their economic situations.

Omnibus Giving should also monitor other changes that will take place within selected corporations. Volunteers should be recruited from these corporations. They should be asked to supply Omnibus Giving's "intelligence analysts" with copies of the periodic newsletter distributed within the corporations. These corporate newsletters often report on important personnel changes including promotions of key executives, recognition wards, and the contemplated retirement of senior officers.

These changes should not only be monitored by Omnibus Giving intelligence analysts. Executives who contemplate promotions, special recognitions, and/or cashing in their chips are typically vulnerable to solicitations. But you must remember that not all, or even a majority, of these changes take place within the month of September. Thus Omnibus Giving should consider campaigning among the affluent throughout the year.

Omnibus Giving should also assign at least one of its volunteers to collect information about "insider trading." Each Monday Gotham's local newspaper publishes selected intelligence about such activity.

> "Insider Trading" reports stock transactions involving owners of 10 percent or more of the stock of a publicly held company and the top officers and directors of such a company. Transactions were compiled by Invest/Net, Inc. in North Miami, Florida, and reported by Bob Gabele.

You may wish to contact Invest/Net directly and inquire about the feasibility of obtaining a more customized and timely database. The local newspaper typically reports activities that took place four to six weeks earlier. Nevertheless, it may be useful to attempt to solicit "right from the newspaper reports." Of course, not all of the people involved in insider trading are euphoric. Some are selling stock because of economic adversity. But you should certainly be targeting those who have recently sold substantial shares or stock as listed by Invest/ Net. Just as an example do you think Mr. Dring is euphoric/ susceptible to a request for contribution?

Major-National Corp., Gotham; building and paper products. Murray W. Dring, vice president, sold 6,528 common shares at $43.38 a share on Feb 4 and now directly holds 16,048 common shares.

The only way to determine for certain whether Mr. Dring is susceptible to solicitations is to have one of your volunteers ask him to make a donation to Omnibus Giving.

Relating to Affluent Minorities

I understand that support for Omnibus Giving among and within major corporations and other large organizations has been your strength. Also, Omnibus Giving often finds that corporate leaders willing to donate money act as important role models and volunteer their time and prestige. Major consulting, accounting, and law firms and other members of the area corporate elite are Omnibus Giving's apostles and advocates in terms of donating money as well as human resources.

Certainly, Omnibus Giving of Gotham is the envy of many other charitable organizations. Your organization probably has more representation from the Gotham corporate elite than any other. This corporate link is a major advantage in gathering funds from the employees of represented corporations, leading professional organizations, and the general population.

However, heavy/exclusive representation from the so-called Gotham elite does have several distinct disadvantages in terms of attracting funds and volunteers from the affluent community. The affluent market in the Gotham trade area is similar to the affluent market in America in general. It is composed of owners of small and medium-sized businesses. Most millionaires who own their own businesses are not part of the so-called elite.

From my observations, Omnibus Giving of Gotham has

attracted few, if any, volunteers/board members/patrons from the "nonelite" millionaire/business owner population. Many members of this population are members of ethnic and racial minorities, including blacks, Koreans, and Jews. How likely are nonelite millionaires, especially minority members, to contribute their time and money to an organization in which they are not represented? The answer is clearly reflected in the contributions given by the very affluent members of these minorities to your charity, that is, very little or nothing at all.

An objective observer examining the composition of key volunteer groups as well as Omnibus Giving's executive staff may conclude the following:

1. Omnibus Giving is managed and directed by the elite establishment in Gotham.
2. Omnibus Giving pays only lip service to demonstrating sincere interest in including minorities in key management and volunteer positions.
3. Omnibus Giving has recently further alienated affluent members of minorities. Asking affluent minorities for significant contributions, but at the same time excluding them from sharing in the glory of the cause, is unconscionable.

Omnibus Giving is truly interested in and committed to generating sizable donations from minority groups. To do so, however, it must make these groups feel that they are part of the first team.

Despite their best intentions, charitable causes, often become symbols of prestige for their managers and volunteers. Ideally, the cause of giving should be paramount. However, the most efficient way to raise funds is to allocate resources toward those segments of the donor market that will give the greatest amounts. These resources must go beyond merely asking prospects for donations. Omnibus Giving must aggressively recruit members from affluent minorities as key players in the organization.

Most charitable organizations that attempt to target the affluent do not fully comprehend how the concepts of giving and recognition are interrelated. Stated simply, the interrelation means: "He who distributes receives the praise and recognition." Distributors of funds are often viewed as the major donors. Omnibus Giving has not been able to attract donations from affluent minorities because of this recognition issue. These potential high donors reason that their gifts will be distributed by the "elite core." They further reason that the members of the elite core will receive recognition from the press and public for donations actually given by affluent minority members. They fear that the elite core will be given the credit for controlling, fund-raising, distributing, and donating.

Omnibus Giving does give recognition to donors. However, it needs to give more recognition to affluent donors by granting them an active part in distributing funds. In other words, affluent minority donors need to be part of Omnibus Giving's control system and, correspondingly, its distribution team.

The concepts of giving and recognition can be appreciated by examining a case study. An exclusive country club in Westchester County, New York, encountered a recurring problem. Its parking lot attendants stayed on the job on average for less than one month. Employees in the club's other facilities remained with the club for much longer periods. Some had worked at the club for 20 years or more.

Why did so many parking lot attendants feel impelled to resign their positions? The answer related directly to giving and recognition. In studying the "parking lot problem," it became apparent that those who gave were not recognized.

During weekends and special events days, the parking lot at the country club filled with hundreds of cars. Almost all the members and guests of the club had attendants park their cars. Upon leaving the club, these members and guests would have their cars delivered to the main exit. The parking lot attendants at the club were required not only to possess a good personality and a clean driving record but also to be quite athletic. Speed in retrieving cars for departing members and guests was a critical dimension in the club's overall image of excellent service. A parking lot attendant on one special events day at the club was required to retrieve upwards of 100 automobiles. The attendants had to run to cars located 100 yards or more from the main exit.

As soon as an attendant delivered a car to the main exit, he would be greeted by the parking lot manager. The manager would open the door on the driver's side and hand the attendant yet another set of keys for yet another car. Thereupon, the breathless attendant was instructed to "hurry, hurry, hurry" and "quickly, quickly, quickly" retrieve the car. Shortly after the attendant departed for the parking lot, the owner of the car would appear. The manager would stand next to the car. Typically, he would hold the door open for its owner with his left hand and hold out his right hand in anticipation of a "well-deserved tip." Rarely did a club member or guest fail to place a tip in his hand.

In discussing the operation of the parking lot with selected members, it was found that most of the club's members regarded the car distributor (the parking lot manager) as the retriever of their cars and believed that he should therefore be given recognition in the form of a handsome tip. More perceptive members realized that it was the athletic parking lot attendants and not the manager who accounted for the high-speed, high-quality service. These members believed that the manager would share his tips with the attendants.

In reality, not one penny of the tips that the manager received was ever given to the actual givers/donors of this excellent service. This accounted for the vast majority of the resignations among the parking lot attendants. These attendants were quick to recognize the scam perpetrated on them by the manager.

Why so much concern about parking lot attendants? What role could they play in the overall operation of an exclusive country club? Unfortunately for the country club and its members, disgruntled attendants quit their jobs just prior to a three-day golf and tennis tournament at the club on a Fourth of July weekend. Members and their guests had to wait up to one hour for their cars to be delivered. It seems that the day before the holiday weekend, all of the attendants abruptly told the parking lot manager that they were no longer interested in "giving without receiving recognition."

Later, a similar situation took place during the club's Memorial Day festival and its Founders' Day celebration. This time, however, a new manager of the parking lot remedied the situation by acting as an apostle to both the club's members and his employees. This approach resulted in consistently high-quality service within his domain. Thus both donors and recipients benefit from a change based on recognition.

What can fund-raisers learn from the parking lot case? Stated simply, donors/givers want to be recognized for their contributions. The public often views fund distributors as the actual givers. Therefore, to attract more donors, especially members of affluent minorities, allow them/encourage them/ recruit them/ask their key members to play the roles of both donor and distributor. As a result, they will probably feel that others are not taking credit for their contributions.

Targeting Affluent Business Owners

Most successful fund-raisers feel that affluent business owners as a market segment have the greatest potential in terms of donations. However, most marketers of charitable causes do not organize their human resources to take full advantage of the opportunities that this segment provides.

Along these lines, Omnibus Giving should reorganize and develop what I call the "task force/affiliation concept." Industries that produce a disproportionate number of prospective affluent donors should be assigned to specific task force groups, each of which has at least one member from the industry. This member does not necessarily have to do any soliciting; however, his tasks would be equally important. One of his tasks would be to identify high-income/high—net worth individuals within the industry. Another would be to determine the firms in the industry and the owners of the firms in the industry that are euphoric because of current or contemplated upswings in their cash flow. This task force member would also keep abreast of periodic changes in the industry. By reading the industry's trade journals, he can identify euphoric prospects. For example, the Gotham area's edition of *AdWeek* lists all of the advertising agencies that are in contention for sizable contracts as well as the winners of these contracts.

Omnibus Giving should immediately contact the winners of these contracts as well as the winners of contracts in a variety of other fields. It should send a letter to the principals of the identified firms, the first paragraph of which should congratulate them on their success. The next paragraph should outline Omnibus Giving's commitment to acknowledging the successes of businesses in the Gotham area and to obtaining donations for worthy causes. The efficacy of such a message cannot be overstated.

Omnibus Giving will find this method successful for at least three reasons. First, the targeting is not random. Omnibus Giving focuses on people whose income and wealth has increased significantly. Second, Omnibus Giving tells prospective donors that it is aware of that increase. Thus it is difficult for the targeted donors to state that they are unable to contribute. Third, many affluent prospects who are encountering socioeconomic success feel obligated to share the increase in their income and wealth.

There are a variety of affluent industries that Omnibus Giving should consider targeting. These include electrical, mechanical, and civil engineering firms; architectural firms; plumbing, heating, and air-conditioning contractors; construction contractors; highway paving contractors; law firms; accounting firms; and consulting organizations. A task force should be assigned one or more of these industries. Each of these task forces should determine which firms in the assigned industry or industries are encountering upturns in business. For example, by studying the publication of record and related trade publications of the legal industry, the task force to which that industry has been assigned will be able to identify the firms and principals in the industry that have won major judgments and/or out-of-court settlements on behalf of their clients.

Prospecting Physicians

Two important issues relate to the problem of generating donations from physicians. First, most physicians are compelled by their status to be heavy purchasers of consumer goods. Given their relatively high incomes, physicians as an occupational category are among the least likely to accumulate any sizable amount of wealth. They tend to be cash poor but consumer product rich.

Second, Omnibus Giving has used ineffective methods of marketing to reach this group. Omnibus Giving should target specific medical specialties. It should view each one of these specialties as a distinct market segment. The median annual income of physicians in general is approximately $140,000. However, many of the specialist groups have a median income that greatly exceeds this amount. Omnibus Giving should concentrate on anesthesiologists, neurosurgeons, orthopedic surgeons, radiologists, and cardiologists. It should contact the most respected and qualified physician within each of these groups. Identify these outstanding professionals by asking dozens, even hundreds, of physicians for their opinions about "who's best." And when you contact those physicians who have been identified as the best, what should you say to them? Try this: "According to your colleagues, you're the very best in your field. That is why we need your help." The credibility and integrity of these physicians underlie their potential role as opinion leaders in the channeling of donations to Omnibus Giving. It is imperative that they act as role models for others in their specialist group. Each of them should be asked two basic questions: "Will you contribute to Omnibus Giving and thus act as an important role model for others in your profession?" and "Will you write letters to your colleagues asking them to support Omnibus Giving?" It is important that Omnibus Giving recognize that intraindustry or intraprofession endorsements by opinion leaders are among the very most powerful inducements for giving.

I hope that my recommendations will become productive components of your campaign. Thank you for your interest in my research.

Regards,

Thomas J. Stanley, Ph.D.
Chairman
Affluent Market Institute

CHAPTER 6

THE PUBLICIST

"Why do influential people endorse him? Because he helps them gain recognition and credibility via favorable press coverage."

FIRST PROMOTE SIGNIFICANT OTHERS

DR. STANLEY:

Why did the local network station broadcast a news item about you and your accounting practice?

MR. MORGAN:

It's a long story. Two years ago, I read about the top scrap metal dealer in our region. He's a local boy who made the front page of *Scrap Metal News*. I got a copy from a supplier to the scrap business. I called the dealer and said, "Congratulations." I asked him if he had ever been featured in the local press. . . . He never was.

DR. STANLEY:

And then what happened?

MR. MORGAN:

I called the business reporter at the TV station. I suggested that he do a piece or two on Mr. S. M., that is, Mr. Scrap Metal. And they ran a feature story on him. He loved it. . . . It was the first time in his life that local people recognized him as a celebrity. Now he is a client.

DR. STANLEY:

What does this have to do with being on TV yourself?

MR. MORGAN:

I gave that TV station a half dozen or more good leads on local businesspeople. It's a great way to approach prospective clients. I guess the TV people felt that I would stop giving them stories if they ignored my own firm's case history. And they were right. So they told my story on television. But I received more business from getting prospective clients on the local station than from being on TV myself.

ENHANCING THE IMAGE OF OPINION LEADERS

A young attorney has a problem. Susan recently resigned from a well-established law firm to go it alone. She graduated from a fine law school in the top quarter of her class. Currently, however, she is just about "breaking even." She does wills, some contracts for small businesses, house closings, and some divorce work. But, in her words, she is "barely making it."

This country has an overabundance of intelligent and well-trained attorneys who can't make a living. These attorneys are competent in terms of the legal services dimension, but most of them, probably as many as four out of five, do not know how to market and sell their services. So what if Susan attended a top law school and graduated high in her class. Such achievements mean zip if you don't know how to relate them to your target market. And from what Susan told me, she was not relating to, not focusing on, the market opportunities that existed. House closings will not pay her rent.

What is really interesting is the fact that some of the most successful attorneys in America graduated from average law schools in the bottom quarter of their classes. These folks, however, knew how to market themselves. They didn't rely on class rankings and so-called prestige diplomas to generate business.

Ah, but Susan is proactive. She recently attended a seminar on marketing professional services. Did she learn anything? The instructor apparently told her to target centers of influence. These opinion leaders influence the patronage habits of successful business owners and other types of affluent prospects.

Although Susan followed her instructor's advice, she is still struggling. What strategy has she been using? The instructor told her to target the owners of small businesses after first gaining endorsements from their accountants. This may sound like a good idea. But CPAs are often reluctant to give endorsements unless they can benefit from doing so.

Susan called on at least one senior partner of each of the top 20 independent CPA firms in her trade area. She asked these CPAs for referrals to clients of theirs who were incorporating. She figured that helping business owners to incorporate would be a nice way to introduce herself to owners of growing businesses. But none of them gave her any referrals. Her lack of success in this regard is not surprising, even though she was not asking for endorsements to major clients.

A Rationale for a Turndown

Susan offered to swap referrals, to share her clients with some of the accounting firms she visited. But this offer was turned down. Clients involved with house closings and divorce settlements are of little interest to a typical senior partner of a CPA firm. Such people will usually tell you that they want business from business owners and high-powered professionals. In most instances, whether you're selling legal services or accounting services, clients who own their own businesses are much more profitable than clients in the so-called consumer or retail market.

I'm not saying that Susan has nothing to trade. But she has to be more creative. She has to consider what CPAs want in exchange for making referrals on her behalf. They want more clients like the ones they have and perhaps bigger clients than the ones they have. They may want recognition and empathy.

How can Susan enlist the assistance of CPAs if her own clients are not big revenue generators? She can give CPAs more than her own clients. How can she do this if she is having difficulty in capturing new clients of her own? Sometimes it's easier to promote the services of others than it is to promote your own! Allow me to explain by reflecting on a recent newspaper article. The headling of the article reads as follows:

Black Female Public Relations Expert Hired as Partner
by Major Law Firm

What is the significance of this article? No, it's not that the new partner is black, not that the new partner is a woman. This article is significant because it reports that for the first time in its long history this major law firm hired a partner who was not an attorney. The article is also significant because it reports that the new partner was a public relations (PR) expert.

All professional service firms, whether they be law firms or accounting firms, need marketing and promotional help. If someone like Susan wanted to prospect the partners of the law firm, what theme would sell? Before that firm hired a PR expert, PR would sell. Reverse the players in this case for a moment. Assume that a CPA was calling on this law firm. Why would it do business with a CPA whose clients were of the same caliber as Susan's current clients? What if the CPA could get the law firm "good press," "exposure," "increased visibility"? Then the CPA might gain a new client and that client's referrals. So what I'm saying is that Susan should offer PR help. This overture would open the door to the CPAs she's prospecting. Most accounting firms do not know how to get good press.

This system will work. I told Susan to ask the next CPAs she called on this important question: "What are your goals, and what are your problems?" Of these CPAs, 9 out of 10 told her that they wanted more clients and better clients. They also said that they didn't know how to attract new clients without breaking their marketing budget.

But how will Susan attain PR skills? Certainly, she can't acquire them overnight. Susan doesn't need PR skills. She just needs to find a PR professional who will do a joint venture with her. As an illustration of this strategy, I related a case study to Susan.

A young financial consultant who, like Susan, was targeting CPAs had a problem similar to Susan's. He had no truly affluent clients to share with the CPAs he approached. As with Susan, these CPAs very nicely, but very firmly, turned down his request. They saw no benefit, no profit from endorsing him to their affluent clients. Like many other sales professionals who have attempted to gain favor with opinion-leading CPAs, he was focusing on his own needs and not on the needs of his target.

How did the financial consultant change the opinion of the CPAs he approached? He told them:

If you will give me referrals to your clients, I will have articles published about you and your firm. These articles will enhance your growing reputation. They will appear in the trade and professional journals that your target audience reads.

A Moonlighting Ghost

At this juncture, many readers may be thinking that they have no interest or skill in writing articles for clients. But think again. The young financial consultant in this case did not write any of the articles that he had published about the CPAs in his network. He hired a ghostwriter to do so. And given the referral business he received from the CPAs he publicized, the fees he paid the ghostwriter were a very profitable investment.

Instead of hiring a high-priced professional writer/publicist, he hired a "moonlighter." What is a moonlighter, and how do you find one? The moonlighter in this case, Ms. "PR Writer," was a highly skilled publicity director at a small college. The financial consultant followed my advice to the letter. I told him to examine the local newspapers, even the neighborhood newspapers, in his trade area. I said,

> Always look for articles that say nice things about a school or college. You will typically find that one or two schools in your area receive most of the good press. I have seen situations where the same local school or college is given good press on an almost weekly basis. This is no accident. I do not believe that some schools are so outstanding that good press just comes naturally. In most cases, good press goes to those schools that have outstanding public relations personnel.

In the case at hand, Ms. PR Writer wrote all of the articles that were published about the college she promotes. She even supplied the local newspapers with corresponding pictures and transcripts of interviews. However, her name never appeared as the writer because she is the perfect public relations/ghostwriting professional. She does all or most of the work, but she allows someone else to get all of the credit. And who received the credit? Typically, the vice president of the college or reporters and writers at the newspapers and professional journals that carried stories about the college.

Ms. PR Writer is more than a ghostwriter. She is a Publicist for her employer and to reporters. This is precisely why she was so very valuable a find for the financial consultant in this case.

Remember, that your probability of getting good press is greatly enhanced if you provide a complete, well-written manuscript to a writer, reporter, or editor. Then allow that person to edit the material and place his or her name on it. Ms. PR Writer is able to get outstanding press coverage because she focuses on the needs of writers, reporters, and editors. Deadlines, deadlines, deadlines and ego, ego, ego.

Since Ms. PR's name never appeared on the articles she wrote, how did the financial consultant find out who she was? He telephoned the college that was constantly receiving great local press coverage and asked to speak to the person who was responsible for that coverage. In less than 60 seconds, he was talking with Ms. PR Writer.

Recruiting Ms. PR Writer

How did the financial consultant persuade Ms. PR Writer to moonlight for him? He started out by acknowledging her achievements in generating good press for the college. Then he asked her to tell him her story—her background and experience in publicity. This conversation was followed by an invitation to "do lunch." And at lunch the financial consultant outlined his marketing strategy.

He told Ms. PR Writer that he wanted to network with high-grade CPAs/influential people by becoming their Publicist. He wanted to give them something in addition to investment products and services. He also told Ms. PR Writer that most of the influential CPAs whom he was targeting were in the Dark Ages when it came to public relations. Then he proposed that Ms. PR Writer moonlight for him—that she ghostwrite articles for selected members of his influence network, that is, CPAs.

The financial consultant promised Ms. PR Writer that "if this thing works as well as I believe it will, I can give you all the business you can handle." Ms. PR Writer agreed to help him. It turned out to be a wonderful relationship. As part of her first assignment, Ms. PR Writer interviewed the financial consultant's top prospect, a senior partner at a major independent accounting firm. Then she wrote articles based on his ideas concerning "business valuation" and "taking the money out of the privately held/small corporation."

Whose name was given as the author of the articles? The name of the prospect, that is, the senior partner of the CPA firm! How did the prospect respond? He is no longer a prospect. He is now a client of the financial consultant.

But this result was not the primary aim of the financial consultant. Nor was it the primary aim of Susan, the young attorney who was unable to gain the endorsements of CPAs. Both Susan and the financial consultant wanted CPAs to refer their accounting clients to them. This is an excellent way to network. What will happen if you get good press for your targeted CPAs? Good press will lead to revenue enhancement via increased exposure and credibility. Every quality CPA firm lusts for good press. And good press is a unique favor that you can bestow on centers of influence. It is a much better gift than a basket of fruit or a mundane appointment calendar.

A Dramatic Impact

What effect did publishing articles for the CPA have on the financial consultant's business? Shortly after the first article appeared in an important trade journal, the "designated author," that is, the senior partner of the CPA firm, received several calls from prospects who had read the article. One of the callers became the CPA firm's largest account. Not long thereafter, the senior partner of the CPA firm began to make referrals on behalf of the financial consultant. In fact, the financial consultant received more high-quality leads from the CPA than did any of the other financial consultants who had been networking with the CPA firm.

Did these referrals translate into business for the financial consultant? Absolutely. The very first referral was the financial officer of a trade association. The financial officer had read the CPA's article. Eventually, the trade association became a client of the CPA firm. The same financial officer recently asked the CPA for a recommendation. "We have over $3 million to invest. Do you know someone that would do a good job helping us with our investment?" Not surprisingly, the CPA recommended the financial consultant. He was asked to manage a little over $3 million of the association's money. But that was only the beginning. He was told that if he did a good job, he would be given all of the association's business!

Endorse Only Quality Professionals

But what happens if the CPA in this case misjudged the financial consultant's ability to make prudent investment decisions? The fact that the financial consultant is an expert in networking does not mean that he is a high-quality source of investment ideas.

A CPA should never make a referral on behalf of a professional just because he can deliver good press. That would be a breach of the client's trust. Then why did the CPA give his endorsement to the financial consultant? The financial consultant in this case was not an investment expert, and he never positioned himself as such. However, he was, and still is, an expert in judging the ability of investment advisors. He studies the track records of more than 100 of this country's asset/investment managers and several hundred quality mutual funds. In essence, he brokers asset managers and funds. He asks only the very best to join his client/influence network. This system allows him to concentrate on networking and studying the performance characteristics of mutual fund investment managers. And he will tell you that he is much more interested in networking than in becoming an investment expert.

The Question of Money

How much did Ms. PR Writer charge the financial consultant for getting good press for his prospects and clients? To date, Ms. PR Writer, has ghostwritten three articles for the members of the financial consultant's network and has had several news items published. Her fee was $1,500, of which one half was paid up front and the other half was paid only after the articles were published. As a result of the business ultimately generated through referrals, this $1,500 investment brought the financial consultant commissions totaling more than 20 times what he paid Ms. PR Writer.

Implications for Susan

Susan the struggling attorney, desperately wants referrals from "well connected" accountants. What should she do to gain referrals from these important centers of influence? She should follow the pro forma case of the financial consultant that I have described. I'm sure she will be able to find a Ms. PR Writer within her trade area. More often than not, the public relations writer who is successful in promoting schools or colleges, hospitals or charitable causes is underpaid or not paid at all. Moreover, this writer is usually underappreciated by his or her employer. So take note, all of you sales professionals out there—the PR Writers in your town are waiting for your call.

But just how many CPAs could Susan help by generating good press? How many CPAs can become stars within one trade area? She could not possibly make more than one or two CPAs media celebrities. *Au contraire!* There are more than 600 trade, professional, and other types of affluent affinity groups within her trade area. Two thirds or more of these groups have some form of publication. So she's looking at a market with about 400 affluent subsegments. If four of these subsegments are allocated to each targeted CPA, there are 100 potentially happy CPAs. How many does Susan want? She can't have all of them. But 5 or 10 good accounting clients can help her generate business with hundreds of their best clients.

Susan, Go beyond CPAs

It would be possible for Susan to get press for other potential clients. Think of all the successful affluent business owners that could benefit from "Susan's Total Service Package," in which she acts as the legal department for small and medium-sized businesses and they receive good press as a bonus. If she follows the pro forma case described above, the "big fish will chase her boat." That's what marketing, selling, and networking with the affluent are all about. Develop a strong favorable image. Offer revenue enhancing via public relations as collateral services. Then prospects, important prospects, will seek you out. These prospects probably don't care about Susan's class standing or the pedigree of her law school. What they care about is the pedigree of Susan's influence network. Her influence network will generate increased revenue for clients, revenue that will more than offset her charges to clients for legal fees. It's all part of a networker's total service package.

CREATING AN INFLUENCE NETWORK FROM GROUND ZERO

DR. STANLEY:

Developing a network takes time. You must be patient. But in addition to that, you must bring something to the table.

MR. MICHAEL:

You have to bring something to the table. You just said it. What if you're just starting out, Tom?

DR. STANLEY:

Well, again, that is a very good question. How do you start networking from ground zero today?

MR. MICHAEL:

You don't know anybody. You don't have a network. You don't have a client base.

DR. STANLEY:

Exactly. Let's say, for example, that you visit an accountant or a lawyer and they say the same thing to you. "Young man, young woman, you're 25 years old. You're wet behind the ears. You're 30 years old. You have no clients."

"That's true, sir. However, I have a list here of people that I will be visiting. I have confirmed appointments with these people. When I do visit with them, I will ask them about how satisfied they currently are with their accountant, with their lawyer, and so forth. Would you mind if I mention you as a potential supplier?"

This proposal places you in a different league. You can be 25 and wet behind the ears. You can be 25 and have no clients. But if you walk into a seasoned professional's office and say, "I know how to play the game. I'm street smart. I want to be your Publicist. I want to enhance your revenue. That's my deal. That's how I'm succeeding."

MR. MICHAEL:

I understand. But how does a person wet behind the ears choose the professionals he's going to target?

DR. STANLEY:

There are no hard-and-fast rules. There are, for example, a lot of business newspapers in different cities that will list the top 20 to top 50 to top 100 independent accounting firms. Of course, you could start with the yellow pages. But walk in and talk with these people. Call these people, make an appointment with them and find out if they're street smart. In other words, are they sensitive to the whole concept of networking? If you find out that these people are not sensitive to the networking concept, you will essentially be going nowhere unless you can educate them about the values and how to's of networking. It's also very, very important that your own accountant be a networker. Your accountant should know how to play the game by rewarding people that help the network.

In *Selling To The Affluent,* I mentioned David Cariseo. He would go to the water department every morning. He would look at its records to find out who just moved into Boca Raton, Florida, who started a business, and so forth. Then he would visit these newcomers.

Ever since I wrote about Mr. Cariseo, many people have been going to their water departments. But many of them forgot the major ingredient. David was so very successful not only because he identified the wealthy prospects that were moving into the community but because he also had a very important message. It was the network message. It wasn't only going to the water department and getting their names. What did he say to these people?

MR. MICHAEL:

Let me guess, Tom. "What do you need?"

DR. STANLEY:

"What do you need?" Exactly! In other words, what's the message? Do you need a financial consultant? That's not the message. Dull, dull, dull. Me, me, me. No empathy for the prospect's goals. What do you need? Do you need an accountant since you've moved here from Chicago? Do you need a lawyer since you've moved here from Fresno, California? Do you need a landscape architect since your lawn is a mess? Do you need a home builder? Do you need a roofer because you have a hole in your roof? Do you need a family physician?

What is the key to the Cariseo system? He acted as a word-of-mouth publicist for important opinion leaders. And remember that he started from ground zero. He would call surgeons. He would call accountants. He would call lawyers. He would call roofers. What would he say? "Would you find it presumptuous if I mentioned your name to the affluent individuals moving into Boca Raton and the business owners that are opening businesses here? Would you find it presumptuous?"

They don't find it presumptuous. They want to know where this guy has been hiding for the last 20 years. He's the first person ever to come to them and say, "Look, first I'm going to do a favor for you, and then maybe you'll do a favor for me." That's essentially why it works so well. Because it tells people that David is extraordinary. He's a Publicist. He's a networker. He's out there promoting clients and prospects before they buy from him.

MR. MICHAEL:

Let me play the devil's advocate role one more time, Tom, especially for some of those who might be doubting Thomases out there. How did he pick which surgeon to call, which lawyer, which builder, whatever, to say that he was going to do the selling for them?

DR. STANLEY:

Well, it's interesting. Let me tell you in a broad sense how that could be done. Essentially, you can contact surgeons and accountants and ask them who they think are the cream of the crop within the industry. It's a little sociometric design that they teach in sociology classes. And what you'll find is that eventually you'll talk to 50 surgeons. They'll point to two or three. You can call those people and say you'll put them on a preferred list because they've been endorsed by their colleagues. Same with accountants. It's not just saying to prospects, "I will provide you with the name of an accountant." You should do your homework, and you should find out who the best people are. But, most importantly, find out who the specialists are. For example, who is the best accountant for surgeons to deal with? Which accountant really understands the specialized needs of surgeons?

MR. MICHAEL:

Who is the best tax lawyer? Who understands the changes in the corporate tax laws as they occur?

DR. STANLEY:

That's right. Who is the best estate planning attorney to contact for someone who's just moving into the community? Who is the best accountant for contractors?

MR. MICHAEL:

And he will know the best life insurance agent that might help out in this estate planning situation?

DR. STANLEY:

Exactly. But again, and most importantly, it just tells the people with whom you're talking that you're a highly intelligent person because you understand their fundamental need. And their fundamental need is more business, more revenue enhancement via publicity, aka "work-of-mouth endorsements." On the other side, they need an entire set of new suppliers.

Now, again, we go back to the concept that I was mentioning before. Let's say a construction contractor moves his entire business from the slow-moving Midwest to the red-hot, let's say, Dade County, Florida. He may need 360 suppliers. And who shows up within 24 hours of this perceived need? David, with a list not only of commercial suppliers but also of personal suppliers. You can't help but like people like that. And he started from absolute ground zero. No previous clients. He walked in the door and took off and was the number one producing broker in that major branch within one year.

PUBLICITY FIRST, ACCOUNTING SECOND: A LETTER TO A STRUGGLING CPA

Dear Professional:

Don't view your recent journey into selling to high-income insurance agents as a failure. Obviously, you have the fundamental characteristic that all outstanding marketing professionals, new business executives, and sales professionals possess. You have courage. It is not easy going out on your own. Success is a result of effort. I'm sure that in the long run you will prosper. You have demonstrated considerable courage by cold-calling on, as you say, dozens of top-ranked insurance sales professionals and agencies in your community. These professionals are an excellent target. However, I think you need to modify your promotional message.

Many top-performing insurance agents are well known in their respective communities. Often, their success is widely publicized in the local newspaper and various popular business publications. The current trend among sales professionals who market luxury automobiles, vacation homes, custom suits, and even investment products and services is to target top-performing insurance agents.

Frequently, these agents are very patient and empathize with those who target them. However, a growing number, as you have found, are losing their patience. Sales and marketing professionals focusing only on their own needs, their own products, their own services, their own fees and commissions, and not on those of their targets, will not be successful in this arena.

You must offer your targets more than conventional accounting services. If you do, you will attract these top-performing agents. These agents are often important patronage opinion leaders for their affluent clients. Therefore, you can expect to gain access, via referrals and endorsements, to their best clients. However, you claim you have nothing to offer but accounting services. You also indicate that you have "only a very few" wealthy clients. So you conclude that "trading client referrals" may be one-sided and, thus, not beneficial to your targets. Perhaps, but being young and having "only a few" wealthy clients is no excuse for not using your marketing intellect. Nor should you abandon your goal of capturing "a significant portion" of the insurance agent market at this time.

Allow me to reflect on a case study. In this situation, Mr. Robert Dean, a young fellow about your age, decided to target a well-known top-producing life insurance agent. Mr. Dan Speaks, the agent whom Mr. Dean targeted, had a net income of nearly $400,000 annually. And he, like many of his counterparts, was growing increasingly impatient with the insensitive sales professionals who called on him. Ninety-nine percent of those who targeted him focused on me-me-me, or their exclusively personal needs. He grew frustrated with these callers, hanging up on some and throwing a few out of his office. Ninety-nine percent of the solicitors played the role of antagonist to Mr. Speaks. Ninety-nine percent of those unannounced, uninvited cold callers were not networkers. But 1 in

100 callers played a different role. He played the role of Mr. Speaks's Publicist.

One sales professional, and only one, transformed this affluent insurance agent into a client. And Mr. Dean, the fellow who made the sale in this situation, had a much more difficult service to sell than you do. He was a securities broker selling investment products and services. Many others had tried to sell this same product to this top-producing insurance agent with absolutely no success.

How did this caller succeed while at least 99 others failed? The answer relates to understanding and capitalizing on knowledge of the target's needs. There are thousands of sellers of investment services in the town where this case took place. And I'm sure that there are hundreds of CPAs who compete with you in your trade area. But very few say what the prospect wants to hear. Would any top-producing insurance agent prefer to discuss your core services before discussing how to increase his client base, enhance his sales revenue, and gain him exposure to affluent prospects?

Most, if not all, top insurance agents prefer to talk about nurturing their own sales revenue and not someone else's. And you can enhance your target's revenue. Follow the lead of Mr. Dean, the investment sales professional in this case. The top-producing insurance agent, Mr. Speaks, was kind enough to share this experience with me. He gave me the details of the conversation with Mr. Dean that captured his business. Mr. Dean walked into Mr. Speaks's office one morning. This cold call became warm very soon after Mr. Dean asked Mr. Speaks a simple question.

Mr. Dean:

> Hello, Mr. Speaks. Since you're a top sales professional, I wonder if you would be willing to give a speech on how you market to millionaire business owners and other wealthy individuals?

Mr. Speaks:

> How did you hear about me?

Mr. Dean:

> I read about you. . . . You're a legend when it comes to marketing and selling to affluent business owners and other wealthy individuals.

Mr. Speaks:

> Oh, well, listen, I'm flattered that you called. Who will be in the audience?

Mr. Dean:

> About 200 of the top independent certified public accountants . . . who either own their own firms outright or are partners in one!

Mr. Speaks:

> Well, what would you like me to talk about?

Mr. Dean:

> The audience would love to know how to market to wealthy business owners and professionals.

Mr. Speaks:

> I can do that. That's how I make a living, a very good living.

Mr. Dean:

> That's why I called. They would be delighted and honored to have someone of your stature address them. They would really learn a lot from you.

Mr. Speaks:

> It is very kind of you to spend your time looking for a speaker for your colleagues. How long have you been in the accounting business?

Mr. Dean:

> I'm not in the accounting business. I'm a stockbroker.

Mr. Speaks:

What is a stockbroker doing recruiting speakers for an accounting group?

Mr. Dean:

Well, accountants make great clients in my business. They are often big savers and investors. They are also very strong centers of influence in regard to endorsements and referrals to their clients. So I approached them as a group. I'm now the de facto chairperson of their speaker selection committee. If this works out, I'm sure I will generate some business out of it. Even if I can invest the association's money, I figure to break even at least.

Mr. Speaks:

You're not only kind, you're very clever. You're an apostle to CPAs. I will bet that nobody in the membership wanted that task. Am I correct?

Mr. Dean:

You are right. That's where I came in. I read about the CPAs having monthly meetings in the local business paper. I called the president of the association cold. He agreed right away since he was given the privilege not only of being president but also of being a one-person committee for selecting speakers. Nobody wanted the job. So I volunteered. He promised to mention my contribution to all the attendees at the next meeting. Also, I will have an acknowledgment in their newsletter next month. This will make it much easier to make appointments to call on the members of the association. By the way, can you send me your biographical sketch and a black-and-white photo of yourself? We will want to publish it in the *CPA Letter*. The letter goes out to over 1,000 members.

Mr. Speaks:

This is great, really. I will be happy to speak. I'm sure I would benefit from the exposure. And I can tell you that I really appreciate your effort. This is a win-win-win situation. I'm looking for new business; you're targeting CPAs, and the CPAs have you as their speakers bureau.

Mr. Dean:

You're right. Everybody wins. It's a very good way to network with prospects and associations.

Mr. Speaks:

I can't tell you how many of your colleagues have asked me to do business with them. Many, many have tried during the past few years. I turned them all down. Each and every one of them. But you're the first one to make me an offer I can't refuse. I have plenty in CDs and annuities. I do my own investing. But I'll tell you, if I get any business from my exposure to the CPAs, I'll give you one half of the revenue to invest any way you wish. How about it?

Mr. Dean:

I can deal with that. You meet the nicest people when you operate your own speakers bureau! I'm so excited about this speakers thing, I can't sleep at night. Just think about the opportunities to come into contact with important people. This beats the daylights out of cold calling—you know, smiling and dialing on the telephone.

As a CPA who targets high-income insurance agents, you can use the same win-win-win approach that Mr. Dean employed in this case. Network with affluent affinity groups. Then expose your prospects and clients to the members of these groups. Become a Publicist to your targets. Also solve one of the major problems confronting local and state associations, that is, the inability to attract qualified speakers.

There are more than 100 affinity groups in your trade area that target wealthy business owners and affluent professionals. Call several members in each of these groups and ask for the names of the best sales professionals. Then call on various insurance groups. Ask whether they would like to have you act as their supplier of speakers. Those accepting your offer will probably reciprocate via endorsements. Select as speakers the best sales professionals from the industries that target the affluent. If you assist insurance groups in recruiting speakers, they will be in your debt. They will usually return the favor. How? By giving you and your services acknowledgments and endorsements.

You can further leverage the presence of large numbers of affluent affinity groups (trade and professional associations) in your area. Since there are over 100 such groups, they probably need as many or more speakers for their meetings, conferences, and seminars. They target the affluent, and so do many top-producing insurance agents. So why not contact the cream of the crop from the insurance industry? Ask each of these selected agents whether they would like you to act as their speakers bureau. I'm sure that most, if not all, would be delighted to accept your offer. They should respond just as did the top-producing insurance agent in the case scenario given above.

But I certainly would not focus only on insurance agents. Your practice should be broader than one industry. You can select other market opportunities from the industries that are represented by the trade and professional groups you will identify as needing speakers. Where can you find information about local and state trade and professional associations? One of the best sources of affiliation groups is Gale Research Company's *Regional, State, and Local Organizations Encyclopedia of Associations.*

Under the heading of Health Care, I would suggest that you send information about your speakers bureau and the speakers you represent to your state medical association. In addition, you might find it advantageous to send individual solicitations to subcategories of the medical profession. These would include the affiliation groups of anesthesiologists, radiologists, cardiologists, and neurosurgeons. Under the heading of Doctors of Dental Surgery, specifically target the affiliation groups of orthodontists. And you might be interested in sending information about your speakers bureau to veterinarian medical associations.

Let me also strongly recommend that you send information to your local and state bar associations, your local and state associations of certified public accountants, and associations of mechanical engineers, electrical engineers, and architects.

Under the heading of Sales and Marketing, I would suggest that you send information about your speakers bureau to your state's association of independent insurance agents, your state's organizations of sales and marketing executives, your state's sales clubs, your state and local boards of realtors, and your state's advertising and public relations organizations.

Also, it would be valuable to include the trade associations that represent such groups as scrap metal recycling entrepreneurs; general contractors; developers; highway, street, and paving construction entrepreneurs; plumbing, heating, and air-conditioning contractors; real estate management organizations; beer wholesalers; wine and distilled alcoholic beverage wholesalers; manufacturers associations; your state's automobile dealers association; your state's builders council; your state's investment dealers association; building material supply associations; retail trade associations; your state's consulting engineers council; associations of personnel consultants; trade associations that represent funeral directors in your state and your local community; trade associations that represent printers, restaurant associations, manufacturer's agents, and sales agents; roofing contractors; associations that represent the executives of associations; and associations that represent meeting planners. These are just a few of the important affiliation groups that would like to hear about your speakers bureau. (Portions extracted from Thomas J. Stanley, *Selling to the Affluent* [Homewood, Ill.: Business One Irwin, 1991].)

Don't attempt to master all of these targets at once. Begin with your favorite target, namely insurance agents. As you develop more understanding of the process, you can begin to target other market segments. But always remember that you will succeed in marketing if you focus on the needs of your targets. These needs typically transcend traditional accounting services. Help your prospects and clients increase their client base. You will be rewarded with their patronage, endorsements, and referrals. Prospects will begin to seek you out because you are more than an accountant. You are an aspostle to your clientele.

I wish you the best of luck in your endeavors. Keep me posted about your continued success.

Regards,

Thomas J. Stanley, Ph.D.
Chairman

CHAPTER 7

THE FAMILY ADVISOR

"Help his family, and he will patronize and endorse your business."

ON BECOMING A FAMILY ADVISOR TO THE AFFLUENT

For nearly 30 nonstop minutes, Barbara told me:

> I am considered by many experts in the financial planning industry to be an authority on helping affluent households (families) reach their investment goals and objectives.

> I have some of the very best ideas about how clients should invest in order to provide for their children's education.

> I have state-of-the-art software for formulating customized investment strategies.

> I am a member of all the important associations that represent financial planners.

> I am certified. . . . I am a member of Phi Beta Kappa. . . . I graduated at the top of my undergraduate class. I hold an MBA degree from _____ . It's a top 20 business school.

> I give my clients access to the very best mutual funds and/or insurance providers in America.

Given Barbara's credentials, one might think that she has no problems marketing her financial planning services. But Barbara, like many of her peers, has a classic marketing problem. She assumes that her ability with regard to financial products and services will automatically translate into new business.

Barbara is a talented and highly qualified professional, but she is product oriented. She is a master of her product, but she is not master of marketing. To be an expert in any area of business, one must meet two requirements. First, as Barbara does, one must have superior skills that are product based. Second, one must be viewed as an expert by market prospects and clients and even by the relevant media.

Barbara is perceived as an expert by her peers. But her peers are neither her clients nor her prospective clients. Interestingly, many of Barbara's competitors who do not possess her product skills but do possess superior marketing and selling skills have several times the client base that she has.

After Barbara completed her self-analysis, I asked her, "Barbara, are you now ready to tell me about your problem?" She became remarkably candid after a while. She stated, "My business has been declining. Each year for the past three years, the number of new clients that I have attracted has decreased. Yet I now know more about financial planning than ever. I study every mutual fund offering. I can tell you about the character of most insurers and their offerings. I know more about tax laws than most tax attorneys."

Barbara's business has declined because she views the world of professional services along product and product knowledge dimensions. When her business began to decline, she intensified her study of product and financial information. She assumed that superior knowledge of products would automatically make her offerings more attractive. Clearly, this logic was flawed.

Barbara would be better off if she had allocated more of her time to cultivating clients. She must be able to relate to the needs of her clients and her prospects. Those needs often transcend financial planning fundamentals.

Dear Barbara:

Your financial planning services will not sell themselves. You must reach out to your target market. To this point in your career, you have not developed a viable marketing system. How do I know about your orientation toward the affluent? I examined the contents of your Rolodex. Do your own frequency count of the categories of cards it contains. Your Rolodex will, and did, "tell on you." It is filled with the names, phone numbers, addresses, and affiliations of only three major categories of characters.

Category One: Your Rolodex is filled with the cards of suppliers of financial products and services. In fact, you have more Rolodex cards for this category than any other. Suppliers are important, but clients are more important. Given your Rolodex, one may assume that you place more importance on your suppliers than on your clients!

Category Two: Clients and, I assume, soon-to-be clients make up the second category. But here again your Rolodex does not lie. You do not have a focused approach. You have clients and prospects from over 100 industries/professions. Is it any wonder that you receive so few of those all-important industry-specific referrals?

Category Three: Generic suppliers of business-related products and services. This list contains the names of suppliers from the office products to dust control industries. Fewer than 1 in 10 are your clients. Don't you believe in reciprocity? Ask those whom you patronize to patronize you.

Keep the Rolodex that you have. I also suggest that you obtain a second one. This "other Rolodex," or Rolodex II, should contain those important people whom you will wish to add to your influence network.

Allow me to give you an example of how to influence influential people. You have superior skills in designing plans for families that wish to fund expensive educations for their children and grandchildren. But how have you addressed the number one objection to your solicitation, that is, "I don't think my son/daughter will be able to get into college." A response of "too bad" is not appropriate. More than half of the affluent people with children under 18 years of age have some concerns about the academic performance of their offspring. Don't ignore this problem; capitalize on it. Remember, you can't sell a financial plan for tuition funding to a client who believes that his child cannot get into college. So design your own demand for such service.

There are well over 100 educational consultants, testing specialists, psychologists, and guidance counselors listed in your yellow pages. They can help your clients and prospective clients whose children are not performing well in school. Begin to network with these people.

How can you tell who the truly outstanding education specialists are? Call the guidance counselors in your local high schools. Ask them whom they would recommend. Call the admissions directors of several area colleges and universities. Ask them for the names of professionals in educational/psychological consulting whom they endorse. Also ask your clients with children who have excelled in college whether they ever used the services of an educational advisor. Call those listed in the yellow pages. Ask them for a list of references and accomplishments.

What's in this effort for you? Consider the following scenarios. You call, for example, a highly qualified psychologist with two possible messages. The first message reflects your current theme, that is, product orientation.

A Product-Oriented Message

My name is Barbara. I'm an expert financial planner. I have a Phi Beta Kappa key. I'm certified. I can design a tuition-funding program that will assure that your children will to go college. I have access to America's leading investment organization. Etc.

This theme is not very productive in today's competitive environment. It demonstrates no empathy for the needs of your target. Your product-oriented message suggests that you have a bad case of the me-me-me's. There is no duller, less imaginative theme.

Change your orientation and your theme. Become proactive. Develop a market-oriented approach. This approach is one that focuses on the real, broader needs of both the psychologist and the affluent families that both of you wish to target. Once again, you want to enhance the sale of your tuition-funding system. Yours is a strategy for families that anticipate spending significant amounts of money for the college and graduate school educations of their children and grandchildren. But these people need more than basic financial planning. They need a financial planner who also acts as a Family Advisor. And what about the psychologist in this case? What does he need? He needs a financial planner who can refer dozens of affluent clients to him.

A Family Advisor/financial planner should help assure that the children of clients will, in fact, be admitted to college. Your role in this regard is that of a financial planner, Family Advisor, and networker. Ideally, you should network with other professionals, such as the psychologist in this scenario, who will assist the children of your clients in reaching their educational goals.

Use a market-oriented approach. Call on the leading psychologist who specializes in helping solve the academic underachieving orientation problems of the children of many affluent families.

Your purpose in contacting the psychologist is threefold. *First,* you wish to network with him. In other words, you want to refer to several of your clients and prospective clients to him—those who have children whose "heads" need to be reoriented. *Reoriented* in this case means creating the desire in children to perform better in preparatory school. This will enhance the demand for your tuition-funding planning package. It will also demonstrate to your target audience that you are more than a generic financial planner. You're an important family resource. You will help them achieve two of their major goals in life. Yes, you will help them with the financial aspects of tuition funding. But even more important, you will help their children "get into college." They will now go out of their way to make referrals on your behalf!

Second, you want the psychologist to refer his clients to you. Almost by definition, his clients are affluent. They will probably need financial planning, especially your tuition package. Remember, even the affluent often have difficulty in funding the education of their children.

Third, you would enjoy having several psychologists as clients. After all, one of these professionals may be the president of your state's psychological association. This may give you a foot in the door to another affluent affinity group.

A Market-Oriented Message

Hello, Dr. Harris. My name is Barbara. Several of my clients are concerned about their children's academic achievement. They fear that their children will not be able to enter high-quality colleges or universities.

I'm a certified financial planner. In spite of the fact that my clients are typically well off, they do have need for my services. One of my specialties is providing clients with a tuition-funding strategy. Of course, if their children are not college material, they won't need my planning package. That is why I'm calling you.

I wonder if it would be appropriate to refer several of my affluent clients to you. This may help your business. And I'm sure it would help mine. I have several hundred clients, and I can tell you that at least several dozen have children who are academic underachievers. I understand that you have considerable experience in helping families in this regard.

I'm sure that your own financial planner refers many of his wealthy clients to you. It's just part of the service that professional planners provide their clients. How many referrals has your financial planner made on your behalf?

I hope someday to earn your patronage as well as your endorsements. Most of my business comes from referrals made by my clients.

Barbara, this theme will sell. Before you ask for this professional's patronage and endorsement, recruit him as a network member. Tell him of the strong need for his services among your own clients. He should be included in your Rolodex II, for he is a potential supplier of wisdom to your clients. He is a highly skilled professional who will be indebted to you. He will probably do business with you. More important, he will refer his clients to you.

You need to be recognized as both a valuable Family Advisor and a financial planner. Thus you must ask this question: What characters should be included in my Rolodex II? In order to answer this question, you must first ask yourself two others. What problems face the affluent family? What resources are available to clients/prospects that can help solve these problems?

Problems	Resource Categories (Rolodex II)
• Children who are currently academic underachievers in preparatory school	• Psychologists with experience in reorienting underachievers
• Children nearing college age who are having difficulty in being admitted into college	• Admissions/educational consultants • Admissions directors of selected colleges/universities • Representatives of fifth year (high school preparatory programs), i.e., preadmittance to college boot camps
• Children who wish to move back home after completing their undergraduate/graduate programs	• Psychologist with experience in reorienting "dependent" children
• Children and/or other family member with drug or alcohol dependency	• Representative/physicians associated with drug/alcohol abuse treatment programs
• Grandparents who wish to move into son's/daughter's home	• Third-party professionals, such as family counselors and clergy, who can take the sting out of saying no

- Adult children with demonstrated inability to provide for the education of their offspring

- Children/grandchildren who are at odds over the future allocation of the dollar proceeds from the liquidation of the family business

- Retirement living professionals, including selected clergy, counselors, and family-oriented psychologists

- Trust/estate planning specialists with experience in developing educational funding programs that bypass adult children

- Family business consultant who is either engaged in a private practice or affiliated with a local college or university

Within one year from this date, you should have at least 50 characters listed in your Rolodex II. That list would represent 50 or more members of your influence network. Each one of these characters can make important referrals on your behalf. Many of them will also make excellent clients for your planning services. There is no secret to building an influence network. It will take time and effort. But it will pay large dividends to you.

Make an effort to debrief all of the clients and prospects with whom you come into contact. Ask them about problems that go beyond financial planning. Take time to find qualified sources/professionals who can assist your clients. Ask all of those with whom you talk whom they would recommend as the best sources of supply. In this way, your Rolodex II will soon be filled. It will contain the top-rated sources of supply in a variety of categories.

Why will affluent families wish to deal with you? They will seek you out because you bring more to the table than do other planners. You help solve their problems. These problems are often more significant than mere financial issues. They relate to the most important goals and needs of affluent familes. Start

writing your book today. What book? <u>Solutions to the Problems
Facing Affluent Families</u>.

Please keep me posted about your influence network.

Regards,

Thomas J. Stanley, Ph.D.
Chairman
Affluent Market Institute

RE: LIMO DRIVER AND FAMILY ADVISOR

Dear Program Executive:

Are you still in search of high-grade limousine services?
If so, I have a name for you: Carmine Stardust.

Carmine's core service is outstanding. You will not find a
more skillful driver. He is always on time, and his limousine
is immaculate. He is very personable. But this core service is
only part of the story.

I am going out of my way to endorse Carmine because
he delivers much more than the basic service elements just
mentioned. Let me share with you this scenario.

During a visit to southern California, Carmine drove me
to and from my hotel. This was my first experience with his
limousine service. Due to the riots in Los Angeles, I was a
bit worried about my safety. When I arrived at Los Angeles
International Airport, Carmine met me at the gate.

He said, "Welcome to Los Angeles. I don't want you to
worry about anything. We will not be going near the area
where the riots took place. Anyway, I'm a retired California
police officer and have a permit to carry a pistol. No one will
bother us, I can assure you."

Carmine's confident attitude did calm my fears. His assur-
ance added an extra element to the service dimension. But, as
I learned during my ride, his extraordinary level of service had
reached a new high several days before I met him.

Carmine told me that he had not refused to accommodate

the needs of his clients during the recent unrest in Los Angeles. On one occasion, Carmine picked up a client in Los Angeles and drove him to his home 70 miles south of the city. The client was very concerned about the riots because his two daughters were scheduled to take their final exams the following day at a college located in the middle of the riot area. Both girls lived at home and commuted to school.

Because of the college's decision to remain open during the unrest, the two young women needed to take their exams or they would not graduate with their class. Carmine's client refused to let his daughters drive to school, nor would he be available to drive them there.

Did these college students miss their final exams? Did they fail to graduate with their class? The answer, of course, is *no* to both questions. Acting as a Family Advisor, Carmine provided a solution to his client's problem. He advised his client as follows:

> I do have a full day tomorrow after taking you to LAX, but I can move some of this business to my colleagues. There is no reason for your girls to miss their exams. Have them ready when I pick you up tomorrow. I'll take you to the airport before I drive them to school. I will escort each one to her classroom. And I'll wait until each one finishes her exam. Then I'll drive them right home. No one will harm them, not as long as I'm around. And, remember, I'll be armed and so will all the campus security people. It would be my pleasure to help you out. Standard rate, no extra charge. It's all part of the service.

Carmine's client was at a loss for words after listening to this proposal. Of course, he was thrilled when his daughters were returned home safely the following day. This influential executive now makes proactive referrals on Carmine's behalf.

As a "million mile" traveler, I can assure you that there are many outstanding limousine drivers. Yet most of them, even in this category, provide only a core set of services. However, the Carmines of the service industry are the ones whom opinion leaders/authors like yours truly go out of their way to endorse.

I hope you do not feel that publishing this letter is presumptuous of me. Carmine is likely to benefit from such publicity. His revenue may be enhanced by the influence network composed of the readers of this material. Carmine is based in Laguna Niguel, California. Call him before he is booked solid.

Sincerely,

Thomas J. Stanley, Ph.D.
Chairman

CHAPTER 8

THE PURCHASING AGENT

"He helped a client save $70,000 on the purchase of a new home. The client then told a dozen influential people about the 'fringe' benefits of dealing with this enlightened networker."

THE ACES OF ACES OF NETWORKING

There is one professional who networks like no one else I have interviewed. I designated him the Ace of Aces of Networking. One might logically conclude that this professional must be a high-performance securities broker or life insurance agent. No, he is not a distinguished member of a President's Sales Council for investment or insurance professionals. In fact, when I reveal the occupation that is printed on his business card, you will probably be very surprised. His occupation, as printed on his card, is Certified Public Accountant. Yes, he is a CPA!

Most sales and marketing professionals think that CPAs are more interested in number crunching and bean counting than in networking. In reality, however, more and more CPAs have been adopting this modern, proactive marketing approach. Still, CPAs are usually not very aggressive in selling their services. However, the CPA I am about to describe is by far the very best networker that I have come across. His case study will open the eyes of those who seek a more productive way to attract and retain affluent clients.

Mr. Art Gifford is the influence network Ace of Aces. He is the senior partner of a highly successful privately held accounting firm. He founded the firm just 11 years ago. Initially, it employed three CPAs. Today it employs 34 CPAs along with a support staff that comprises nearly 20 other types of employees. It has over 800 clients, and in addition it conducts 50 major corporate audits and more than 300 tax-consulting projects. The firm continues to grow and to attract affluent clients. The bulk of its clients are either owners of highly successful small and medium-sized businesses or high-performance, self-employed professionals.

ON BECOMING A NETWORKER

How did Mr. Gifford attract this business? All of his current clients became clients because of his network system. He has never had to make a sales call. He has never had to knock on doors. All of his clients were referred to him by members of his influence or referral network.

During the month prior to my first interview with Mr. Gifford, 37 affluent business owners and/or self-employed professionals were referred to him by members of his network. By the time my interview took place, 34 of those prospects had become his clients. Yes, networking has been very productive for Mr. Gifford. So productive, in fact, that he developed his own computer program to track his success in closing prospects and converting them into clients. It's a rather simple, but effective, program. There are six columns, labeled as follows: Prospect Name, Type of Business or Profession, Name of Person Who Made Referral (that is, the name of the person in the influence network), Referrer's Business and/or Occupation, Potential Income (the annual income that can be generated from the prospect), and Converted (whether or not the prospect has become a client). The program reflects Mr. Gifford's commitment to attracting new clients and making them members of his influence network.

Who are the members of that network? Mr. Gifford's current clients provide him with most of his referrals, but many other people with high credibility also make referrals on his behalf. The endorsements of these opinion leaders are very important in influencing the patronage habits of their friends and business associates. These opinion leaders include such categories as attorneys, physicians, psychologists, loan officers, business brokers, securities brokers, financial planners, insurance agents, real estate brokers, contractors, subcontractors, and owners of automobile dealerships. In all, Mr. Gifford's network, the Arthur 80 Network, comprises 80 or more categories.

Why do so many people go out of their way to make referrals on an accountant's behalf? No, Mr. Gifford does not buy products or services from all the members of his influence network. Actually, he buys from only a minority of these suppliers of products and services. He has gained an ever-increasing number of endorsements, referrals, and new clients because he provides more than core accounting services.

What is the meaning of the term *core accounting services*? For Mr. Gifford, it means the following: (1) high-quality accounting advice, consultation, and preparation; (2) rapid response to needs and inquiries; (3) timely answers to pressing problems; and (4) competitive prices.

One might think that Mr. Gifford or any other CPA who provides these services should have no trouble in attracting a large number of affluent clients. Yet this is not the case. Most of the CPAs in America provide high-caliber core accounting services. Thus the provision of core accounting services does not explain the wide variations in the number of prospects that CPAs are able to attract, convert to clients, and retain as clients.

OFFERINGS BEYOND THE CORE

To be successful in networking with the affluent, you do need high-quality core offerings. But you also need to offer members or potential members of your referral network something else. What is this "something else"?

Eight faces or dimensions underlie influence networks. Many outstanding networkers employ only one or two of these faces. However, Mr. Gifford employs all eight. The eight faces of networking are as follows:

1. *The Purchasing Agent.* Mr. Gifford is a skilled and experienced negotiator. He often negotiates the purchase of homes, automobiles, and other expensive items for members of his network.

2. *The Revenue Enhancer.* Mr. Gifford often sells products and services on behalf of his clients, his prospective clients, and other members or prospective members of his network.

3. *The Loan Broker.* Many people dislike shopping for loans. However, this Ace of Aces of Networking enjoys this task. He especially likes finding suitable credit sources for members of his network.

4. *The Talent Scout.* Most successful business owners and self-employed professionals are constantly searching for and screening new sources of supply. Mr. Gifford has a list of high-quality suppliers that is available to members of his influence network.

5. *The Publicist.* Mr. Gifford is more than a self-promoter. He often helps his network members to gain visibility, recognition, and credibility.

6. *The Mentor.* Mr. Gifford often acts as a Mentor to clients who have various career- and business-related problems.

7. *The Advocate.* How many accountants write unsolicited letters of support for the causes of their clients? Mr. Gifford does this all the time.

8. *The Family Advisor.* Many accountants tell their clients what it will cost to send their children to college. But first things first. Will these children have the high school credentials that they need in order to get into college? Mr. Gifford helps his clients with this problem.

In essence, Mr. Gifford provides advisory and referral services to clients, prospects, and other participants in his network. These services are particularly valuable to those clients who are achieving economic success. Economic success has many correlates, including the choice of a new home, the choice of a new car, the choice of a new boat, the choice of a private school and college, the choice of starting a new company, a new factory. In these regards, Mr. Gifford often plays the role of a skilled Purchasing Agent for the members of his network.

In many instances, as affluent people progress in life, they are in constant search of new opportunities to enhance their revenue and of suitable suppliers to help them achieve both business and personal goals. They refer business to Mr. Gifford because he helps them to solve more than their accounting problems. Remember that eight kinds of issues confront many successful people. That is why Mr. Gifford's network system has eight faces of offerings.

To fully appreciate how this system operates, one must look inside the minds of the clients, prospects, and other members of Mr. Gifford's network. The system has eight faces. In addition to providing the core accounting services, Mr. Gifford helps people along eight dimensions. These dimensions range from acting as a Purchasing Agent for network members to playing the role of Loan Broker for trusted clients.

Why does Mr. Gifford provide more than the core accounting services? First, he genuinely enjoys helping clients. Second, he discovered that clients will actively give endorsements and referrals to accountants who provide them with more than those services. And third, he has found that clients will remain clients of accountants who help them to solve problems that go beyond accounting issues.

Below are case studies that document Mr. Gifford's extraordinary ability to network. These case studies are organized along the eight faces or dimensions of influence networking.

THE PURCHASING AGENT

Currently, Mr. Gifford's influence network includes several owners/managers of automobile dealerships. Why would the owner of an automobile dealership go out of his or her way to make referrals on an accountant's behalf? Does Mr. Gifford have to purchase his automobiles from all of the dealers who join his network?

Mr. Gifford actually does not have to buy automobiles from every dealer who gives him a referral. This high-performance networker does, however, often act as an automobile Purchasing Agent for his clients. He has found that owners/managers of dealerships are likely to do business with a CPA who refers his accouting clients to them. *But isn't it a bit awkward to be hawking automobiles when you're supposed to be in the accounting business?*

Therein lies the problem: A too narrow definition of the offering. Remember that Mr. Gifford is not just an accountant. He is an apostle to his clients. He offers his clients solutions to problems that go beyond the core accounting services.

Consider the fact that many of Mr. Gifford's high-income clients hate to shop for/purchase/lease automobiles. Yes, they even hate to shop for luxury automobiles. Many of his clients will tell you that they don't have the time to do these things and that they do not have the stomach to play the negotiating game associated with getting a good deal on a luxury automobile.

Given this scenario, how do these people go about purchasing a new automobile? According to Mr. Gifford, the pro forma is very simple:

> Most of these high-income people walk into a showroom and walk out with an automobile. Because they never comparison shop, never do much homework studying the offerings, they typically pay top dollar for their automobiles . . . or they sign leasing deals that are no bargains.

How did Mr. Gifford determine that many of his clients and prospective clients had problems related to the purchase of automobiles? When clients or prospects walk into Mr. Gifford's office, he debriefs them. Before discussing accounting issues, he spends 15 minutes asking all "visitors" about their achievements and about their problems and needs. It's all part of his intelligence-gathering ritual.

As a result of this intelligence gathering, Mr. Gifford learned early in his career that many of his affluent clients, especially physicians with very high incomes, had a real problem in buying/leasing automobiles. Having learned this, what did the Ace of Aces of Networking do to help solve the problem? He acquired the information that he needed to become the Purchasing Agent of these affluent clients. Along these lines, he now maintains a list of selected dealerships that sell luxury automobiles and of the owners, sales managers, and top sales professionals of these dealerships. What dealerships are on this list? Dealerships of luxury automobiles that will give Mr. Gifford's clients significant discounts.

What happens when a client tells Mr. Gifford that he needs a new automobile? Mr. Gifford will either give a copy of the list to the client, or he will actually negotiate the purchase or lease himself—that is, he will do the shopping and the haggling over price on the client's behalf. Although Mr. Gifford offers to include the client in the negotiation via a three-way conference call, most clients prefer that he negotiate the purchase by himself.

> A wealthy client and his wife decided to buy two new Mercedes. . . .
> I said, "Before you do that, where are you buying them and how much are you having to pay for them?" . . . I said, "Let me make a phone call. Maybe I can save you some money." So I called up another dealership in the city and we ended up saving them in the neighborhood of $8,000 on two cars. And so through a phone call [to me], they didn't have to go through any more hassles. They went in and told them what they wanted. And within two or three days they were both in new cars and saved $8,000.

Upon request, Mr. Gifford will tell a client who has an automobile to trade in how much it is worth. For the benefit of his clients, he subscribes to several publications that list the estimated value of used automobiles.

Are all of the automobile dealers on Gifford's list his clients? No. But many are or will soon become clients. Since he "sends them business," most of them reciprocate by making referrals on his behalf.

Assume for a moment that you are the owner of an automobile dealership. You're in an extremely competitive business. More and more brands of luxury automobiles are being marketed. In addition, the tax on such automobiles is curtailing consumer demand for them. You're also very concerned about the future of your business, given the economic downturn our nation has been undergoing. All of these issues race across your mind each day.

In this situation, how would you respond to someone who wishes to share his clients with you? Imagine the impact that Mr. Gifford's message will have on you and on the other owners of dealerships that market luxury automobiles?

> Hello, Mr. Luxury Automobile Dealer. My name is Art Gifford. I'm a CPA with 850 affluent clients, 63 of whom are successful physicians/surgeons. These physicians/surgeons are especially prone to drive luxury automobiles. That's why I'm calling you. Several of them have asked me to negotiate the purchase of top-of-the-line touring sedans.
>
> I hope you don't mind dealing with an intermediary. These clients just don't have the time or interest in shopping.

I would like to work something out with you. I'm always looking for quality suppliers who can help my wealthy clients.

I'm sure your accountant and other suppliers of professional services send you business this way all the time. Am I correct? Well, if not, perhaps you should educate them or find new sources of supply.

If you're an intelligent automobile dealer, you will probably provide price and other concessions to Mr. Gifford's clients. After all, Mr. Gifford is in a power position. He has a significant influence on the automobile dealership patronage habits of many affluent consumers.

But your response to Mr. Gifford's proposal will probably not be limited to price concessions. What else can you do to make certain that he continues to share his clients with you? You can make referrals on his behalf. Think of all the suppliers from whom you purchase products and services. Suppliers provide you with everything from uniforms to cleaning agents. Perhaps they can utilize the services of an enlightened accountant. How many of their accountants ever referred business to them?

As an enlightened automobile dealer, you're likely to ask yourself a very basic networking question: *Why am I now dealing with an accountant who has never taken the initiative of referring his clients to my dealership?*

In his own subtle way, Mr. Gifford encourages the automobile dealers with whom he comes into contact to ask themselves that question. That is why so many of these dealers have recently asked him to supply them with accounting services.

In a follow-up interview, I discovered that Mr. Gifford's role as Purchasing Agent for clients was not limited to automobiles.

DR. STANLEY:

Mr. Gifford, do you ever act as a Purchasing Agent for items other than automobiles?

MR. GIFFORD:

Just this week I helped a client negotiate the purchase of a home.

DR. STANLEY:

Would you explain how this took place?

MR. GIFFORD:

In the process of speaking with a client, a neurosurgeon, I discovered that he was about to be taken advantage of. He was about to cut a deal with a building contractor . . . but he had no experience in dealing with contractors.

DR. STANLEY:

Was there a problem with the agreement that was being proposed?

MR. GIFFORD:

Many . . . many problems. The builder wanted to charge my client cost plus 15 percent for his fee. It's a bit stiff when you're talking about a $1.1 million home.

There were some other problems too. The builder also wanted my client to pay a 5 percent sales commission on the $300,000 lot where the home was to be built.

DR. STANLEY:

Who was the agent? Who owned the lot?

MR. GIFFORD:

The builder wanted to be the agent. . . . He also owned the lot. Nice deal. He proposed to my client that he pay a $15,000 sales commission on the lot. Plus 15 percent of the $1.1 million for his fee. That's $15,000, plus $165,000 for the builder fee.

DR. STANLEY:

Was the builder proposing to make $180,000 on this deal?

MR. GIFFORD:

That's right.

DR. STANLEY:

What advice did you give your client?

MR. GIFFORD:

Well, I told him that there should be no sales commission on the lot. Also, I thought that a 10 percent fee on the home would be more reasonable.

DR. STANLEY:

How did the neurosurgeon respond to your suggestions.

MR. GIFFORD:

He agreed with my recommendations.

DR. STANLEY:

Did he renegotiate the deal with the builder?

MR. GIFFORD:

He hates to hassle . . . doesn't have the time . . . and a lot of people, especially doctors, find it a bit degrading to have to quibble over price. So I offered to negotiate on his behalf.

DR. STANLEY:

Did you cut a better deal than the one the builder had proposed?

MR. GIFFORD:

I enjoy the negotiating process . . . especially when I'm representing a client. I do it all the time.

The first thing I did when I spoke to the builder was to cut out the 5 percent sales commission on the lot. So I saved my client $15,000 with just a few moments of effort.

DR. STANLEY:

What about the other part of the deal?

MR. GIFFORD:

After several conversations, the builder agreed to a fee of 10 percent instead of 15 percent.

DR. STANLEY:

How did you succeed in having the builder reduce his fee?

MR. GIFFORD:

I told him that the client gave me full authority to negotiate. Also, I reflected upon what other . . . ah, competing builders were currently charging in this economy. And added that several of my clients were home builders. They would be pleased, very pleased, to build a home of this value for 10 percent. He agreed . . . saved my client about $70,000.

DR. STANLEY:

Did you charge your client for this service? You did save him a lot of money.

MR. GIFFORD:

No. He is a client. He pays for our accounting and tax planning. Everything else is free. It's just part of our service. But I tell them, send me some business . . . tell your friends about us . . . referrals. That is how we do business.

DR. STANLEY:

One more question. Would a builder work for less than 10 percent?

MR. GIFFORD:

Yes. Especially in this market. But you never want to cut a deal so one-sided that the supplier, a builder or whoever, resents you. They want a fair deal. And remember, if you cut them to the bone, they will likely ignore your request to come back and repair things after the home is completed.

It's just the same as we spoke about auto dealers. Sure, I can cut deals so that they sell cars at cost . . . even below. But they will hate me and my clients. Just try and go back under these circumstances and see what kind of warranty work they will do. Or ask for a free loaner car. You cut them to the bone, and you can just about forget service after the sale. On the other hand, you can't sit by and let your own clients get ripped off. Nobody should have to pay 15 percent to build a home or list price of any automobile. Be fair and be balanced, and everyone will win in the long run.

THE REVENUE ENHANCER

Consider the example of a top-producing sales professional whom Mr. Gifford recently helped. The sales professional, Mr. Henry, was 27 years of age. In the year before he came into contact with Mr. Gifford, he generated a net annual income of approximately $200,000. Certainly, he was delighted with his productivity. But he was not at all delighted about paying nearly $80,000 in state and federal taxes (including social security payments).

Mr. Henry, a self-employed sole proprietor, had little in the way of deductions. His accounting specialist merely computed his tax obligations and filled out the appropriate tax forms. Mr. Henry received the very basic core accounting services. No proactive tax-planning advice was ever given or offered.

Despite his high income, Mr. Henry's heavy tax obligations took all the fun out of being a top producer. He told several of his clients, colleagues, associates, and friends about his dilemma. One of these contacts was a member of Mr. Gifford's influence network. This fellow, who endorsed Mr. Gifford, told Mr. Henry that he needed to deal with an expert in providing tax planning for highly compensated individuals.

But Mr. Henry also expressed another concern. He was worried about being able to match his outstanding sales performance in the upcoming years. Mr. Henry was not alone. Many great sales professionals often question their ability to continue producing record-breaking sales figures. Thousands of sales professionals, especially at the beginning of a new year, are very interested in discovering new ways to enhance their revenues. But who could help Mr. Henry meet/exceed his revenue goals?

Mr. Henry anticipated that Mr. Gifford would be able to help him solve his tax-related problems. But he did not realize that he also qualified for Mr. Gifford's revenue enhancement services.

Mr. Henry was self-employed. He sold financing/leasing packages for expensive medical equipment to hospitals, surgeons, and the like. How was he rewarded for connecting with the Ace of Aces of Networking?

More than 60 of Mr. Gifford's clients were surgeons! Several of his other clients managed and/or owned major health care facilities. *Some were owners of highly successful medical equipment companies!* These equipment companies usually had a difficult time selling their offerings unless they also provided customers with a leasing arrangement.

Mr. Henry became a client 10 minutes after he first sat down to speak with Mr. Gifford. During this initial meeting, Mr. Gifford asked him about all aspects of his business, his goals, and his problems. When Mr. Henry introduced the issue of generating sales of leasing packages, Mr. Gifford interrupted the conversation to telephone an important client of his accounting firm, the CEO and owner of a top-ranked medical equipment company. During the call, the CEO indicated that his company was looking for a high-quality supplier of leasing packages for clients who adopted its medical equipment systems and Mr. Gifford, in response, endorsed Mr. Henry as a quality supplier of leasing packages. Within six months, Mr. Henry generated more than $30,000 in net fees as a result of this endorsement.

But did Mr. Gifford help solve Mr. Henry's tax-related problems? He suggested that Mr. Henry fully utilize the nominal deductions and pension options of self-employed business owners. As a result, he saved Mr. Henry more than $10,000 in state and federal income taxes.

Solving tax-related problems is a core offering of CPAs. Many CPAs are experts in solving such problems. But Mr. Gifford also significantly enhanced Mr. Henry's revenue. If you were Mr. Henry, what CPA firm would you have patronized?

Currently, Mr. Gifford continues to enhance Mr. Henry's revenue. He provides Mr. Henry with endorsements and referrals to many of his surgeon clients. Mr. Henry reciprocates. Remember, Mr. Henry comes into contact with hundreds of highly compensated surgeons each year. What is the number one financial problem of most surgeons? Most surgeons will tell you that it is to reduce their tax liabilities. And many surgeons mention that problem to Mr. Henry. How does Mr. Henry respond? He immediately refers them to Mr. Gifford!

Thus Mr. Gifford recruited Mr. Henry not just as a client but also as an important information conduit and patronage opinion leader for hundreds of surgeons. Mr. Gifford will be rewarded many times over for having enhanced Mr. Henry's revenue. Mr. Henry now sells more than leasing packages. He also sells on behalf of the Ace of Aces of Networking.

Mr. Henry is only one of hundreds of clients/prospects whose revenues have been enhanced by Mr. Gifford. Does your accountant enhance your revenue? If not, you may wish to educate him about the benefits of the helping clients sell their offerings. If he is insensitive to such education, you may wish to find a more enlightened accountant.

How did Mr. Gifford determine that Mr. Henry was a quality supplier? If he proved to be a loser, Mr. Gifford might alienate good clients.

Like most great networkers, Mr. Gifford is a very good judge of character as well as sales performance. He is clearly streetwise. His street smarts first told him that Mr. Henry was a man of character and integrity as well as a very intelligent and productive service provider. He was able to confirm these impressions by closely examining Mr. Henry's financial records and tax data. Mr. Henry's sales figures did not lie, and neither did his tax returns. Moreover, a trusted client had referred Mr. Henry to Mr. Gifford.

During my third interview with Mr. Gifford, I noticed a stack of pictures of a home on his desk.

DR. STANLEY:

Mr. Gifford, from that stack of pictures I see on your desk, one might think you're about to purchase a new home. Am I correct?

MR. GIFFORD:

No. One of my clients, a builder, needs to sell it. It's been on the market for several months. . . . There are not a lot of buyers for a $900,000 spec home [home built and funded by a builder who "speculates" that a buyer will be found near or soon after its completion] in this economy.

DR. STANLEY:

Well, what, may I ask, are you doing with all those pictures of the home?

MR. GIFFORD:

I told the builder that I would try to help him move it. I'm sending [50] pictures of the home to some of my clients, the clients who have the means of purchasing a home of this type. A description of the home will also be enclosed with a little note from their accountant. It's a good home, and the price has been reduced by about $150,000. It will sell.

DR. STANLEY:

Do you mean that you sell homes for clients?

MR. GIFFORD:

I do it all the time. . . . It's part of the service. No charge for this service. The builder is a great client. He has done a lot for my business . . . referred many of his subs [subcontractors] to our accounting practice. I know builders in general are having a rough time. That's why I offered to help. You should have seen his eyes light up when I told him that I would send pictures of the home to my clients.

DR. STANLEY:

How did you know that this builder had a problem selling this home?

MR. GIFFORD:

I regularly call all my clients just to see how they are doing. It's an important part of the service that is provided. Most of my clients have some product or service that they sell. So accounting is not the only thing on their minds.

When a client tells me he needs to sell something and the market is resisting, I try to help. It's part of the service.

DR. STANLEY:

Have you sold many houses for your clients who are home builders?

MR. GIFFORD:

Well, let me put it this way. I have helped them sell at least several dozen homes since I started in this practice. That's millions and millions of dollars. And I'll bet that I have saved them well over a million dollars in the sales commissions.

DR. STANLEY:

Two more questions. How do you find time to do the selling function for others? And why do you take this upon your shoulders?

MR. GIFFORD:

You must make time to help clients. There are no eight-hour days in my business. It's often 9 A.M. to 9 P.M. for a six-day workweek.

And why do I get involved in selling for others? I'm good at it. Anyway, I enjoy helping my clients, and they appreciate what I do for them.

If you help clients "move product," in a down market especially, they will never forget you. They will tell dozens of their associates about our service. That's where all our new business comes from, referrals from clients.

DR. STANLEY:

Other than accounting services and homes, what else do you sell? [*Laughter.*]

MR. GIFFORD:

Everything from pension administration services, payroll services, and printing services to security systems, businesses and roofing contracting services!

Those who aspire to become great networkers must ask themselves this question: "Have I sent any pictures of my clients' products to my other clients in the past year?" It is likely that less than 2 percent of the so-called networkers in America have done so. What a fine opportunity sending out such pictures affords to all of those who aspire to become great networkers!

THE LOAN BROKER

Mr. Gifford's influence network contains more than a dozen credit suppliers. This is yet another reason why so many self-employed business owners and entrepreneurs deal with him. Take the role of a business owner for a few minutes. You're in your mid-50s. You have had a good track record in your business. You have never defaulted on a loan. Yet you are constantly being abused by the credit institutions you patronize.

Your suppliers of credit don't seem to trust you. They often ask for complete updates on your financial position. They demand that you document everything. Some suppliers that you have dealt with for years are now reluctant to lend you money. Other suppliers constantly call in your loans. And your most reliable supplier, the one that you have dealt since you founded your business, has just become a branch of a large national institution. Now the loan officers at this branch don't seem to know you. In fact, they told you yesterday that your application for commercial credit would probably be turned down.

You have discussed your credit-related problems with several colleagues. One of them has suggested that you visit his Loan Broker. The Loan Broker in this case is Mr. Gifford, CPA. Yes, in addition to his accounting duties, the Ace of Aces of Networking also helps his clients acquire credit.

Would you be willing to change accountants if doing so could solve your credit problems? Probably, because none of your suppliers ever helped you obtain a loan or offered to negotiate the terms of a loan for you.

If you're a client or a prospective client of a high-grade networker, ask to see his list of credit suppliers. Mr. Gifford was kind enough to share with me what he calls his "banker stack"—the business cards that make up the credit supply segment of his referral system. The first cards were those of bankers who, according to Mr. Gifford, provided commercial loans to business owners needing to borrow at least $500,000. These cards were followed by the cards of credit suppliers in the $1 million and over category.

How can you, a business owner, increase the probability of qualifying for a loan from one or more of these credit suppliers? While some uncertainty is always associated with obtaining credit, Mr. Gifford's endorsement is very valuable. How does he increase your odds of having a loan approved? He essentially says this to a bank officer:

> John Smith is a valued client of mine. He should be given a loan based not only on his current financial record but also on my estimate of how well he and his business will be doing in the future.

It is very important for credit suppliers to be sensitive to Mr. Gifford's endorsements. If they do not heed his advice and provide loans to selected members of his network, he will expel them from the network and never again refer any of his 850 clients to them. Of course, credit suppliers that are part of his network reciprocate. They often provide significant referrals to Mr. Gifford.

What kinds of credit suppliers may be found in Mr. Gifford's network? One of these credit suppliers is a senior officer of a private bank that provides services from A to Z for affluent professionals. This bank gives the client an opportunity to interact with its most senior bank officers. That's its main selling point.

Another credit supplier in Mr. Gifford's network is an officer of a major bank. This bank has a division that focuses on high-income physicians and surgeons. The bank wants to lend these individuals the money they need for both personal and business purposes.

Mr. Gifford's network also includes officers of major banks that focus on the networking needs as well as the private banking needs of affluent professionals and business owners. The function of such officers is not only to provide credit and trust products but also to help bank clients gain access to other clients who can enhance their revenues.

One of the more interesting kinds of credit suppliers to whom Mr. Gifford refers clients specializes in providing both construction and permanent mortgages to self-employed people. Such people often find it difficult to obtain a mortgage. Most credit suppliers are not proficient in providing mortgage loans to this category of lender.

Other kinds of credit suppliers are also members of Mr. Gifford's network. Several of these credit suppliers are interested in attracting new business clients to their factoring and accounts receivable services.

The more enlightened credit suppliers often take the initiative of contacting Mr. Gifford. They wisely seek his endorsement of his clients' patronage habits with regard to credit institutions. However, Mr. Gifford is proactive. He often takes the initiative of contacting the senior officers of lending institutions. He aggressively recruits to his influence network credit suppliers whose advertisements express their willingness to lend money to self-employed business owners and professionals.

In many cases, such credit suppliers become part of Mr. Gifford's influence network. Some even become his clients. Most of the credit suppliers with whom he interacts will go out of their way to lend money to network members at rates below the norm. I asked Mr. Gifford whether he thought that his endorsement typically enabled his client to obtain a loan. Mr. Gifford's responded as follows:

> Absolutely. Because the bankers are not going to lend to someone who walks in off the street. They are not going to have near the faith and understanding about what's going on. But it's quite different if they would have a qualified professional state on their behalf that they know this person, that he has high ethics, is a blue-chip person, has no credit problem. I know if they [the clients] pay all their bills. I tell them this is the type of person who is going to be making twice the amount of money in three years. This is a blue-chip client.

The concept of loan brokering is very important to all who aspire to become extraordinary networkers. Therefore, an entire chapter (Chapter 9) details this topic.

THE TALENT SCOUT

Step inside the shoes of a very successful entrepreneur. Some weeks ago, you sold one of your divisions. You now have several million dollars in your bank account. So you and your family decide that it's time to build a dream house. But you have never built a home. You don't know a home builder or even a carpenter. But your accountant works closely with many home builders and subcontractors.

Yes. Mr. Gifford has yet another face—the face of the Talent Scout. He maintains a "talent list" made up of suppliers who he feels are qualified to serve his clients. Home builders and their subcontractors are but two of the categories of his talent list. Automobile dealers and credit suppliers, as discussed above, are two other categories. But there are many more.

What other categories of suppliers are part of Mr. Gifford's influence network? During an interview with him, I asked him this question. In answer, he opened the drawer of his credenza. It's a large credenza and a large drawer. That's a good thing because it contains *80*—yes, that is eight zero—stacks of business cards. All of these are the cards of network members, that is, people who, in Mr. Gifford's estimation, are qualified to supply his clients with products or services. Some members of the network are buyers of products and services. Some are both buyers and sellers.

Why so many categories of network members? Mr. Gifford's clients are affluent business owners and professionals. They often need a wide variety of suppliers. Think how many kinds of suppliers you might need if you contemplated building a new home? You would probably need more than 100 kinds.

Like many of Mr. Gifford's other clients, you are pressed for time and you dislike searching for quality suppliers. Since you're thinking about building a home, it is appropriate to focus for a moment on the talent category called residential home builders.

How would Mr. Gifford go about finding the talent you need? Isn't the choice of a residential home builder a risky one? Often, it can be. But, again, Mr. Gifford has three master builders on his talent list whom he recommends to clients. He recommends these builders because they possess the characteristics required in order to be placed on his network list. First, they are in a very sound financial position. Mr. Gifford knows that from their revenue figures and income tax returns. Second, they are held in high regard by other clients in the network who have used their services. Otherwise, they would not be members of the network.

Each of the three master builders works closely with dozens of suppliers and subcontractors. Many of these suppliers and subcontractors were referred to Mr. Gifford by the master builders. But what about your interest in having a new home built? Immediate access to the appropriate suppliers and subcontractors would be a valuable added dimension to the accounting services you're receiving.

What types of suppliers appear on Mr. Gifford's home construction/supply list?

- Appliance dealers
- Architects—residential
- Building construction/ materials dealers
- Cabinetmakers
- Carpet and Rug Dealers
- Driveway paving contractors
- Drywall installers
- Electrical contractors
- Fireplace installers
- Foundation/excavation construction
- Interior decorators
- Landscape architects
- Lawn maintenance specialists
- Lawn sprinkler installers
- Locksmiths
- Mortgage providers
- New construction contractors
- Painting contractors
- Plumbing contractors
- Real estate agents
- Remodeling contractors
- Roofing contractors
- Security system installers/monitors
- Swimming pool dealers/ designers
- Tennis court installers
- Tree surgeons

Several investment service providers are also part of Mr. Gifford's influence network. One is a highly successful financial consultant (FC) whose investment management service provides clients with access to America's top independent investment counselors.

Since Mr. Gifford's network rejects 99 percent of the "applications for admission" from financial consultants and advisors, readers may be interested in learning how Mr. Woodberry, the FC in this case, gained Mr. Gifford's endorsement.

Mr. Woodberry is an outstanding networker. His networking system is so simple, so logical, and so efficient that most of his competitors overlook it. Many of his clients are highly successful self-employed business owners and professionals. He typically asks each of these clients this question: "May I have your permission to send a copy of your monthly investment statements to your accountant?"

Mr. Gifford received one of these sets of statements. Thus, Mr. Gifford and Mr. Woodberry had a client in common even before they networked in concert.

What was Mr. Gifford's reaction when he received the statements? Remember, these statements documented the outstanding track records of the investment managers whom Mr. Woodberry represented.

Mr. Gifford met with Mr. Woodberry shortly after the investment statements were distributed. At the meeting, they discussed three issues and consummated a three-part agreement. First, Mr. Woodberry agreed to open an investment management account for Mr. Gifford. Second, both parties agreed to refer clients to each other. Third, both parties agreed to discount their fees for the services they provided to the clients that were referred to them in this manner.

Being included in Mr. Gifford's network has paid big dividends to Mr. Woodberry. During a one-year period prior to my first interview with Mr. Gifford, he gave Mr. Woodberry many important endorsements and referrals. How many clients with a net worth of more than $1 million did Mr. Gifford share with this FC? On average, 4 per month or nearly 50 in one year.

Almost all of these people eventually became Mr. Woodberry's clients. And, of course, Mr. Woodberry often reciprocated by referring business to Mr. Gifford.

THE PUBLICIST

It's time you played yet another role. You are now Mr. James E. Prince, a self-employed headhunter, also known as an "executive search professional." What are your needs? Certainly, those needs often transcend having your income tax forms prepared.

Head-hunting is a very competitive business, especially in your part of the industry. You make your living finding, screening, and recruiting top-quality sales and marketing professionals for both national and regional corporations. A growing number of headhunters have been attempting to compete with you. At the same time, many firms that in the past often used the types of services you offer are now doing much of their own recruiting.

Four days ago, you told your accountant, Mr. Gifford, about these problems. He listened attentively while you spoke. Did telling a good listener about your problems make you feel better, Mr. Prince? After all, talking about your problems is good psychological therapy.

However, you found out today that accounting services and listening were not the only offerings provided by the Ace of Aces of Networking. You received an important phone call this morning. The pro forma message delivered to you during that call came as a very pleasant surprise.

MR. PRINCE:

Hello. Prince Executive Search. James Prince speaking.

MR. MILLER:

Hello, Mr. Prince. Ed Miller calling. I spoke with your accountant yesterday—Art Gifford. He told me that you're quite an expert in the area of recruiting top sales and marketing professionals. Is this your specialty?

MR. PRINCE:

Yes, it is.

MR. MILLER:

Good. Art suggested that I call you. I'm the president of the marketing and sales managers club. Art contacted me with a great idea. All of our members are sales and marketing managers. We would enjoy having someone talk to us about what we are worth on the market today. Also, we would love to have someone enlighten us about how much we can expect to pay for a top sales professional. And we also need to know where the market is going for sales professionals and sales managers.

Can you help us?

MR. PRINCE:

In other words, you would like me to give a speech to your members. Is that your question?

MR. MILLER:

That is my question. We can have at least 100 managers in the audience. This might be good for your business. A lot of us spend money on recruiting quality sales managers and executives.

MR. PRINCE:

Is this topic some type of annual program theme?

MR. MILLER:

No. In spite of the need for such a program, we have never had someone with your background speak to us. Amazing, isn't it?

MR. PRINCE:

So that I just understand this a little better—whose idea was this whole thing?

MR. MILLER:

Your accountant's! It's a great idea.

MR. PRINCE:

How did you become acquainted with my accountant?

MR. MILLER:

He recruited me . . . asked me and some other salespeople to help raise money for the Little League and the high school's athletic program. We all worked well together. Now I'm a client. But I didn't mean to get off the topic. Are you interested in helping our membership? You will likely pick up some new clients from our group.

MR. PRINCE:

Let's get together and work out the details.

Mr. Gifford utilizes several broadcast media to promote his clients' offerings. These media range from providing speaking opportunities to having case studies published in newsletters. In fact, Mr. Gifford's firm recently established a CEO Breakfast Club. Once a month, several dozen CEOs who head up local or regional firms meet for breakfast and enlightenment. The enlightenment comes from the after-breakfast speeches. Who gives these speeches? Clients or prospective clients of Mr. Gifford's firm. And these speakers have considerable interest in marketing their offerings to the firms represented by the CEOs in the audience. Yes, the benefits of addressing this group can be significant. Perhaps one speaker said it best when he stated:

> It would take me six months to set up, let alone conduct, a sales interview with all of these people. And here they are all in one room. I'm the entertainment. Thank you, Mr. Gifford.

Although Mr. Gifford helps his clients in various ways, his one-on-ones or personal/word-of-mouth endorsements typically have the most influence on the demand for his clients' offerings. Mr. Gifford estimates that he makes several hundred such endorsements each year.

THE MENTOR

Playing the role of Mentor often solidifies the patronage habits that start-up entrepreneurs have with the accountant who guides them.

DR. STANLEY:

> What do you do for clients who are starting a new business from ground zero?

MR. GIFFORD:

> Well, the first thing we do is we have a new business start-up kit that's about a hundred pages long. It takes them through all the applications, many of the elections they need to consider. We make this available in an effort to attract new business to our firm. It's pretty broad and in depth in terms of many considerations that new businesses have. Of course, the first thing is you have to get a lawyer to get you incorporated. You need to get a good banking arrangement. And to be adequately capitalized. Most businesses are not adequately capitalized.

DR. STANLEY:

> Let's say I was starting in business. I'm not sure who I should deal with in terms of office supplies, a computer or copier system, who's

going to clean the office—things like that. Do they ask you for your list of approved suppliers?

MR. GIFFORD:

I take a more aggressive approach in trying to steer them in the right direction. I know a lot of people in these businesses, having been in business in the city for 25 years. And so I just take the initiative and say. I don't wait for them to ask. I just tell them. I tell them who the best suppliers are. They need this, this, and this. These are the people. Oh, you need a copier, a computer. These are the types of people you need to use. Let me tell you what my findings are. I think you can buy computers the cheapest here. If you need somebody, we have people that install, set up, and train—setting up your in-house system. We can sell you software. We can train your secretary or your wife to run it. Depends on what your needs are.

THE ADVOCATE

Mr. Gifford often plays the role of the Advocate. He supports the causes of his clients and his community. As a result, he has enhanced his reputation as well as his client base. Many of Mr. Gifford's clients are real estate developers. A growing number of real estate developers will become his clients.

Assume for a moment that you're a real estate developer and that tax law changes have been major impediment to the success of your business. But who cares about your problems? How many of your suppliers have been proactive in pushing for more favorable legislation?

DR. STANLEY:

Did you write letters protesting the tax laws that are harming real estate development?

MR. GIFFORD:

On several occasions. . . . Whenever it became very obvious to me that our lawmakers were missing the point, I fired off a series of letters . . . to the president . . . senators . . . representatives . . . local and state politicians regarding a number of things I thought needed to be corrected.

DR. STANLEY:

Have you played the role of Advocate for any causes other than those of your clients?

MR. GIFFORD:

I've been heavily involved in youth sports for the last 15 years . . . Little League, Pony League, the high school, athletic associations. I've been involved in the financial part . . . managing and raising funds to support these efforts.

DR. STANLEY:

Could you just give me some idea—when you say raising funds, what is it you actually do?

MR. GIFFORD:

Our Little League program . . . the baseball budget was $120,000 this year. And so we raised funds through the registration, through advertisements, through promotional type of programs. Candy bar sales. The football program had an $85,000 budget.

DR. STANLEY:

How much money do you think you raised in total?

MR. GIFFORD:

Over the years, it's got to be in the neighborhood of, conservatively, $200,000 or $300,000.

DR. STANLEY:

On that basis, did you meet any new clients or people who helped you with referrals?

MR. GIFFORD:

Absolutely. Absolutely. Through rubbing elbows, you come to find out that the people making the money have the interest in participating in the community. Many of those people became clients.

DR. STANLEY:

Could you take me through one or two scenarios of how that happened? You're working with these people, and what happened?

MR. GIFFORD:

Let's take the case of Mr. Edson. We worked together at the high school athletic association. And we solicited funds together for the athletic association for a period of about two years. When it came time for him to form his new business, he asked me to assist him in getting incorporated and handling his financial affairs. And it's been a very good client relationship. We've helped his business grow. We helped him negotiate the sale of the division. We just helped him locate a line of credit with the bank. It's been a good relationship.

THE FAMILY ADVISOR

For a few moments, pretend that you're an affluent business owner and that you have three children. Your oldest, Fawn, is a high school senior. Your youngest, Amy, is a high school freshman. And your son, John, is a high school sophomore.

You have over $100,000 in education funds for each of your children. Yes, you were smart to accumulate that money. But don't be too quick to take all the credit. Ten years ago, you were wise enough to hire the Ace of Aces in Networking as your accountant. During your first meeting, he asked you: "How are you going to finance your children's education?"

You answered in a manner that many others in your position thought appropriate. Your plan was no plan at all. After all, you had a very high income. You felt that you could easily pay for tuition and fees out of your current income. But your accountant quickly disproved your assumption by telling you how much it would cost to educate three children.

Ten years ago, Mr. Gifford estimated that you would need $120,000 to fund the college education of each of your children. You were shocked to learn that you would be unable to fund your children's college education via your current income.

Today you have the money you need to cover the college costs of your children. However, you now have another problem. This problem is quite common among the children of the affluent population. Amy and John are not performing well in high school. Their guidance counselor has even had the audacity to suggest that they "may not be college material."

What good does it do to accumulate funds for college if your children are not college bound? Mr. Gifford has often helped clients who face problems of this type. He is, among other things, a Family Advisor. In playing this role he provides his clients with a list of key contacts at private high schools that specialize in "reorienting students." These schools, which some refer to as "academic boot camps," mold underachieving students into college material. They have outstanding records in "reorienting" academic underachievers. They are part of Mr. Gifford's network.

How did Mr. Gifford's list of academic boot camps originate?

MR. GIFFORD:

Basically, we've had two kids come up through the ropes and we've seen most of the problems parents have. And so we're in tune with these kinds of things and with these parents that are maybe a few years younger and maybe haven't had the experience in dealing with academic problems.

DR. STANLEY:

Did you develop from clients' and your own experience a list of approved schools?

MR. GIFFORD:

We talked to a number of people. We have several contacts . . . a number of sources. The schools are well thought of across the region. We have a lot of experience when it comes to dealing with parents, dealing with children, having been so involved with that over the years. I assess needs and different opportunities. When someone comes to me to do their tax return, not only do I prepare the tax return, but I'm probably going to end up spending an hour or two to explore these other avenues. Those who have already taken the step tell us if they are pleased with the schools.

Mr. Gifford provides yet another service. To illustrate, once again take the role of the affluent client. Several colleges have recently accepted your oldest child, Fawn. However, she was rejected by the college that she listed as her first choice. This scenario, which actually took place recently, demonstrates the benefits of patronizing suppliers who have an affinity with the admissions directors of select colleges and universities. Affinity of this kind, in fact, is a function of the role of such suppliers in helping colleges by providing them with fund-raising support and related assistance.

MR. GIFFORD:

Well, we've had several experiences at _____ _____ University. I had one client who called me and said that his daughter had difficulty getting in. And I wrote a letter down there, and she got accepted.

DR. STANLEY:

Did you write a letter to the admissions director?

MR. GIFFORD:

To the admissions director. And she got accepted about two weeks later.

DR. STANLEY:

Did you call first, or did you just write a letter?

MR. GIFFORD:

Just wrote a letter.

DR. STANLEY:

What did you say? Could you tell us briefly?

MR. GIFFORD:

Basically, I just attested to the quality of the family and the brothers and sisters and what they've accomplished. And indicated that I'd been contributing and I was a professional person, and I gave her a letter of reference highly recommending that they accept her.

DR. STANLEY:

How did this all come about?

MR. GIFFORD:

The client told me he had a problem. He knew where his daughter wanted to go. He called me and asked if I'd be willing to do it. And I said I'd be happy to.

DR. STANLEY:

Have you ever written any letters of recommendation before?

MR. GIFFORD:

Lots of them.

As a Family Advisor, Mr. Gifford provides such services as

tuition fund planning, referrals to academic advisors and boot camps, and endorsements of applicants. It's all part of the service, service beyond the core. And service beyond the core generates significantly more endorsements and referrals than do traditional accounting services.

THE RULES OF NETWORKING

Mr. Gifford's influence network system is based on a set of rules that he developed more than a decade ago. Every sales professional, marketing professional, and new business development officer will benefit from reviewing these rules.

Rule 1: Identify those professionals who already have an influence network composed of the types of people that you want as clients.

Be very selective in choosing the professionals, especially the CPAs, with whom you network. Also, in choosing a CPA or any other supplier with whom to network, interview several before making your final decision. Review their credentials, that is, their core credentials—their ability to provide high-quality services. But equally important, examine the composition of their influence networks.

Many suppliers/professionals, even some successful CPAs, have no influence network. They are purely and simply people who provide core products and services. In today's age of influence and networking, it is critically important that you target people who will provide you with revenue-enhancing potential.

If you wish to sell your offerings to surgeons, for example, consider targeting certified public accountants whose clients include surgeons. Telephone the surgeons you wish to serve, and ask them for the names of their accountants, attorneys, and other suppliers/service providers. Then consider networking with those accountants, attorneys, and so on. What if you are an attorney yourself and you wish to sell your services to real estate developers? Then you should patronize an accountant, such as Mr. Gifford, who has many real estate developers as clients.

Why did I use surgeons and real estate developers in these

examples? Because many of them are among Mr. Gifford's current clients. Early in his career, he developed, almost intuitively, a picture of the anatomy of the wealth/commerce that existed within his trade area. Surgeons and real estate developers were two of the five segments that he targeted at that time.

But how did he attract so much business from these segments? Quite simply, he developed a customized network that contained most of the attorneys/specialists who represented many of the successful surgeons and real estate developers in his trade area.

Your revenue can be greatly enhanced if you interface with professionals who have large numbers of clients that you wish to attract. It pays to shop around. You will find that the very best service providers, whether they be lawyers or accountants, are not only influential members of an influence network but also highly skilled specialists. They offer particular types of specialized services to clients in particular occupational/industrial classifications.

Rule 2: Align yourself with those who will actually make you part of their influence network.

Determine whether the CPA, the attorney, other supplier, and even the physician whom you are considering targeting will make you part of their network. Often, professional service providers are both patronage opinion leaders and conduits of information about the business opportunities encountered by their clients. Most influential suppliers will be delighted to accept your referrals and to have you as a client. But some of these suppliers may be reluctant to place you on their influence team! So it is important to determine right up front whether they will place you in their influence network.

Initially, you should ask selected suppliers, especially CPAs and attorneys, whether you can become part of their influence networks on a conditional or probationary basis. It makes no sense to become a client of high-performing professionals who have marvelous influence networks if you are excluded from those networks. The time to determine that, however, is before you start doing business with these opinion leaders. Therefore, do not be afraid to ask these professionals, or any other potential suppliers, for references. Then take the time to ask their clients whether they have received network-related benefits.

Rule 3: Be willing and able to contribute to the network.
No. You don't have to purchase offerings from each member of your network. But always bring something to the party. Be willing to trade referrals. For every referral your accountant gives you, for example, you should be willing to reciprocate. But what happens if you are just a newly minted sales professional, a newly minted marketing professional, or a newly minted new business development officer? You're at ground zero. What can you do in that case? You really don't have any clients to trade with patronage opinion leaders.

There are numerous instances in which the "Abe Lincoln story" actually works. In fact, it was very effectively utilized by Mr. Gifford in his salad days. Even if you are at ground zero, there is nothing wrong with approaching a highly successful professional who is the kingpin of an influence network. Admit that you are starting out; state that you are honest, that you are hardworking, that you are bright, and that you have no clients. However, also point out that because of your integrity, hard work, and intelligence, you will accumulate clients as you progress through your career life cycle.

Many people who will ultimately become clients of a seasoned networker are in the early stages of their career life cycle. These rookies share your current problem of bringing little to the table. Convince the networkers you wish to influence that you would like to provide these rookies with your service or product—that you will serve them, work with them, and cherish their business despite the fact that they have very little business to give.

You can also use some of the information that you have obtained from the preceding material to teach even seasoned professionals and business owners how to network with other successful people. There is always room to do that. Do not be afraid to educate, persuade, and influence people who are older and more successful than you. You will gain endorsements and much goodwill for doing this.

Some novice sales professionals have gained important endorsements by using yet another novel approach. Before attempting to join an influence network, they schedule several dozen appointments with affluent business owners. Then they visit selected/influential CPAs, lawyers, and other types of professionals. During such a visit, the novice requests endorsements and referrals to the members of the professional's influence network. However, the novice makes this request only after telling the influential professional what he or she wants to hear: *"Here is a list of the affluent business owners with whom I have appointments next month. I plan to visit several dozen of these prospects each month. I would be delighted to endorse you and your firm."*

Perhaps Mr. Gifford said it best when I asked him how he recruits networkers:

> One of the biggest compliments you can give somebody is a business referral. . . . You can see the light in his eyes. I had lunch with a prospect today. I asked him to give me a dozen of his business cards. . . . Told him right up front . . . I'm happy with the professionals I deal with and those who serve my clients. But . . . sometimes, philosophically or personalitywise or whatever, [one of those professionals] may not get along well with a client. If that situation occurs, I'll be happy to give my clients your cards. . . . I'll give you a shot. Of course, this fellow was part of a quality operation. . . . We have checked him out. He's well thought of by his clients and his employer.

Rule 4: Be patient and have a long-term view of the benefits of creating an influence network.

One of the major stumbling blocks for people who are attempting to become members of influence networks relates to what I call "the short-term view versus the long-term view." Most people fail in their attempts to sell via networking because they are impatient. It takes years to develop an influence network, and it takes years to become a viable member of such a network. Keep that in mind. You may see little or no progress for six months or even a year. But if you keep smiling and if you are persistent in persuading members of the influence network, they will respect you. It takes time. But with patience you will become a member.

Rule 5: Spend more time with key centers of influence than you do with your peers, colleagues, and competitors.

Spend more time affiliating with members of important influence networks, with members of key occupational groups such as private practice attorneys and CPAs. Spend more time with these people than you spend with fellow sales professionals. Spend more time with patronage opinion leaders than you spend with the people in your own industry's affiliation group.

There is nothing wrong with reading the literature that emerges from your own industry. There is nothing wrong with attending meetings sponsored by your own industry's trade association. However, most of the salespeople in this country fail to become great sales professionals because they focus more on their own industry, their own competitors, their own literature than on the industry they are targeting.

Why not start reading journals that contain information about the important players in the professions of accounting and law? These are the people on whom you should focus. They can often generate business for you by making just one phone call.

Rule 6: Solicit business on behalf of the members of your influence network.

Solicit and obtain business for members of your influence network. Remember, it is often easier to sell prospects products and services other than your own. When visiting prospects, casually mention the names of one or more of the accountants, one or more of the attorneys, one or more of the loan officers who are members of your influence network. Do not be afraid to make referrals on behalf of these members. Once again, even if you're at ground zero and you don't have any clients, you can still make referrals on behalf of people whom you're trying to influence. And make sure that these referrals are documented by follow-up letters that you send not only to your prospects but also to the people for whom you make referrals. These people will be indebted to you.

This method offers a good way to communicate with these influential people. It implicitly tells them, "I want to be part of your network. I want to help. I understand your need for revenue enhancement, and I know how to play the game of marketing very well." They will view you not only as an intelligent marketer but also as someone who wants to become a solid member of their influence network.

Rule 7: Act as an intelligence officer and publicist for the members of your influence network.

At least once a month, contact selected members of your influence network, including important accountants and attorneys. Write to them. Send them notes. Cut out articles that may help them with their business. Send them case studies from trade journals that identify people who are coming into significant amounts of money. Show them that you understand how euphoria relates to changes in patronage habits among affluent business owners and professionals. In other words, become their intelligence officer.

When you contact a member of your influence network, you may wish to include a copy of a letter that you have sent to local business editors and reporters. What letter? The letter you wrote encouraging them to print stories about that member. Here again, what you're doing is tapping the network member's need to have his achievements, his euphoria recognized by the local business and trade press. The trade press in this case is the press of the trade that the network member is attempting to penetrate.

Rule 8: Entertain network members.

The most productive marketers regularly entertain members of their influence network. You should enjoy interacting with your fellow networkers. You should engage in recreational activities with them. You should find the game of networking not only interesting and exciting but also enjoyable. Too often, people fail in approaching the affluent market because they spend 90 percent of their recreational time, apart from family requirements, with people from their own industry. For example, Mr. Gifford stated:

> Personally, I spend a lot of time with people who are referring opportunities. I go to dinner with them and their wives, play golf with them. I have lunch with them in a business setting. I just get to know them on a personal basis so they have a means to trust my judgment and my way of thinking.

Isn't it better to consider asking members of important influence networks to play golf, fish, hunt, or go to a ball game with you than always to interact on a social level with people in your own affinity groups? These people have little or no influence, and they have no ability to provide you with revenue enhancement.

Rule 9: Interface with several centers of influence.

Do not limit yourself to interfacing with only one accountant or one attorney. Again, you do not have to purchase services from 20 CPAs or 15 attorneys or a dozen auto dealers to gain their endorsements. What you have to do is to make these people aware of the fact that you can enhance their reputation, their business, and their revenue by providing them with new clients. Do favors for them. Many of them would value your participation in trade meetings and conferences at which their own clients may be present. Offer to provide them with speakers. Offer to provide speakers, for example, to the law firms that you are attempting to influence, to their affinity groups, and to the affinity groups that they are prospecting.

Rule 10: Endorse only those who are qualified to provide the core product or service.

Never make a referral with a view only to your own ultimate profit. In other words, never make a referral on behalf of someone who cannot do the job. Otherwise, you will lose your credibility among the members of your influence network and jeopardize your position as a member of the network.

Rule 11: Network for higher causes.

Why not assemble your newfound knowledge about networking and volunteer to donate your intellect? Why not approach some local charities and apply your skills to their fund-raising campaigns or their efforts to attract volunteers? You could tap your own influence network, or you could provide seminars to solicitors for these charities. Many of Mr. Gifford's best clients first came into contact with him via his fund-raising activities.

Remember, you look your very best in the eyes of both prospects and clients when you are giving away your intellect for free. You would be amazed at how many sales professionals never offer their marketing and sales intellect for volunteer purposes. Surprisingly, this continues to be the case despite the fact that the highest concentrations of affluent prospects can often be found in charitable organizations that seek to help those who are far from affluent.

Rule 12: Recruit, recruit, recruit new members to your influence network.

Always be on the lookout for new members for your network. For example, when sales professionals solicit your business, listen to their messages and debrief them. They may be potential clients for you and other members of your network. At the very least, they may be valuable sources of information about new revenue sources and new market opportunities. Mr. Gifford receives much of his information about the top-ranked suppliers via the debriefing process. He regularly debriefs laywers and brokers of various sorts, including business brokers, investment advisors, stockbrokers, and real estate brokers. These people are constantly searching for opportunities throughout the business community.

Recruiting suppliers/clients for the current members of one's network is a professional and productive type of selling. The best way to initiate a relationship with potential clients is to first address their needs—new sources of supply and more customers. Yes, the old adage still holds true: *It is better to give than to receive.*

ENDNOTE

Networkers with Mr. Gifford's skills are rare. So it may be difficult to find such a networker within your trade area. If you can't find one, why not train selected professionals and other types of suppliers to network in the Gifford style? Yes, teach these people to fish. They will reciprocate by sharing their catch. You now have considerable knowledge about how the Gifford network system operates. Offer to share that knowledge with clients, prospects, and other types of potential network members. Teaching is a noble profession. It is also an ideal way of attracting, conditioning, and retaining clients.

CHAPTER 9

THE LOAN BROKER

"He who obtains credit for clients will always have clients."

THE NEED FOR CREDIT

You're a professional. You want to do more for your clients than provide them with your core services. Most of your clients are affluent business owners and self-employed professionals. Many of your most important clients have told you that they have a recurrent need for credit, that they often find it difficult to obtain loans in a timely manner, and that they are now paying high interest rates and related fees on loans.

What you have learned from these clients is in harmony with my own research findings. Affluent business owners and self-employed professionals are typically heavy users of both commercial and personal credit. There is a very clear, positive relationship between income and credit use. The average American household spends about $700 in interest on the money lent to it by various types of business organizations. The average household in the $50,000–$100,000 income category spends over $6,000 annually for interest on loans, while the average household in the $1 million or more income category spends more than $150,000 annually for interest on loans.

The attitude research I have done also documents the importance of credit services to the affluent. In a recent study of millionaires, for example, I found that credit services were rated as the most important services offered by financial institutions. Moreover,

I found that the importance attached to credit services monotonically increases with both income and net worth.

Can you leverage these credit needs and attitudes of the affluent? Yes! You can play the role of informal Loan Broker for your clients and your prospective clients. And you're in an excellent position to play this important role. Accountants, lawyers, financial consultants, insurance agents, financial planners, even physicians and dentists can learn how to play this role. And those who do learn how to help the affluent with their credit-related needs will reap important benefits. They will retain their current clients, and they will attract an ever-increasing number of valuable new clients.

You should provide more than core services. You should go further and proactively make referrals on behalf of clients who need the services of high-grade credit specialists. If you do this, business owners and self-employed professionals will be more likely to patronize your firm than those of your competitors. Why? Because you demonstrate a deeper understanding and make a greater contribution to solving their problems than do your competitors. You find, evaluate, and help secure quality credit sources for your clients. And if these credit sources are truly enlightened, they will refer their clients and associates to your organization. This reciprocity is the highest form of marketing and selling. It is, in essence, high-performance networking.

Where can one find credit sources for clients? Before answering that question, it is important to note that many high-performance networkers have their Rolodexes filled with the names of quality suppliers. Those suppliers include credit suppliers. The credit suppliers in your Rolodex are the ones that are inclined to offer preferred credit terms to the networker's clients.

High-grade networkers should constantly search for quality credit sources. Advertisements of credit providers appear in almost every issue of your local business/commercial newspaper. These advertisements often indicate that the sponsor and its senior executives are strongly committed to lending money to business owners, to professionals, and to other self-employed individuals. As a pro forma of the type of credit-oriented advertisements that the networker should look for, consider the following example:

The River Bank

Many banks promise you good service, and then hand you over to their support staff. But you need credit decisions, not just support. At *The River Bank* you will get decisions. You will work with experienced bank officers—highly skilled and seasoned professionals who will manage all your business and personal accounts.

The River Bank is committed to the business owner and to the self-employed professional. If you're shopping for a line of credit, your account executive will arrange it for you. If your schedule makes it difficult for you to come to the bank, you can conduct business with your account officer at your office.

Whatever it takes, your bank officer will get credit decisions made rapidly and with a minimum of red tape.

The River Bank is owned and managed by local business leaders with a proven track record of helping successful businesses and professional practices grow.

For additional information about this fully customized relationship orientation to banking, contact our president, Lee Ajax, at 963-5521. *The River Bank's* appreciation of your needs is at the very top of this unique organization's philosophy of business.

The theme of this advertisement, which appeared in a locally distributed business periodical, is quite clear. The River Bank wants to lend money to business owners and self-employed professionals. Seven other credit-oriented financial institutions placed similar advertisements in the same issue of the business periodical and six loan brokers placed classified advertisements in that issue.

Thus, despite the strong demand for credit among the affluent, there is often significant competition among lenders to the affluent. Given this situation, how would the typical credit professional (loan officer/broker) respond to your message, Mr. Housham, CPA?

PRO FORMA NETWORKING DIALOGUE

MS. HELEN GROSS:

Good morning. Mr. Ajax's office.

MR. ROBERT HOUSHAM, CPA:

Good morning. I would like to speak with Mr. Ajax. Is he available?

MS. HELEN GROSS:

Well, he is on the phone right now and has another caller on hold. I can have him return your call. Let me take down your name and a few other items of information. He will call you right back.

MR. HOUSHAM:

I am Robert Housham. I'm a certified public accountant here in town.

MS. GROSS:

Most of our clients are either business owners or self-employed professionals. To speed things up a bit, can you tell me if you're facing a deadline in terms of having a loan approved?

MR. HOUSHAM:

Well, not exactly. You see, many of my clients are also either successful business owners or self-employed professionals. Very often they are in need of credit, and just as often they ask me about the best source of credit in our community. Some of these people need $1 million mortgages. Others, in fact, most, need commercial lines of credit for the purchase of equipment and for inventory. That's why I'm calling. I noticed in the latest issue of *City Business* that your organization is committed to serving the credit needs of business owners and professionals. If that's the case, I would like to recommend your services to my clients.

MS. GROSS:

Oh, I see. Mr. Ajax would be very interested in speaking with you. Can you hold? Let me put a note in front of him. Please hold.

MR. LEE AJAX (president, The River Bank):

This is Lee Ajax, Mr. Housham. Ms. Gross, my assistant, tells me that your clients may need a new source of credit.

MR. HOUSHAM:

I have many successful clients. Most are business owners or self-employed professionals. Many need loans for new equipment, inventory, and even construction/permanent mortgage loans. That's why I'm calling.

I saw your advertisement in *City Business*.

MR. AJAX:

Well, by all means have your clients contact me. We are committed to this community.

MR. HOUSHAM:

My clients really hate to shop for loans. In spite of high performance within their own disciplines, they are not very sophisticated when it comes to borrowing money. I'll be honest with you, Mr. Ajax. Many of them have been burned badly by so-called good credit terms. They are really gun shy. So I have volunteered to act as their credit mentor. I promised them that I would find them the best sources of credit available in our community. That's why I'm calling you. They don't have the time to do this themselves.

MR. AJAX:

And, Mr. Housham, you're their accountant?

MR. HOUSHAM:

Yes, that's right. Finding suitable credit sources is just part of my commitment to clients. I do much more for them than their accounting.

MR. AJAX:

I must say you have a novel approach to serving clients.

MR. HOUSHAM:

Your organization will probably fit the criteria for my "short list of preferred credit suppliers" designation. If it does, I can send you several dozen clients a year who have significant credit needs. These are people with integrity. I know my clients. I have their financial data. They are high-caliber people.

MR. AJAX:

We will do anything we can to gain your endorsement. I'm sure that your clients appreciate the effort that you make on their behalf. It's quite unusual for someone to take this much interest in clients.

MR. HOUSHAM:

Well, I'm sure that your accountant, as well as your other suppliers, go out of their way to refer business to you.

MR. AJAX:

I have to admit that the credit mentor role is new to me.

MR. HOUSHAM:

If your current suppliers are not sending you a lot of business on a regular basis, maybe you should be looking for a new set of suppliers.

MR. AJAX:

You may be right.

MR. HOUSHAM:

Well, Mr. Ajax, I know you're busy. Can you send me a dozen of your business cards, brochures, and loan applications. These applications should be for commercial credit lines. But also include a half-dozen construction/permanent mortgage applications. You know, whenever my clients hit the big time, they want to build something. I'll work with a client next week in putting together the proper documentation. Then perhaps the three of us can get together.

MR. AJAX:

I would be delighted to work with you and also earn your endorsement. I'll have the materials couriered over to your office today.

MR. HOUSHAM:

I look forward to it. I'll be back to you next week.

MR. AJAX:

It will be my pleasure. I appreciate your interest.

The How-To's of Becoming a Loan Broker

In order to benefit from your role as Loan Broker for clients, you should give several factors serious consideration. Just calling yourself a Loan Broker and promising clients access to special credit deals are not sufficient. You must deliver on your promises. And you should leverage your role as Loan Broker aggressively in terms of retaining current clients, attracting new clients, and generating an increase in referrals and endorsements among your targeted audience.

1 *Be proactive.* Be aggressive in seeking the best sources of credit for your clients and your prospective clients. This activity should be part of your overall job description.

2 *Play the role of an intelligence officer.* Train yourself to find credit sources. Become a focused reader of advertisements for credit sources that appear in business periodicals. Also examine the yellow page directories for your trade area. You are likely to find more than a hundred credit-oriented organizations that propose to lend money to business owners and self-employed professionals.

Most important, debrief your clients, prospects, and other key informants about their views concerning the "really big question." What organizations/loan officers have you found that are serious about lending money at competitive rates? This question should be part of your prospecting dialogue when you're speaking with dozens, even hundreds, of clients and potential clients each month. Those who express an unfulfilled need for credit are likely candidates for your loan brokerage service.

3 *Keep names and scores.* A top-notch networker may have several dozen credit sources filed in his Rolodex. In addition to the names, addresses, and phone numbers of these sources, other information is important. Such information includes the types of loans that the credit source provides—for example, accounts receivable loans, commercial loans under $500,000, commercial loans over $500,000, commercial mortgages, equipment leasing, jumbo mortgages, construction loans/permanent mortgages, swing loans, and unsecured lines of credit.

It is also important to keep score. A highly skilled networker will use his Rolodex entries as score cards. For each credit source, he will indicate on its Rolodex card the number of referrals (clients/ prospects) that were made to the source and the number of loans that were approved by the source. Keeping score is very important in maintaining and enhancing one's influence network. Score keeping is the basis for rewarding those credit sources that agree to lend money to clients. Reward them by referring an increasing number of clients to them.

4 *Act and think like the head of a trade association.* Both trade associations and professional societies often provide their members with access to special price agreements with selected suppliers. It is not unusual for members of these affinity groups to receive discounts on the purchase of office supplies, magazine subscriptions, and rental cars. Yet rarely do these affinity groups help their members obtain credit. Networkers can capitalize on this void.

You're a private practice accountant, a financial consultant, or a life insurance sales professional who has been in the business of targeting the affluent for five or more years. You probably have a hundred or more clients, and you may have as many as several hundred clients. Begin to think of yourself as the head of your clients' trade association. You now have power, the power to represent many of the "members" of this trade association in their negotiations for preferred loan rates and the like.

This is your bargaining chip. You explain to credit suppliers that you have a great many clients with a strong propensity to borrow and that your referral, your endorsement can generate considerable business for "trade association approved" credit suppliers.

5 *Be competitive and street smart.* Most successful credit suppliers respect high-quality networkers. Why? Because these credit suppliers immediately see the benefit of relating to those networkers who will bring them a steady stream of referrals. They also understand that you're street smart. You will ultimately benefit from your efforts to help clients find quality sources of credit. Clients will be attracted to people who help them meet their credit-related needs. By the same token, credit suppliers will feel obligated to, even dependent on, networkers who act as opinion leaders for their own affinity group, that is, their client base.

But be competitive. Tell each credit supplier in a subtle way that you have a *list* of preferred credit suppliers. It is absolutely essential for you, the enlightened networker, to explain to credit suppliers that your Rolodex contains the names of several of their competitors. The issue of competition is just as important in gaining good credit terms for clients as your ability to act as a patronage opinion leader for dozens, even hundreds, of successful business owners and self-employed professionals.

6 *Succeed even from ground zero.* So what if you're just starting out in a career called "in the service of the affluent"? Begin to
network with credit suppliers early in your career. Call or visit them
in person. Tell them that your goal is to serve the same affluent
clients that they target. Show them your appointment book, an
appointment book that documents your commitment to prospecting
affluent business owners and self-employed professionals. Legiti-
mize yourself by leveraging the prestige of your prospects.

Ask each credit supplier for a dozen or more of their brochures/
business cards. Why? So that you can share them with your prospects who express a need to borrow! This practice will demonstrate
to both prospects and credit sources that you are a gifted and
professional networker. Yes. Revenue enhancement is precisely
the theme credit suppliers wish to hear. And how unique it is to
speak of the credit needs of prospects instead of only your me-me-
me message.

7 *Focus on prime targets.* Newly established credit suppliers
are often the most likely to say yes to requests for loans. The term
"newly established" can designate a start-up organization or one
that has recently expanded its operation into your geographic terri-
tory. Such credit suppliers are often willing to "go the extra yard"
in order to gain a foothold within a community. Just think how you
would respond to a call from a networker if your organization were
starting from ground zero. Start-up credit suppliers would probably
feel obligated/indebted to a networker who calls and offers them an
endorsement and access to his clients. They may even lend money
to clients of such a networker who have only marginal credit ratings!
Read advertisements and news reports in your local business periodicals that identify credit suppliers that are in the start-up mode.

8 *Understand the value of reciprocal references and endorsements.* Focusing your networking energy and resources on start-up
operations has its drawbacks. First, it is always uncertain whether
any great number of these operations will appear in your community. Equally important, start-up credit operations typically have
(almost by definition) no referral base. In other words, they may
not have any contacts/clients in the community to refer to you and
your business.

Most of the top-notch networkers who act as loan brokers
target both new and well-established lenders. How do they ap-

proach a well-established credit organization? In addition to the strategies discussed elsewhere in this chapter, they employ one other strategy. Initially, they establish rapport with the credit organization by being very selective in making referrals. In other words, early in the courtship they refer only their most creditworthy clients. Once trust has been established, they refer other clients as well. Remember, successful networking requires a long-term view of relationship building.

9 *Document your endorsement.* Each time you endorse a client as being creditworthy, document your support in writing. Send a letter supporting your client's application for credit to the targeted organization/credit officer. Also send a copy of that letter to the client. And by all means, show these pro forma letters of endorsement/support to prospective clients. Such letters are strong and tangible evidence of your special brand of service and commitment to your clients. And always ask your prospects this all-important question: How many of your current set of professional service providers ever wrote a letter like this on your behalf? "Zero" is the most common response.

10 *Leverage your networking activity.* Yes, to succeed in networking, you must give before you expect to receive anything from your efforts. However, once you have given, don't be shy about asking your network members to reciprocate. Ask them to endorse you and your organization. For every five referrals that you make to a credit institution, it should return the favor at least once. What if the credit institution is not wise enough to begin endorsing you on its own? Ask for its endorsement. What if it continues to ignore your needs? In a nice but firm tone, tell the credit institution that you can't continue to help it generate business without reciprocity.

Your current clients whom you have helped obtain loans can be an excellent source of referrals. When they have had a loan approved via your endorsement, contact them. And just after they thank you for your special type of service, ask them these key questions:

"Whom do you know that might benefit from my services?"
"May I tell them that you're a client of mine?"
"May I tell them that you suggested that I call them?"

But what if the credit source that you recommended turns your client down for a loan? There are several possible solutions to this problem. These include:

- Reminding the credit source about how many of your clients are credit prone.
- Asking the credit source to reconsider the application. It should reconsider when you explain that you can't send future business its way in light of its rejection of your client's loan application.
- Expressing to the credit source your need, given the current circumstances, to deal with its competitors.
- Finding another credit source.

Those with the power to network must express it. Power that is hidden is often useless.

MR. P. W. CHARLES

Mr. Charles is a highly successful financial consultant. He is also a very skilled networker. Part of his marketing philosophy is to target segments that others ignore. One of his prime targets consists of senior bank officers and loan officers

During the early stages of his career, Mr. Charles found out that none of his colleagues ever prospected the so-called bank market. Hypothesizing that many small banks had no in-house investment experts, he proposed to become their investment expert. Using this hypothesis and proposal as an introductory theme, he called on a number of small banks within his trade area. The initial reaction of their officers to his proposal was less than positive.

Although most of the bankers whom he prospected agreed with Mr. Charles's concept, they felt that he was too young and too inexperienced to handle their investment requirements. However, Mr. Charles was not discouraged by his initial lack of success. More than a year later, he called on the same banks and submitted the same proposal.

The second time around, however, Mr. Charles was successful in gaining considerable business from many of the banks. As a result, he helped many small banks to manage their investments and also generated a considerable number of new clients among the bank officers whom he contacted. In other words, he acted as both an institutional financial consultant and a personal financial consultant.

Why was Mr. Charles's second campaign more successful than the first? Yes, he was more seasoned. But more important, the second time around he offered the small banks revenue enhancement as well as investment advice.

Mr. Charles acted as a patronage opinion leader for many of his affluent clients and prospective clients who owned businesses. He made a habit of contacting his clients periodically to discuss their needs with them. And he did not limit the discussion to investment-related topics. When clients and prospective clients needed to borrow money from a bank, he helped them satisfy that need.

According to Mr. Charles, more than one half of the business owners among his clients were dissatisfied with their current sources of commercial credit! My own research findings are in complete harmony with this contention. Mr. Charles offered to act as a Loan Broker for his clients and prospects. This offer greatly increased the number of his clients among the business owners within his trade area.

In light of this added dimension of service, several small banks within Mr. Charles's trade area were delighted to have him manage their funds. Mr. Charles sent each of these bank clients dozens of referrals each year, and these banks made referrals of their own clients to Mr. Charles. Interestingly, several senior officers of these banks opened accounts with Mr. Charles.

Thousands of licensed brokers operate in the state where Mr. Charles is based. But of these brokers, it seems, only he views banks as members of his influence and client network and not as part of the competition.

Mr. Charles's perception of banks as members of his network is no longer limited to small banks. Senior loan officers of two of the largest commercial banks in his region have accounts with him and refer many of their affluent credit clients to him. I asked Mr. Charles why these loan officers directed business to him and not to their own investment/trust departments. His answer was as follows:

> The investment/trust departments rarely, if ever, send any business to my clients who are involved in commercial lending. Also, these senior loan officers are competing for resources with other divisions

within their respective banks. And they worry about the track record that their own banks' investment people have established. It has not been very good at all. And the fees are quite high.

Webster's defines *symbiosis* as the close union of two dissimilar organisms in a mutually beneficial relationship. So does Mr. Charles—except that he calls it "networking."

INDEX

MORE BOOKS IN THE AFFLUENT LIBRARY

Dr. Thomas J. Stanley's *Affluent Library* is a reference for attorneys, doctors, accountants, real estate brokers, financial advisors, fundraisers, and others to help them find, talk to, and network with the affluent. As a group, the *Affluent Library* gives readers the complete advantage of a total system for influencing wealthy customers—an advantage that puts them far ahead of their competition. Stanley shows anyone who sells—from insurance salespeople to luxury product dealers—how to gain the respect of top clients and turn them into long-lasting, top accounts.

Marketing to the Affluent
Thomas J. Stanley
Finalist, 1989 Benjamin Franklin Award, Business Books

> "RE: The technique of proactive marketing. Dr. Stanley is right on the mark. Right up my sales training managers' alley."

> Gerhardt Blendstru, Vice President of Sales and Marketing, Porsche Cars North America

The first book of the series, this premier guide reveals an accurate picture of who the affluent are *and* are not. Readers will find the true demographics, psychographics, buying, and patronage habits of the wealthy. Includes in-depth interviews with some of the nation's top sales and marketing professionals who have successfully identified affluent prospects.
ISBN: 1-55623-105-9

Selling to the Affluent: The Professional's Guide to Closing the Sales that Count
Thomas J. Stanley

> "By using Dr. Stanley's techniques, an individual or an organization can gain reputation, wealth, and instant credibility within that industry."

> Sidney A. Friedman, Million Dollar Producer, Top of the Table Member, Million Dollar Round Table, Corporate Financial Services, Inc.

After readers have found their potential group of affluent clients, they can use the second book to land those prospects. Stanley shows readers the key indicators that reveal when a prospect is about to make significant dollar transactions. *Selling to the Affluent* shows everyone who targets the wealthy buyer how to improve their closing percentage and improve their income.
ISBN: 1-55623-418-X

Available at Fine Bookstores and Libraries Everywhere.